Field Guide
to the Natural
World of
New York City

Field Guide
to the Natural
World of
New York City

LESLIE DAY

Illustrated by
MARK A. KLINGLER
Foreword by
MICHAEL R. BLOOMBERG

*In association with the New York City
Department of Parks & Recreation*

THE JOHNS HOPKINS UNIVERSITY PRESS

BALTIMORE

© 2007 The Johns Hopkins University Press
All rights reserved. Published 2007
Printed in China on acid-free paper
9 8 7 6 5 4 3

The Johns Hopkins University Press
2715 North Charles Street
Baltimore, Maryland 21218-4363
www.press.jhu.edu

Day, Leslie, 1945–
Field guide to the natural world of New York City / by Leslie Day; illustrated by
Mark A. Klingler; with a foreword by Michael R. Bloomberg.
    p. cm.
    Includes bibliographical references and index.
    ISBN-13: 978-0-8018-8681-2 (hardcover: alk. paper)
    ISBN-13: 978-0-8018-8682-9 (pbk.: alk. paper)
    ISBN-10: 0-8018-8681-3 (hardcover: alk. paper)
    ISBN-10: 0-8018-8682-1 (pbk.: alk. paper)
    1. Natural history—New York (State)—New York—Guidebooks. 2. New York
(N.Y.)—Guidebooks. I. Title.
    QH105.N7D39 2007
    917.47'0443—dc22   2007006288

A catalog record for this book is available from the British Library.

All watercolor plates © 2007 Mark A. Klingler

Photographs of trees and shrubs by Leslie Day

Book design by Kimberly Glyder Design

CONTENTS

FOREWORD

NEW YORK, OUR BELOVED CITY of 8.2 million, is many things: a leading cultural center, a place of history and myth, the financial capital of the United States, and the melting pot of the world. When I tell visitors about its parks and its wildlife, however, they often look at me with surprise—or think that I am referring only to Manhattan's magnificent Central Park. But New York City has a wealth of open space, and is one of the greenest cities in America, and perhaps the world.

Our "Emerald Empire," as the New York City Department of Parks & Recreation calls it, comprises over eleven thousand acres, and includes forests, woodlands, freshwater wetlands, and salt marsh ecosystems. When one adds to this the natural areas managed by the state and federal government throughout the five boroughs, the City contains over twenty-five thousand acres of natural parkland. This book, written by a local environmental educator and naturalist, looks deeply at the secret and not-so-secret green spaces that help make our City a rare gem.

In these pages, Dr. Leslie Day takes us into New York's "forever wild" sites, and along the curves of our City's long shoreline, but she also reveals the nature that is right in front of us, for example, outside coffee shops, restaurants, and theaters on one of our "green streets." This book is our guide to unveiling a hidden New York that we might not have noticed before, helping us investigate and identify the butterflies, wildflowers, birds, embankments, and other features of our landscape and ecosystem that we pass by every day on the way to somewhere else.

The City and its Parks Department are hard at work protecting our natural heritage. These efforts help ensure that all New Yorkers and visitors have access to the natural wonders that bring such sparkle to our great City. Using this book you, too, can discover the "Natural World of New York City." I hope you enjoy the journey.

Michael R. Bloomberg

Mayor

KEY TO THE PARKS DESCRIBED IN THIS BOOK

1. CENTRAL PARK
2. INWOOD HILL PARK
3. RIVERSIDE PARK
4. PELHAM BAY PARK
5. VAN CORTLANDT PARK
6. FLOYD BENNETT FIELD

7. MARINE PARK
8. PROSPECT PARK
9. ALLEY POND PARK
10. JAMAICA BAY WILDLIFE REFUGE
11. MOUNT LORETTO UNIQUE AREA
12. WOLFE'S POND PARK

ACKNOWLEDGMENTS

THE BEAUTY OF THIS BOOK lies in the contributions of the talented artists and photographers who shared their work with me. First and foremost is Mark Klingler whose splendid paintings have given this book its charm and made it come to life. Second would be Jean Steins who so kindly let us use the detailed and elegant maps by her late husband, the cartographer Mark Stein. Thank you to George Booruji for his beautifully illustrated map of New York City. I am indebted to Mike Feller, Don Riepe, David Künstler, Marjorie Pangione, and Clodagh Green for their stunning photographs. A special thank you to Cathy Klingler for her support and assistance.

I would like to thank the following people who helped with this book: Commissioner of Parks Adrian Benepe; New York City Department of Parks and Recreation, Natural Resources Group: Bill Tai, Alexander Brash, now with the National Parks Conservation Association; Mike Feller, Marge Gargiullo, Janine Harris, and Ellen Pehek, all helped check the parks' and species' descriptions for accuracy. Van Cortlandt Park and Pelham Bay Park: Margot Peron, David Künstler; William Schiller, American Museum of Natural History. Riverside Park: Crista Carmody, Sal Trento, Margaret Bracken. Riverside Park Fund: Jim Dowell, Terry Cohen, Sabrina Dukes, Jeff Nulle. Central Park Conservancy: Sara Cedar Miller. Mount Loretto Unique Area: Betsy Ukeritis, New York State Department of Environmental Conservation. Staten Island Protectors of Pine Oak Woods and Dick Buegler. Jamaica Bay Wildlife Preserve: Don Riepe: New York Littoral Society; Robert Cook, PhD. Floyd Bennett Field: Ron and Jean Bourque. Prospect Park: Peter Dorosch and the Brooklyn Bird Club.

Over the years, the following people and organizations have helped with research in the following areas: Fish: Tom Lake, Hudson River Estuary Naturalist, N.Y. State Department of Environmental Conservation and Christopher Letts of the Hudson River Foundation. Amphibians, reptiles, and mammals: Robert Cook, PhD, U.S. Department of the Interior, Cape Cod National Seashore; Lori Cramer, New York Turtle and Tortoise Society. Birds: Peter Dorosch and the Brooklyn Bird Club; E. J. McAdams, Joseph Giunta, and Ron Bourque of the New York City Audubon Society; Alison Evans Fragale, Edgewater Parrots. Invertebrates: Randy Mercurio,

American Museum of Natural History. Mycology: Howard Goldstein, MD, New York Mycological Society; Vladamir Schuster. Wildfloers: Aril Lowry, New York Botanical Garden; Jean Bourque, New York City Audubon Society. Trees: Wayne Cahilly, New York Botanical Garden. Geology: Pamela Brock, PhD, Patrick Brock, PhD, and Alan Ludman, PhD, Queens College; Jay Holmes, American Museum of Natural History; Guillermo Rocha, Brooklyn College. I also thank Sidney Horenstein, Environmental Educator Emeritus of the American Museum of Natural History, whose marvelous geological tours of New York City on land and on water are so enlightening.

I am so grateful to those who walked the parks with me and taught me so much. In particular, Jill Benzer, whose love and knowledge of the natural world of New York City is inspirational, and Sanda Cohen, who showed me the wonderful "backyard" world of her childhood: Brooklyn's Prospect Park. I thank educators Sharon Seitz, who has spent years researching and writing about the history of New York City's islands and shorelines, and Regina McCarthy, who has devoted her adult life to educating teachers about New York City's parks and the natural world. I am grateful to Lincoln Karim for his beautiful photographs of, and dedication to, Pale Male, the red-tail hawk of Central Park, which continue to inspire me.

I thank my family and friends who have walked miles with me exploring the beauty of the five boroughs: my wonderful husband, Jim Nishiura, a biologist by trade and soul mate in our love of nature; my son Jonah Nishiura and Gina Auletta; my brother, David Wohl, and my dearest friend, Trudy Smoke, and let me not forgot my companion on many of these walks, our little dog, Sadie.

I thank Alan Robbins, Leslie Robbins, Nancy Leff, and Beth Weinstein for their support. I am grateful to my brilliant and loving stepmother, Faith Wohl; my sister and brother-in-law, Jennifer and Michael Zinn; my cousins Nancy and Gary Peters and Jon Goldstein and Lela Cocoros; and my brothers Bill Wohl and Mike Wohl and their families and my friends Virginia Johnson and Electa Brown for their encouragement. I thank my upstate neighbors, Corinna and Gail Peckham, who have taught me so much about the natural world on their Prattsville, New York, farm.

I thank my neighbors at the 79th Street Boat Basin who showed up at my door to tell me of the harp seal that had hauled out on ice one magical winter night in the marina and my neighbors of more than thirty years at the marina, particularly Ray Stephens, Raquel and Werner Buhrer, Jane Clegg, Ed and Regina Bacon, Wayne Gryk, Simone DiBagno, Doug Hynes and Teri Walsh, Nat Lichtwar and Linda Mays, Glavey-Weiss and Hayama-van der Lande families, who love the natural world and have shared many of their river animal sightings and findings with me. I thank the marina staff: Nate Grove, Marc Brown, Joe Burck, Pedro Miranda, Troy Porter, Chris Vallozzi, Otto Malloy, and Jasmine Rios, who, over the years, have shared their interest in wildlife and saved the lives of injured waterfowl and countless freshwater snapping turtles, painted turtles, and red-eared sliders, who have found their way into the brackish waters of the Hudson. Thank you to Greg Smith for hauling out the enormous Atlantic sturgeon that washed up at the Boat Basin so that I and others would have a chance to see this beautiful animal.

I thank my dear friends Cindy Kane, who inspires me with her beautiful bird paintings; Meg Berlin, who shares her love of botany with me; and Kaare Christian and Robin Raskin who, over a decade ago, encouraged me to create a city naturalists website.

I appreciate the support of my colleagues at The Elisabeth Morrow School, particularly my headmaster, Dr. David Lowry, and principal, Germaine DiPaolo; our technology wizards Sarah Rolle, Marianne Malmstrom, and Micah Malmstrom; my fellow science teachers, Carolyn Milne and Gail Weeks; our librarian, Eleanor Schuster, our writing club teacher, Lisa Nicolaou; and our music teacher Ann Winze who can whistle down titmice and chickadees. I thank Chris Jurgenson, Gil Marino, Gerry Mulholland, Al Mulle, Osberto Martinez, Vito Liza, and Craig Smith for preserving the wildlife habitats on our campus and my wonderful students and their families who have been so excited about this book.

I thank my mentor and friend Professor Sal Vascellaro at Bank Street College of Education and my mentors at Teachers College Columbia University: Professor O. Roger Anderson, chair of Science, Math and Technology; Professor Angela Calabrese Barton; and Professor Elaine Howes, now at the University of South Florida.

I owe everything to my editor, Vincent J. Burke, PhD, who gave me the incredible opportunity to write this book. His intelligence, humor, and nurturing have sustained me. I also thank Vince's capable assistants, Brendan Coyne and Bethany Ross. I am grateful to Susan Lantz and Andre Barnett, the copyeditors on this project, whose patience, hard work, and keen eyes have made this a better book for the reader.

A WORD ABOUT MY CHOICE of organisms: For the most part, I selected species that the readers are most likely to see. Therefore, there are many more birds because birds are abundant year-round in New York City. I also chose some organisms that live their lives beneath the soil and are not easily found, such as the tiny centipede, *Nannarrup hoffmani*, a newly discovered species found nowhere else in the world but Central Park.

When I started this book, I was a child of Manhattan, born on the island and familiar only with its parks. Now, at the end of this journey, I am connected to many more parks and living organisms of my city. I hope you, the reader, will also develop connections to the natural world, wherever you live in our city. The splendor and history of the parks and their animals, plants, mushrooms, and rocks are out there and in here, within this book for you to explore.

FOR MY FATHER, HOWARD WOHL, WHO TAUGHT ME TO CARE.

AND FOR JIM, WHO MAKES EVERYTHING POSSIBLE.

ACKNOWLEDGMENTS

16

the
natural
history
of
new york
city

FOUR HUNDRED MILLION YEARS AGO, towering mountain peaks loomed where New York City now stands. Over hundreds of millions of years, the peaks eroded, leaving boulders and rocky outcrops of gneiss, marble, and schist. New York City was part of the great supercontinent of Pangea that came together about 250 million years ago. Approximately 135 million years ago, Pangea started to separate into the continents we know today. We can now see the remnant mountaintops and the testimony of these tectonic events scattered throughout the city. The ocean advanced and retreated over the dwindling mountains, depositing layers of sediment over the city's hard bedrock. More than a million years ago, the age of glaciation began, cycling with the earth's climate. The glaciers came and went and came again, ultimately molding present-day New York. At least four separate ice sheets advanced and retreated across the city. About seventy-five thousand years ago, the Wisconsin Ice Sheet advanced southward at the rate of one foot per day, deepening the bed of the Hudson River and covering what is now Manhattan and the Bronx. With much of the earth's water supply trapped in glaciers, sea levels were lowered by hundreds of feet, creating terrestrial habitats around the city. Mastodons, wooly mammoths, saber-toothed tigers, and the giant sloth were able to walk across a dry Long Island Sound from Queens to Connecticut.

Turtle Pond, a small kettle pond in Alley Pond Park.

As the glacier retreated about seventeen thousand years ago, it changed the course of the Bronx River, severing that river's connection to the Hudson and forging a new channel into the Long Island Sound. Alluvial deposits of sand and gravel—carried by the glacial meltwaters—poured into the unglaciated parts of what would later be Brooklyn, Queens, and Staten Island. The meltwaters filled depressions in the earth, forming "kettle ponds" such as the twenty-foot deep Oakland Lake in Alley Pond Park, Queens.

Over centuries, the morainal sand deposited by the glaciers accumulated along the coastlines of Brooklyn, Queens, and Long Island and created a chain of barrier island beaches, such as the Rockaway Peninsula. Salt marshes were common along these alluvial coastlines.

Plant life was virtually destroyed by the advancing ice sheets but returned as each ice sheet retreated. At the close of the last Ice Age, the region became heavily forested. Scrubby pines and small birches thrived in the sandy sediments in what is now Alley Pond Park. As

the climate warmed, new plants took root in New York, replacing the Arctic willows and grasses. Conifers such as spruce, pine, and fir trees dominated the area until seven thousand years ago, when hemlocks and broadleaf deciduous trees such as oaks and chestnuts created mixed forests. Humans first arrived in the area about this time and, with the warming climate, the Ice Age mammals disappeared. Five thousand years ago, about the

A pair of wild turkeys foraging in a Pelham Bay Park woodland.

same time that human villages became more common, hickories replaced the hemlocks, and holly and birch grew in the oak and chestnut forests.

The first human inhabitants of the land that would become New York City lived among bears, mountain lions, wolves, beaver, muskrat, mink, otter, dolphins, seals, whales, and abundant fish and shellfish. Birds were plentiful, including bald eagles, wild turkeys, and dozens of species of waterfowl. So numerous were the wild turkeys that full-length feather cloaks were worn by the native people as protection from the rain. Wildflowers were so abundant that their scent could be detected miles out at sea. Grapes, huckleberries, cranberries, plums, raspberries, and strawberries were everywhere.

During the sixteenth and seventeenth centuries, Europeans were drawn to the region by the lucrative trade in otter, mink, muskrat, and beaver furs. Dutch and then English settlements grew at the foot of Manhattan Island. Soon their villages spread to encompass the surrounding areas of the Bronx, Brooklyn, Queens, and Staten

Island, replacing, sometimes brutally, the tribal villages that had occupied the area for the previous five thousand years.

With the influx of people from around the globe, this small community of traders expanded to become the largest metropolis in the United States. Humans poured into New York City during the 1800s, and many of the larger species of wildlife retreated. However, invertebrates, birds, snakes, frogs, toads, salamanders, and rats, squirrels, and other small mammals thrived in the region even as the city expanded. In the late 1800s, concern that the city was growing so fast that soon there would be no access to nature led to the creation of Central Park, the first public park in America. It was designed by Frederick Law Olmsted and Calvert Vaux as a place where people could enjoy the natural world. Park planners of the day commonly populated the parks with exotic plants and animals from faraway lands. New York City was a hotbed of such introductions; trees and birds from Europe and shrubs from Japan were transported there. Many other species just caught a ride with the waves of immigrants and the ocean vessels. The natural world of New York City changed dramatically with the arrival of Europeans, as some species disappeared and other new ones arrived.

Today the city is a complex ecosystem; the result of its tumultuous history. Hundreds of species of birds inhabit its streets, parks, and waters. Insects, worms, crustaceans, fish, amphibians, reptiles, trees, wildflowers, and mushrooms are within walking distance of virtually every apartment building, house, and hotel. The city has more than five hundred miles of coastline, some fringed with saltwater marshes, such as the islands of Jamaica Bay in Queens. New York's thirty thousand acres of parks contain hundreds of species waiting to be discovered, identified, and appreciated by the reader. This guide is designed to make the natural world of New York City accessible by revealing the diverse, living, and ancient geological treasures the city has to offer.

CHAPTER 2

the
parks

THE BRONX

Pelham Bay Park

LOCATION
Bordered on the north by Park Drive; on the west by the Hutchinson River, Amtrak, and the Bruckner Expressway; on the south by Middletown Road and Watt Avenue; and on the east by Eastchester Bay and the Long Island Sound.

TELEPHONE
(718) 430-1890

SIZE
2,765.5 acres

HABITATS
forest, meadows, rocky shoreline, creeks, sound, bay, lagoon, river, mudflats, salt marshes

Natural History   The formation of the area that is now Pelham Bay Park was a result of over fifty million years of mountain building and erosion, melting and cooling rocks, and glacial scouring. The exposed bedrock along the shore is Hartland schist. There are scattered outcroppings of Fordham gneiss as well. Look closely to see small red garnets, mica, and quartz embedded in the Hartland schist. The coastline of Pelham Bay sits on the southern-most part of New England's rocky shore, which extends all the way north to Maine. Part of this metamorphic bedrock, principally along its eastern shore, was exposed roughly fifteen thousand years ago during the last age of glaciation. As the massive ice receded, it left irregular coasts as well as giant boulders called *erratics*, which means "wanderer." The advancing glacier carried boulders from the Connecticut and Westchester areas and deposited them along the shore of Hunter Island. Native Americans, who lived in the area for nearly five thousand years, used these erratics for ceremonial meeting places. At the northeast end of the island sits a huge boulder known as Lion Rock, or The Sphinx. The rock

"Bronx" carved into the exposed gneiss bedrock on the shore of Pelham Bay Park.

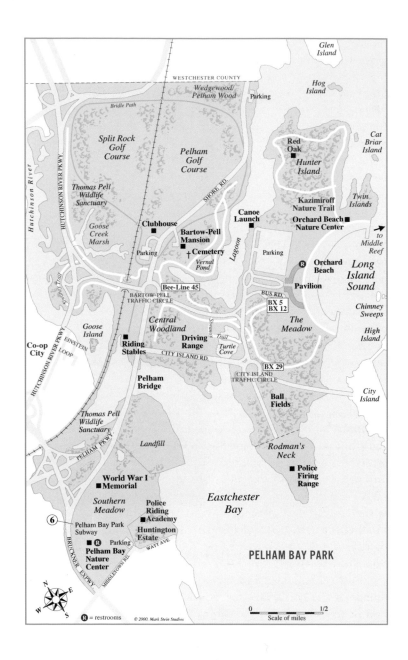

WESTCHESTER COUNTY

Glen
Island

Wedgewood/
Pelham Wood   Parking

Hog
Island

Bridle Path

Split Rock
Golf
Course

Pelham
Golf
Course

Red
Oak
■
Hunter
Island

Cat
Briar
Island

Thomas Pell
Wildlife
Sanctuary

Kazimiroff
Nature Trail

Twin
Islands

Goose
Creek
Marsh

Clubhouse
■

Bartow-Pell
Mansion
† Cemetery

Canoe
Launch
■

Orchard Beach ■
Nature Center

Parking

Vernal
Pond

Parking

Ⓡ Orchard
Beach

Pavilion

Long
Island
Sound

to
Middle
Reef

Bee-Line 45

BARTOW-PELL
TRAFFIC CIRCLE

BUS RD.
BX 5
BX 12

Chimney
Sweeps

Goose
Island

Central
Woodland

Riding
Stables
■

Driving
Range

The
Meadow

High
Island

Co-op
City

Turtle
Cove

CITY ISLAND RD.

BX 29

Pelham
Bridge

CITY ISLAND
TRAFFIC CIRCLE

City
Island

Ball
Fields
■

Thomas Pell
Wildlife
Sanctuary

Landfill

Rodman's
Neck

■ Police
Firing
Range

World War I
■ Memorial

Southern
Meadow

Police
Riding
■ Academy

Eastchester
Bay

6
Pelham Bay Park
Subway

Huntington
Estate

■ Ⓡ   Parking
Pelham Bay
Nature
Center

WAIT AVE.

PELHAM BAY PARK

N
W   E
S

Ⓡ = restrooms   © 2000. Mark Stein Studios

0   1/2

Scale of miles

Hutchinson River

HUTCHINSON RIVER PKWY.

SHORE RD.

Lagoon

Strome

Trail

Siwanoy Trail

EINSTEIN LOOP

HUTCHINSON RIVER PKWY.

PELHAM PKWY.

BRUCKNER EXPWY.

MIDDLETOWN RD.

remained here for over ten thousand years with a smaller boulder balanced on top. In the 1990s, however, the top section broke away and now lies near the larger piece. Early colonists noted that the Indians revered this boulder as they did other erratics.

Human History The Siwanoy, members of the Lenape tribe, inhabited the land of Pelham Bay Park and the Long Island Sound until they sold the land to the Europeans in the mid-1600s. The Siwanoy lived off the land and the sea, gathered fruit and nuts, and hunted animals in the forests and fish and shellfish in the sound, bay, inlets, and rivers. The shores provided sacred ceremonial sites, particularly the giant boulders. From quahog shells, the Siwanoy made *wampum*,

Rocky shoreline at Pelham Bay Park.

the ornamental beads they used for trading with Europeans. The Dutch West India Company purchased the land from the Siwanoy in 1639 and named the area Vreedelandt, meaning "land of freedom." Despite years of attempts by Europeans to settle there, the Siwanoy continued to control the area. In 1654, the Englishman Thomas Pell signed a peace treaty with the Siwanoy leader, Chief Wampage. Pell settled the land, including the area that is now Pelham Bay Park. This began the British control of the region. During the Revolutionary War, Pell's land was a buffer between the British-held Manhattan and Patriot-held Westchester. Concealed behind stone walls, six hundred Massachusetts Patriots held the British forces and stopped them from going north. Remnants of these walls can be found in the Split Rock Golf Course.

In the 1800s John Mullaly, a resident of the Bronx and the founder of the New York Parks Association, advocated the preservation of natural areas in the Bronx. In 1888, several estates were merged into Pelham Bay Park. (Pellham—"land of Pell," was the name given to this area by the Dutch.) Poor children from the lower east side of Manhattan were brought to the park, and in 1911, a children's retreat was established on Twin Island in a mansion leased by the city to the Jacob Riis Neighborhood Settlement House, founded by Riis, the activist and photojournalist, to help poor city families.

With the construction of Orchard Beach in the 1930s, Park Commissioner Robert Moses joined Rodman's Neck to Hunter Island, adding 115 acres of land to the park. Using over three million cubic yards of sanitation landfill, construction crews brought in white sand from the Rockaways, Queens, and Sandy Hook, New Jersey.

Turk's-cap lilies and mountain mint in the Meadow in Pelham Bay Park.

Today Pelham Bay Park, consisting of thousands of carefully restored and protected acres and a multitude of habitats, is a place of incredible biodiversity and beauty.

Orchard Beach During May and June, horseshoe crabs emerge from Eastchester Bay and the Long Island Sound onto Orchard Beach, where they mate and lay thousands of eggs. In winter look for waterfowl, hawks, and falcons such as the American kestrel hunting from trees along the beach.

The Meadow Consisting of twenty-five acres of open grassland, the Meadow hosts a variety of wildlife. Plants include switchgrass, goldenrod, little bluestem, wild strawberry, and threatened northern gamma grass. The Meadow has long been known for its high concentration of rare plants. Birds visiting the Meadow include the ring-necked pheasant, and the American woodcock. One of the few remaining grasslands in the city, the Meadow lies between Orchard Beach and Rodman's Neck. The forest adjacent to the Meadow is filled with bayberry bushes and white poplar, black cherry, pin oak, crab apple, smooth sumac, and dogwood trees.

Hunter Island The Kazimiroff Nature Trail has a forty-five-minute-long (blue) trail, or a thirty-minute-long (red) trail through 125 acres of Hunter Island's wetland perimeter, exposed bedrock shore, and deep inland forest. Follow the numbered posts marked red or blue. In 1986, this trail was named for Dr. Theodore Kazimiroff, a Bronx historian who helped preserve the park. During winter, the forest of Hunter Island is a good place to find a pair of great horned owls in the larger deciduous trees, and the tiny saw-whet owl roosting in small white pines. The lagoon is a sheltered wetland that attracts osprey in the fall, and loons, pied-billed grebes, black ducks, and bufflehead ducks in winter. As you follow the trail toward the Long Island Sound, you will see a large boulder, or glacial erratic, protruding from the water. The Siwanoy Indians called this sacred ceremonial site the Gray Mare.

Hunter Island Marine Zoology and Geology Sanctuary is located on the northeastern corner of Hunter Island and Twin Island. The exposed rocks along the shore are Fordham gneiss, composed of the characteristic light and

Great horned owl fledgling clinging to a white poplar tree in Hunter Island forest.

dark banding and swirls. In the warmer seasons at low tide, exposed tide pools teem with small fish, barnacles, clams, and oysters.

Thomas Pell Wildlife Sanctuary The salt marshes of the Thomas Pell Wildlife Sanctuary include the sixty-nine-acre Goose Creek Marsh and the Hutchinson River marshes. Although much reduced in size, the city's salt marshes are extremely valuable natural resources. Called "transitional zones" because they sit between the land and sea, between saltwater and freshwater rivers and streams, salt marshes filter and trap pollutants that would contaminate the sounds, bays, and oceans. They absorb fertilizers, improve water quality, reduce erosion, and provide habitat for invertebrates, fish, amphibians, reptiles, birds, and mammals.

The lagoon is home to a wide variety of wildlife that live in the salt marsh and mudflats. Although few plants can survive in salt water, the salt marsh is calm enough for saltmarsh cordgrass to flourish in the sand and silt flooded twice a day by the tide. As this grass spreads, it traps floating debris such as sediment and particles of decaying plant and animal material, which build up to form nutrient-rich muck. Red-winged blackbirds, marsh wrens, egrets, and herons are commonly observed, as are raccoons that fish the marsh. The inlets provide habitat for breeding marine fish. Rabbits, skunks,

Tide pools and the Long Island Sound, Pelham Bay Park.

raccoons, owls, hawks, and other animals feed within the wildlife sanctuary's woodlands, wetlands, and marshes. Follow the Split Rock Trail through the sanctuary.

Some of Twin Island's salt marshes were restored in the mid-1990s. Gamma grass, a salt-tolerant grass, grows here. This grass is the only host plant for the larvae (caterpillars) of a rare moth known as *Amphipoea erepta ryensis*. Pelham Bay Park contains one of the few known populations of this moth species in the Mid-Atlantic region. In winter look for loons, grebes, cormorants, bufflehead, and common goldeneye ducks on Long Island Sound. Using a spotting scope, during low tide, you may see harbor and harp seals hauled out on a long line of rocks far out in the sound, known as Middle Reef.

Bartow-Pell Mansion Museum Grounds   The grounds of the Bartow-Pell Mansion Museum are a good place to find wintering saw-whet owls, which roost in the lower branches of conifer trees such as white pines. Look for the signs: "whitewash" (white droppings) on the branches, trunk, and ground, and owl pellets (indigestible hairs, feathers, bones, teeth, and claws) vomited up by the owls and found on the ground.

GETTING THERE

By Bus and Subway   From Manhattan, take the Bronx-bound #6 train to the last stop: Pelham Bay Park. The footbridge will take you to the southern section of the park where there are athletic fields, picnic areas, and some special areas such as the Meadow. For the northern section of the park, the BX5 and BX12 stop next to the footbridge in summer. Take either bus to Orchard Beach. After Labor Day until spring, take the BX29, which stops downstairs from the subway platform and across the street. Ask the driver to let you off at the City Island traffic circle. It is a mile walk from the circle north to Hunter Island.

By Bus   From Queens take the QBX1 bus across the Whitestone Bridge to the Pelham Bay Park subway station. Follow instructions above for bus routes to the park.

By Bus   From Westchester, take the Bee-line #45 or #45Q to the Bartow-Pell Mansion Museum and the park subway station. For Bee-line bus information, call (914) 813-7777 or go to http://bee-linebus.westchestergov.com/.

By Car   From the south, take the Bruckner Expressway, I-95 north, to the southern section exit 7C, Country Club Road / Pelham Bay Park. Take the service road. Turn right at the second traffic light onto Middletown Road and park in the lot on the left.

From the north, take the Bruckner Expressway, I-95 south, to exit 8B, Orchard / City Island. Cross Pelham Bay Bridge, and turn right at the traffic light. Turn right to the City Island traffic circle. Stay on the right, and take the third turn to Orchard Beach. Or cross the Pelham Bridge and go straight to Shore Road. At the Bartow traffic circle, the first turnoff will lead to Orchard Beach. The second turnoff takes you to the Bartow-Pell Mansion. You will pass the Pelham / Split Rock Golf Courses on your left.

Winter along Twin Island's shoreline.

Van Cortlandt Park

LOCATION

Van Cortlandt Park South (West 240th Street) and West Gun Hill Road to Westchester County line; Broadway to Jerome Avenue and Van Cortlandt Park East

TELEPHONE

(718) 430-1890

SIZE

1,146 acres

HABITATS

forests, meadows, grassland, ridges, ancient gneiss outcroppings, marsh, lakes, ponds, streams

Natural History   Van Cortlandt Park's steep ridges, hillsides, and open meadows were carved by glaciers. The 1.1 billion-year-old Fordham gneiss outcroppings are the bedrock of ancient mountains worn away by glaciers, wind, and water. The high, forested upland of the Northwest Forest drops suddenly to the east over high cliffs toward the Tibbetts Brook Valley. Before it was dammed around 1700 to power a Dutch gristmill and form the Van Cortlandt Lake, Tibbetts Brook meandered south into the Harlem River. John Kieran, Bronx naturalist and author of *The Natural History of New York City*

Van Cortlandt Park Lake in autumn.

(New York: Fordham University Press, 1959) remembers swimming in the pools of Tibbetts Brook as a child. He writes: "Tibbetts Brook ran above-ground through cattail marshes and wet meadows all the way from the (Van Cortlandt Park) Lake outlet to the old northern loop of the Harlem River, crossing Broadway at about 240th Street en route and providing several good swimming holes to which I gave my patronage as a schoolboy."

Human History   The Wiechquaeskeck Indians, members of the Lenape tribe, lived in the Van Cortlandt Park area, hunted the forested uplands, fished Tibbetts Brook and its wooded swamp and cattail marsh, farmed on what is now the Parade Ground, and for-

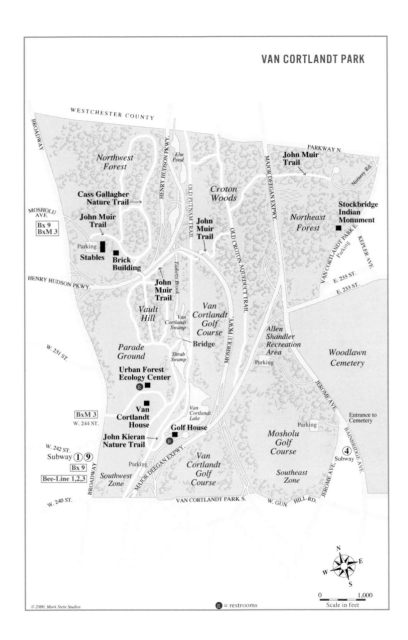

VAN CORTLANDT PARK

WESTCHESTER COUNTY

BROADWAY

Northwest Forest

Elm Pond

HENRY HUDSON PKWY.

OLD PUTNAM TRAIL

PARKWAY N.

John Muir Trail

Nursery Rd.

Cass Gallagher Nature Trail →

MOSHOLU AVE.

Bx 9
BxM 3

John Muir Trail

Croton Woods

John Muir Trail

MAJOR DEEGAN EXPWY.

Northeast Forest

Stockbridge Indian Monument

VAN CORTLANDT PARK E.

Parking

KEPLER AVE.

Parking

Stables   **Brick Building**

HENRY HUDSON PKWY.

Tibbett's Brook

OLD CROTON AQUEDUCT TRAIL

E. 235 ST.

E. 233 ST.

John Muir Trail

Vault Hill

Van Cortlandt Swamp

Van Cortlandt Golf Course

MOSHOLU AVE.

Allen Shandler Recreation Area

Woodlawn Cemetery

W. 251 ST.

Parade Ground

Shrub Swamp

Bridge

Parking

Urban Forest Ecology Center
ℝ■

JEROME AVE.

BxM 3
W. 244 ST.

Van Cortlandt House
■

Van Cortlandt Lake

Mosholu Golf Course

Parking

Entrance to Cemetery

BAINBRIDGE AVE.

Golf House
ℝ

John Kieran Nature Trail →

W. 242 ST.
Subway ①⑨

Bx 9

Bee-Line 1,2,3

BROADWAY

Parking

Southwest Zone

MAJOR DEEGAN EXPWY.

Van Cortlandt Golf Course

Southeast Zone

④ Subway

JEROME AVE.

W. 240 ST.

VAN CORTLANDT PARK S.

W. GUN HILL RD.

© 2000, Mark Stein Studios

ℝ = restrooms

N W E S

0   1,000

Scale in feet

aged for nuts, berries, and edible plants in the meadows and forests. In 1639, the Dutch West India Company purchased most of today's Bronx County from the Wiechquaeskeck. In 1646, the governor of New Netherlands gave the land of what is now the Bronx and southern Westchester to Adriaen Van der Donck, the man who helped create the Dutch colony on Manhattan Island. Van der Donck, who had developed a good relationship with the local Indians, cleared the land and built a house and a sawmill. (Today the Saw Mill River Parkway is named for his sawmill.)

Van der Donck's unofficial title as lord of this huge tract of land was Yonkheer, which, in Dutch, means a young gentleman of property. His land was known to English speakers as "the Joncker's land," and after his death was shortened to "Yonkers." In 1655, Van der Donck was murdered by Indians from the "South River" (Schuylkill River) area. After his death, the land changed hands several times until 1693, when Frederick Philipse, a wealthy English merchant, purchased it. In 1694, Jacobus Van Cortlandt married Philipse's daughter Eva, and over a thirty-eight-year period, Jacobus, a future mayor of New York City, purchased the entire area of the present-

Compound leaves of the staghorn sumac turn a brilliant red in fall.

day park. In 1748, Jacobus's son Frederick built the Van Cortlandt House and the family burial grounds on Vault Hill where, at the outbreak of the American Revolution, city clerk Augustus Van Cortlandt hid the city records from the British Army. George Washington stayed at the Van Cortlandt mansion in 1783, the night before he returned to New York City to reclaim the land from the retreating British. In 1837, the forty-one-mile-long Croton Aqueduct was built on the Van Cortlandt land to bring water from Westchester County to a reservoir in Manhattan. The former site of the reservoir is currently occupied by the main branch of the New York Public Library at 42nd Street and 5th Avenue. In the 1880s, two railroad lines were laid across the parkland. The Van Cortlandt family farmed and lived on the land through the 1880s. The city of New York took title to Van

Cortlandt Park in 1888. The first municipal golf course in the country opened here in 1895; a second golf course, the Mosholu Golf Course, opened in 1914. The Parade Ground was created in 1901, and the National Guard used it for training exercises until the end of World War I. In 1906, the Bronx chapter of the Daughters of the American Revolution dedicated a memorial to Chief Daniel Nimham and the seventeen Stockbridge Indians who were murdered there during the Revolutionary War. In 1913, the cross-country running course, used by middle schools and colleges and universities today, opened, featuring five-mile and three-mile loops. The Tortoise and the Hare sculpture sits on a stone pedestal just outside the finish line of the cross-country track.

Highway construction in the 1940s and 1950s cut through the park, and the fiscal crisis of the 1970s wreaked havoc on its upkeep. In 1983, the Van Cort-

The silvery checkerspot butterfly.

landt and Pelham Bay Parks Administrator's Office was created to oversee the park. This office established a natural resources crew that increased children's programs, volunteer activities, and special events. In 1992, Friends of Van Cortlandt Park was established to promote public partici-pation in the Park and fund-raise for renovation projects and special programs.

John Kieran Nature Trail Named for the journalist, naturalist, and author, the trail starts at the Lake, under the branches of maple, oak, and ash trees. In summer, ferns dot the trail. On the left is Tibbetts Brook, which widens into a swamp with yellow flowering spadderdock water lilies, arrow arum, phragmites, and snapping turtles. Native grasses, such as little bluestem and switchgrass, intermingle with Virginia rose.

Over sixty species of butterflies have been observed in this area. In early summer, look for spicebush swallowtail, eastern tiger swallowtail, American copper, coral hairstreak, banded hairstreak, hickory hairstreak, striped hairstreak, and great spangled fritillary. Van Cortlandt Park has one of the largest populations of silvery

Van Cortlandt Park's Northwest Forest with Fordham gneiss outcroppings.

checkerspots in North America, and Vault Hill Meadow is often called the best butterfly habitat in New York City.

Northwest Forest   With its Fordham gneiss rock outcroppings, black oaks, and lofty tulip trees, this forest is home to the great horned owl, various bats, eastern chipmunks, the red fox, white-tailed deer, wild turkeys, and coyotes, who likely follow the Old Croton Aqueduct Trail from Westchester down into the park. In wet depressions, red maple, white ash and sweet gum trees shade the ground, where skunk cabbage, cinnamon ferns and lizard's tail grow.

John Muir Trail   This trail begins at the Northeast Forest. Enter at Van Cortlandt Park East and Katonah Avenue and follow the road past the Arthur Ross Nursery. Named after the great Scottish-American conservationist who founded Yosemite National Park and the Sierra Club, the trail passes through forests of hundred-foot-tall trees, wetlands filled with frogs and salamanders, and grasslands alive with songbirds, wildflowers, and butterflies. The 1.5-mile-long trail heads west through the Northeast Forest, Croton Woods, and the Northwest Forest. During spring migration, a wide variety of birds can be observed along the way, including woodpeckers, flycatchers, vireos, warblers, thrushes, tanagers, and grosbeaks. In the Northeast Forest a phragmites marsh is filled with the sounds of the red-winged blackbird and the spring peeper.

Cass Gallagher Nature Trail   Named for a local environmentalist and park advocate, this trail leads through the Northwest Forest, 188 acres of deep woods sitting atop a north–south rocky ridge. Enter from the western side of Broadway and Mosholu Avenue or on the John Muir Trail from Croton Woods. (On the John Muir Trail you enter the Northwest Forest after you cross the bridge that spans the Henry Hudson Parkway.) Northwest Forest is a hundred-year-old wood, filled with oaks, sweet gum, tulip trees, and understory trees and shrubs such as sassafras, spicebush, and mapleleaf viburnum. American chestnut saplings, an important and widespread tree before the chestnut blight destroyed millions in the early 1900s, occasionally grow from old stumps. In June 2006, an American chestnut, a large and healthy specimen by today's standards, was found deep in the woods. Owls, bats, eastern chipmunks, eastern cottontail rabbits, raccoons, and opossums can be seen in this mature forest. In early spring before the trees leaf out, you may come across ephemerals such as spring beauty, Dutchman's breeches, and trout lilies.

Urban Forest Ecology Center   Run by the Urban Park Rangers, the center is at West 246th Street, east of Broadway at the southern end of the Parade Ground. It houses exhibits on forest flora and fauna, urban forest preservation, and meeting rooms for the Junior Bird and Nature Club for children. Call (718) 548-0912 for further information and to learn about Ranger-led tours of the tremendous biodiversity of this city park.

Sunlight-dappled forest along the Cass Gallagher Nature Trail.

GETTING THERE

By Car   From any New York City borough, take the Major Deegan Expressway, which has two park exits: Van Cortlandt Park South, serving the south and eastern portions of the park, and East 233rd Street, serving the north and eastern sections of the park. The Henry Hudson Parkway's Broadway exits lead to the park's west side.

By Subway   From Manhattan and the Bronx, take the IRT #1 train to West 242nd Street, which will put you near the Parade Ground. From Brooklyn and Manhattan, take the IRT #4 to the train's last stop at Woodlawn, which will put you at the park's southeastern section.

BROOKLYN

Floyd Bennett Field

LOCATION
Gateway National Recreation Area, Flatbush Avenue South before
Marine Parkway Bridge

TELEPHONE
(718) 338-4306 / (718) 338-3799

SIZE
1,448 acres

VISITOR CENTER
Ryan Visitor Center, open year-round, 8:30 a.m.–5 p.m. Most
guided visitor programs start from the visitor center.

HABITATS
grasslands, freshwater pond, beach, salt marsh, runways, woods,
shrub thickets, pine forest, community gardens, campgrounds

Maintained pathways of the North Forty Nature Trail make it easy to walk and observe wildlife in Floyd Bennett Field.

Natural History   Seventeen thousand years ago, when the Wisconsin Ice Sheet receded from our area, deposits of sand and gravel carried by glacial meltwater poured along the shores of present-day Brooklyn, Queens, and Staten Island. These morainal deposits formed a five-mile-wide delta known as an outwash plain. Over centuries, the morainal sand accumulating along this coastline created a chain of barrier island beaches within what is now Jamaica Bay, including Barren Island. Vast salt marshes characterized the coastline.

Human History   Until the late 1800s, Jamaica Bay was essentially a wilderness area, providing fish and shellfish for the Native Americans and settlers. In 1909 New York City began dumping its refuse here, and today, as you walk along the beach at low tide, you will find the sand studded with pottery shards and colored glass from that era. In 1930 numerous small islands were connected for the construction of a naval air station, which would later be enlarged to create Floyd Bennett Field. Barren Island, a 387-acre marsh, along with 33 small islands, was chosen as the site for New York City's first airport. Six million cubic yards of

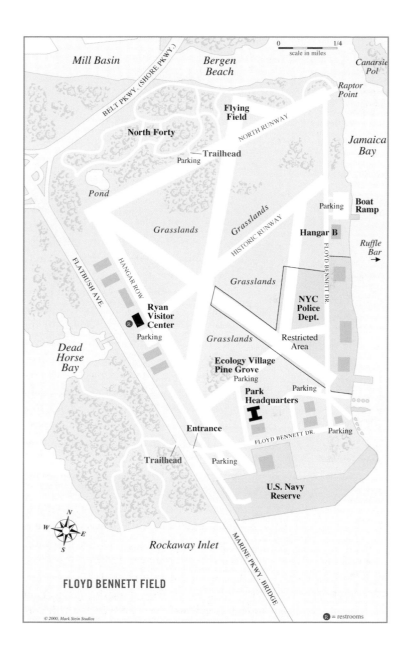

Mill Basin

Bergen Beach

0   1/4
scale in miles

Canarsie Pol

BELT PKWY. (SHORE PKWY.)

Raptor Point

Flying Field

North Forty

NORTH RUNWAY

Jamaica Bay

—Trailhead
Parking

Pond

Grasslands

Grasslands

HISTORIC RUNWAY

Parking

Boat Ramp

Hangar B

Ruffle Bar →

FLATBUSH AVE.

HANGAR ROW

Grasslands

FLOYD BENNETT DR.

Ryan Visitor Center
Parking

NYC Police Dept.

Grasslands

Dead Horse Bay

Grasslands

Restricted Area

Ecology Village Pine Grove
Parking

Parking

Park Headquarters

Entrance

Parking

FLOYD BENNETT DR.

Parking

Trailhead
Parking

U.S. Navy Reserve

N
W   E
S

Rockaway Inlet

MARINE PKWY. BRIDGE

FLOYD BENNETT FIELD

© 2000, Mark Stein Studios

🅿 = restrooms

sand were pumped from Jamaica Bay to connect the islands and raise the site to sixteen feet above the high-tide mark. Mayor Jimmy Walker named the airfield for Floyd Bennett, the aviator who piloted Admiral Byrd across the North Pole in 1926.

Transcontinental, transatlantic, and round-the-world records were set from Floyd Bennett Field in the 1930s by aviation's early

Grasslands of Floyd Bennett Field during winter.

heroes, including Amelia Earhart, Howard Hughes, and "Wrong Way" Corrigan. In 1941, the field became a naval air station, remaining very active throughout World War II. The field was expanded in size from 387 acres to 1,288 acres. Several miles of roads were added and long concrete runways were installed, along with facilities for large Navy flying boats, before the airfield was decommissioned in 1950.

The National Park Service took over Floyd Bennett Field and made it part of Gateway National Recreation Area in 1971. The Ryan Visitor Center, headquarters for Gateway National Recreation Area and housed in the original air control tower, was named for Congressman William Fitts Ryan, who helped establish this urban national park.

Grassland Habitats for Wildlife Because their fields are mowed, airports unintentionally provide habitat for grassland birds, which is what happened at Floyd Bennett Field. However, when the airfield was decommissioned, this habitat disappeared as shrubs and trees grew up between the runways. In 1985, thanks to the work of Ron and Jean Bourque and the New York City Audubon Society, a grassland restoration project reversed the natural succession in 140 acres of the field. Today, the National Park Service and the New York City Audubon Society manage this grassland. Tree and shrub growth are suppressed by annual mowing in August.

Pine Groves and Deciduous Trees Ladybird Johnson, as part of her "Beautify America" program, helped plant a grove of Japanese black pine trees at Floyd Bennett Field. Today many of these black pines are dying from blue stain fungus, which is carried by the black turpentine beetle. These pines are being replaced by the native eastern white pine. The pine groves provide shelter and night roosts for Cooper's and sharp-shinned hawks, and day roosts for occasional owls. The pine groves are also the site for camping grounds at the Field. Deciduous trees and shrubs at Floyd Bennett Field include bayberry, black cherry, willow, cottonwood, crabapple, gray birch, groundsel, and winged sumac. Winter birds such as golden-rumped warblers feed on the bayberries, and migrating tree swallows depend upon the bayberries and winged sumac berries.

Queen Anne's lace and red clover, Floyd Bennett Field.

Butterflies and Flowering Plants During spring, summer, and fall, the grasslands are full of colorful wildflowers, including black-eyed Susans, Queen Anne's lace, golden asters, evening primrose, camphorweed, bush clover, wild lettuce, and blue curl.

The fields abound with grasses such as windmill grass, fall witchgrass, purple lovegrass, little bluestem, weeping lovegrass, tall redtop, dune grass, switchgrass, and foxtail grass. Wildflower and grass colors and hues of green, red, blue, white, and yellow change almost every week and every season. These wildflowers also attract numerous butterflies, including the coral hairstreak. The overgrown runway strips near Flatbush Avenue are home to populations of cobweb skipper and dusted skipper butterflies in April and May. Common checkered-skippers, checkered whites, and pipevine swallowtails are here in August and September. Black swallowtails, common buckeyes, and red-banded hairstreaks can be found on the sumac blossoms. In September, monarch butterflies nectar on the perennials at the community gardens and the buddleia (butterfly bush) outside the Gateway Center for Science and Environmental Studies.

Birds Floyd Bennett Field is known for its grassland birds, wintering hawks, and year-round raptors. Spring migration brings American kestrels, bobolinks, eastern meadowlarks, grasshopper sparrows, northern harriers, upland sandpipers, and woodcocks.

Emergent marsh grasses along the Jamaica Bay shoreline at Floyd Bennett Field.

During fall migration, as many as fourteen kestrels have been seen sitting along the police helicopter runway fence. Populations of grassland birds have been declining in the northeast, and this is reflected in the loss of their breeding populations at Floyd Bennett Field, where the grasshopper sparrow and the meadowlark no longer breed. However, the savannah sparrow still breeds here. The northern harrier has also been an occasional breeder at the Field and is often seen hunting over grasses and shrubs year-round. Winter residents include red-tailed hawks, Cooper's hawks, sharp-shinned hawks, American kestrels, merlin, and northern harriers. A pair of peregrine falcons living year-round on the Marine Parkway Bridge occasionally hunts the Field. They have been observed bathing in rainwater puddles on the runways. Some occasional winter visitors include the short-eared owls and snowy owls.

Birds that commonly nest in the Field include northern flickers, woodcocks, ring-necked pheasants, brown thrashers, catbirds, common yellowthroats, and white-eyed vireos. Twenty-five to thirty species of nesting birds summer in the Field. During spring, summer, and early fall, the many tree swallow nesting boxes throughout the Field are active, and tree swallows and barn swallows hawk insects over the grasslands. In October, thousands of tree swallows gather and feed on bayberries before they embark on their southern migration. Along the beach in summer you can observe herons, egrets, geese, and double-crested cormorants. Throughout winter a variety of wintering ducks can be found.

Beach Walk Jamaica Bay surrounds Floyd Bennett Field on its north, east, and south shores with sand beaches and remnants of the marshes upon which Floyd Bennett Field was constructed. From the park entrance, drive straight down Floyd Bennett Drive until it turns sharply to the left. Make the first right and follow the road to a parking area near the bay. There are times when this beach is closed to the public, but when open, particularly in the winter, this is a good place to observe birds. Low tide exposes rocks, a jetty, and a row of concrete pilings where cormorants, black-backed, laughing, herring, and ring-billed gulls, and common terns and various shorebirds perch. In spring, look south to the beach and marsh for resting waterfowl and oystercatchers. Although you are permitted to walk on this beach, it is recommended that you use binoculars and observe birds from the bulkhead area as moving onto the beach will only flush the birds. From this bulkhead area, you have a good view of Canarsie Pol on the left and Ruffle Bar on the right. These uninhabited islands, about a mile away, host winter raptors that can be observed through binoculars and spotting scopes.

NORTH FORTY

A grassland management plan (GRAMP) was initiated in 1986 to maintain habitats for open-country birds. The North Forty Nature Trail winds through open shrubland, dense shrubland, and stands of phragmites to a man-made two-acre pond called the Return-a-Gift Pond. (When you check "Return a Gift to Wildlife" on your income tax form, the money goes for projects such as this.) Wildlife on the pond can be observed through the open windows of a wooden bird blind. The beginning of the trail through the shrubs is habitat for rufous-sided towhees, catbirds, brown thrashers, robins, northern cardinals, common yellowthroats, and mockingbirds who feed on

Return-a-Gift Pond viewed from the bird blind on the North Forty Trail, Floyd Bennett Field.

rosehips of the multiflora rose. Common waterfowl on the pond are black ducks, gadwall, glossy ibis, green-winged teal, hooded mergansers, mallards, northern shovelers, pied-billed grebes, spotted, least, and solitary sandpipers, and wood ducks. Be aware that dog ticks and deer ticks might be in the tall grasses and take precautions.

Ecology Village Campgrounds Floyd Bennett Field is the only place in New York City where you can legally camp. There are campsites at the field's Ecology Village and within the pine grove, including an accessible campground for wheelchair users. Contact Ecology Village at (718) 338-4306 for information.

Gateway Greenhouse Education Center Community Gardens
The park is also home to the largest community garden in the country, with 480 plots. Schoolchildren, families, neighbors, and friends care for these gardens. The Gateway Greenhouse Education Center is a volunteer program that prepares trees, shrubs, and plants for life in city public spaces by growing them to a size more likely to survive urban conditions. For more information about the garden or the education center, contact the Floyd Bennett Garden Association at (718) 338-4255.

Other Users of the Field   The New York City Police Department and the New York City Sanitation Department use the runways of the Field for training. The Sanitation Department's training site has a compost area where seeds from nearby gardens and lawns have germinated. Watermelons, squash, zucchini, all kinds of gourds, cosmos, and morning glory are some of the plants that have taken hold here. Ring-necked pheasant have been observed near this site.

GETTING THERE

By Subway and Bus   From Manhattan, take the #2 subway to the last stop: Brooklyn College at Flatbush and Nostrand avenues. At the subway stop, take the Q35 bus from Nostrand Avenue in front of Lord's Bakery, which will take you south on Flatbush Avenue. Ask the bus driver to stop at the main entrance to Gateway National Recreation Area at Floyd Bennett Field. Cross Flatbush Avenue South at the traffic light. Walk into the Field past the booth at the entrance. Walk the long road on the left until you reach the Ryan Visitor Center on the left, which has an air control tower on its roof. There you can pick up some maps of the area. Floyd Bennett Field is a very large area to walk. Be prepared with good shoes, water, a sun hat in summer, and some food. In winter, dress warmly. It is practical to drive from area to area and walk small parts of the field. If you take public transportation, be aware that you will walk long distances.

By Car   From the Long Island Expressway, take Woodhaven Boulevard, which becomes Cross Bay Boulevard after crossing Rockaway Boulevard. Continue on until you reach the Belt Parkway. Take the parkway west to exit 11S, Flatbush Avenue South. Take Flatbush Avenue South about a mile to the light right before the Marine Parkway Bridge. Go left into the entrance to the Gateway National Recreation Area and Floyd Bennett Field. Drive past the entrance booth, turn left, and on your left you will see the Ryan Visitor Center where you can pick up additional maps.

From the Brooklyn-Queens Expressway get onto the Belt Parkway going south. Take Exit 11S to Flatbush Avenue South. Proceed about one mile to the traffic light right before the Marine Parkway Bridge. Go left into the entrance to the Gateway National Recreation Area and Floyd Bennett Field. Drive past the entrance booth, turn left and on your left you will see the Ryan Visitor Center.

Garden plots filled with summer blooms, nectaring bees, and butterflies at Floyd Bennett Field make up the largest community garden in the country.

Marine Park

LOCATION
Avenue U (south side) between Burnett and East 33rd streets

TELEPHONE
(718) 421-2021

SIZE
798 acres

HABITATS
salt marsh, Jamaica Bay, beach, Gerritsen Creek, wildflower meadows, sand dunes, beach plants, shrub and vine thickets

Natural History   Marine Park sits on the westernmost inlet of Jamaica Bay. The outwash plain of this area was formed by meltwater from the glacial ice sheet to the north. The barrier beaches of the Rockaway Peninsula protected the slowly forming Jamaica Bay from the Atlantic Ocean. Shallow saltwater inlets, such as the Gerritsen Inlet, pushed up into the marshland. Gerritsen Inlet is also fed by upland freshwater streams.

A great egret fishing in Gerritsen Creek at low tide with a backdrop of autumn-hued marsh grasses.

Human History   The brackish Gerritsen Inlet, created by fresh water mixing with salt water, supported oysters, Atlantic sturgeon, striped bass, and blue crabs, which were harvested by the local Canarsee Indians, who also hunted deer, waterfowl, and other animals of the marsh. With the arrival of the Dutch, this area became known for its wampum: cylindrical purple and white beads drilled from quahog shells. Valued by the native people and used by the European settlers as currency in exchange for beaver pelts, the abundant supply of quahog led to this area becoming the earliest permanent European settlement on Jamaica Bay. By 1624 the community was known as Nieuw Amersfoort, named after a city in Holland. The Dutch settlers raised livestock and farmed maize, squash, beans, and tobacco. In 1645, the Dutch farmer Hugh Gerritsen built the first tide-powered mill in North America. When George Washington's army was in Brooklyn, this mill ground flour

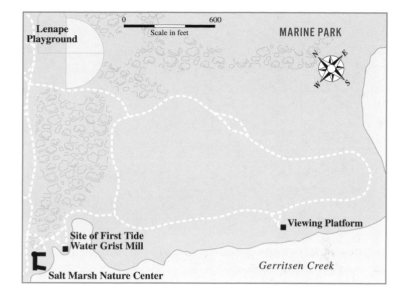

Lenape Playground

MARINE PARK

0 ————— 600
Scale in feet

Viewing Platform

Site of First Tide
Water Grist Mill

Gerritsen Creek

Salt Marsh Nature Center

for his troops. The mill operated until 1889. In 1935, it was burned by arsonists. The wooden pilings you can see crossing the creek at low tide are the remains of Gerritsen's mill. By 1900 there were plans to turn Jamaica Bay into a major shipping port. In 1917 two local men, Frederic B. Pratt and Alfred T. White, fearing that the Gerritsen Creek marshland would be completely developed, donated 140 acres to the city for a park. By 1937 the park, now called Marine Park, encompassed 1,822 acres.

In 1974, when the National Park Service created the Gateway National Recreation Area, the city transferred 1,024 acres of Marine Park to Gateway. Today the 798-acre Marine Park constitutes a natural preserve for a wide variety of wildlife throughout the seasons.

The Salt Marsh Nature Center at Marine Park   This environmental education and community center is managed by the New York City Urban Park Rangers. Its purpose is to educate the public about the natural and cultural history of Gerritsen Creek. Educational events, public programs, conferences, and community group meetings are held here.

View of Gerritsen's Inlet from the Salt Marsh Nature Center at Marine Park. Wooden pilings are remnants of the dam that created Dutch farmer Hugh Gerritsen's mill pond. Gerritsen's mill, the first tide-powered mill in America, operated from the seventeenth century until the late 1800s.

Nature Trail This one-mile-long trail will take you about forty minutes to walk. There are arrows and numbered post stops along the way. The salt marsh stretches out, green in summer, and brown in winter. Two salt-tolerant grasses, saltmarsh cordgrass and salt meadow cordgrass, thrive along the shore of Marine Park. At low tide, look for fiddler crabs as they emerge from their burrows to feed. In spring, summer, and fall, shorebirds such as least sandpipers, willets, ruddy turnstones, sanderlings, and greater yellowlegs probe the mudflats with their long bills for snails, shrimp, and crabs. From the platform at stop 6, you can view birds throughout the seasons. In winter, waterfowl such as common loons, Canada and brant geese, buffleheads, and red-breasted mergansers visit this protected inlet, which stays free of ice. During May and June, horseshoe crabs can be seen along the shore, mating and laying thousands of eggs, which migrating shorebirds feed on. In summer, great blue herons, great egrets, and black-crowned and yellow-crowned night herons fish the creek. Along the trail bloom abundant wildflowers such as seaside goldenrod, common milkweed, butterfly weed, and marsh elder. Marsh wrens weave their nests in the giant phragmites reeds. Cottontailed rabbits and ring-necked pheasants live in and around the creek.

By Car From the Long Island Expressway take the Woodhaven Boulevard exit toward the Rockaways. Woodhaven Boulevard turns into Cross Bay Boulevard. You will be on Woodhaven / Cross Bay Boulevard for five miles until you reach the Belt Parkway. Take the parkway west to exit 11N, Flatbush Avenue North. Take Flatbush Avenue North to Avenue U. Make a left onto Avenue U and continue west for ten blocks. Pass East 33rd Street and enter the parking lot on the right. You will see the Salt Marsh Nature Center directly across Avenue U. Or going east on the Belt Parkway, exit at Kings Plaza / Flatbush Avenue (11N), then follow the above directions from Flatbush Avenue North.

Yellow-crowned night heron near the nature trail along Gerritsen Creek in Marine Park.

By Subway and Bus From Brooklyn, take the M or D train to Avenue U station, then the eastbound B3 bus to Burnett Street and Avenue U. From the Bronx, Manhattan, or Brooklyn take the D train to Avenue U Station, then follow bus directions above.

By Bus From Brooklyn, take B46, B2, or B41 to Kings Plaza. Transfer to westbound B3 bus to Burnett Street and Avenue U.

Prospect Park

Natural History Fifty thousand years ago, the land that is now Prospect Park lay buried under one thousand feet of ice. When the ice retreated it left the terminal moraine—a long, hilly ridge that

A shaded, rocky perch overlooking Binnen Falls near the Boathouse in Prospect Park.

runs through Brooklyn, Queens, and Long Island. Prospect Park's northern border sits on this steep ridge, which over millennia formed rich forests, steep ravines, and rolling meadows. The southern border of the park sits on crushed rocks deposited by the retreating glacier and was used as the site for Prospect Park's sixty-acre lake. The retreating Wisconsin Ice Sheet left behind depressions created by submerged chunks of glacial ice that melted and formed kettle ponds. The planners of Prospect Park used these natural ponds as part of the watercourse, which also includes Fallkill Falls, the Ravine, the Lullwater, and Prospect Lake. Brooklyn is the most sparsely forested borough in New York City, and Prospect Park claims 150 acres of its last remaining native forest. This forest was preserved because park designers Frederick Law Olmsted and Calvert Vaux incorporated these woods into their plan. The Midwood, the forest sitting below the terminal moraine, was left mostly intact. The other forested area is the Ravine, which sits on the moraine and includes hills and kettle ponds with a stream that cuts through a steep valley.

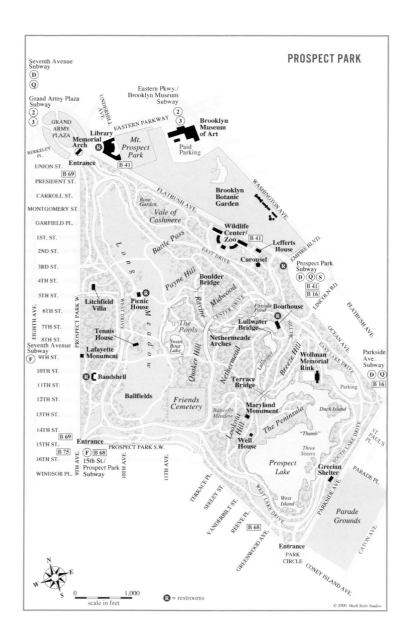

PROSPECT PARK

Seventh Avenue
Subway
Ⓓ Ⓠ

Grand Army Plaza
Subway
②
③

GRAND
ARMY
PLAZA

UNDERHILL AVE.

Eastern Pkwy./
Brooklyn Museum
Subway
②
③

Brooklyn
Museum
of Art

Paid
Parking

EASTERN PARKWAY

BERKELEY PL.

Library
Memorial Ⓡ
Arch

Mt.
Prospect
Park

UNION ST.   Entrance

B 41

PRESIDENT ST.

CARROLL ST.

MONTGOMERY ST.

GARFIELD PL.

1ST. ST.

2ND. ST.

3RD. ST.

4TH ST.

5TH ST.

6TH ST.

7TH ST.

8TH ST.
Seventh Avenue
Subway
Ⓕ 9TH ST.

10TH ST.

11TH ST.

12TH ST.

13TH ST.

14TH ST.

15TH ST.

16TH ST.

WINDSOR PL.

B 69

FLATBUSH AVE.

Rose
Garden

Vale of
Cashmere

Battle Pass

EAST DRIVE

Brooklyn
Botanic
Garden

WASHINGTON AVE.

Wildlife
Center/
Zoo   B 41

Carousel   Ⓡ

Lefferts
House

EMPIRE BLVD.

Prospect Park
Subway
Ⓓ Ⓠ Ⓢ
B 41
B 16

Long

Payne Hill

Ravine

Boulder
Bridge

Midwood

CENTER DRIVE

Pagoda
Pond   Boathouse

Lullwater
Bridge   Ⓡ

WEST DRIVE

Litchfield
Villa

Picnic
House   Ⓡ

Tennis
House

Meadow

The
Pools

Swan
Boat
Lake

Quaker Hill

Nethermeade
Arches

Nethermead

Lullwater

HILLTOP

LINCOLN RD.

FLATBUSH AVE.

OCEAN AVE.

Breeze Hill

East Lake Drive

Wollman
Memorial
Rink

Parking

Parkside
Ave.
Subway
Ⓓ Ⓠ
B 16

EIGHTH AVE.

PROSPECT PARK W.

Lafayette
Monument

Ⓡ Ⓒ Bandshell

Ballfields

Friends
Cemetery

Terrace
Bridge

Butterfly
Meadow

Maryland
Monument

Lookout Hill

The Peninsula

Duck Island

"Thumb"

Three
Sisters

ST.
PAUL'S
PL.

B 69

B 75   Ⓕ B 68

Entrance
PROSPECT PARK S.W.

15th St./
Prospect Park
Subway

9TH AVE.

10TH AVE.

11TH AVE.

TERRACE PL.

SEELEY ST.

VANDERBILT ST.

REEVE PL.

Well
House

Prospect
Lake

West
Island

Grecian
Shelter

SOUTH LAKE DRIVE

PARADE PL.

PARKSIDE AVE.

CATON AVE.

Parade
Grounds

B 68

WEST LAKE DRIVE

GREENWOOD AVE.

Entrance
PARK
CIRCLE

CONEY ISLAND AVE.

N
W   E
S

0   1,000

scale in feet

Ⓡ = restrooms

© 2000. Mark Stein Studios

PROSPECT PARK

53

Human History   A century before the park was created, it was the setting for the first major battle of the Revolutionary War. In August 1776, George Washington's army protected passes along Flatbush Avenue, on what is now the Park Drive, against the British, who controlled Manhattan Island. Although they lost the battle, they held the British long enough for Washington's troops to escape to New Jersey. The Maryland Monument at the base of Lookout Hill commemorates this "Battle of Long Island."

During the mid-nineteenth century the urban park movement reached Brooklyn. In 1866, Olmsted and Vaux, the architects of Central Park in Manhattan, submitted a plan for Prospect Park. The principal features included the Long Meadow, the Ravine, a sixty-acre lake, rolling green meadows, winding carriage drives with scenic lookouts, woodland waterfalls and springs, and a rich forest. Rustic shelters, arbors, bridges, and arches were constructed throughout the park. The Concert Grove House and Pavilion were built adjacent to the lake so that park visitors could enjoy music in a pastoral setting that included a wellhouse near Lookout Hill and a

The gentle Ambergill Stream, designed to look like a mountain stream, cuts through the Ravine and is shaded by recently planted native shrubs.

dairy with milking cows. When the park was completed in 1868, two million people came to enjoy what would become known as "Brooklyn's Jewel." Over the next thirty years, the Boathouse, the Tennis House, Picnic House, and Model Yacht Club were constructed. Parks Commissioner Robert Moses commissioned a zoo in 1935, a bandshell in 1939, and multiple playgrounds around the park's border. During this period of expansion, the park was overused and not cared for properly. In 1987 a group of concerned citizens formed the Prospect Park Alliance, which, along with the local community, the Parks Department, and private donors, has been doing remarkable work restoring Prospect Park. One of the truly significant accomplishments has been the completion of the landmark project at the Ravine. It is one of the largest restoration projects of public parkland in the country. As part of this work, they unearthed the waterfall that had been buried under ten feet of eroded soil. They prepared the ground for extensive native plantings selected by botanists. They removed much of the phragmites, thereby expanding the water area of the pools, and replaced them with cattails, water lilies, and other aquatic plants. The country's first urban Audubon Center opened in 2002 in the restored Boathouse on the lake.

Woodlands   Prospect Park is home to the only forest in Brooklyn. The enormous diversity of trees combined with wetlands provided by the watercourse attracts a wide range of wildlife, including thousands of migratory birds who stop in the park during spring and fall on their journey through the Atlantic flyway.

The Prospect Park Alliance has planted over twenty thousand mostly native trees and shrubs so that the ecosystem will become self-sustaining and even more valuable to local wildlife. There are trees in the park that date back from the time of the Revolution. The oldest tree is a 220-year-old black oak in the Ravine. The Alliance has designated these trees as "heritage trees." The park's most famous tree is the Camperdown Elm, a dwarfed, weeping elm planted in 1872 near the Boathouse and made famous by Brooklyn poet Marianne Moore. The genetic nature of this tree causes it to grow horizontally instead of vertically. Perhaps more than any other site in New York City, the Prospect Park woodland is a place to take in the grandeur of these native trees.

The Vale of Cashmere   Built around a natural kettle pond, the Vale, a formal, sunken garden, is located near Grand Army Plaza at the northeast corner of the park. Steps lead forty feet down to the pond. Birds that have been observed here include the worm-eating warbler, northern waterthrush, Louisiana waterthrush, and hooded warbler.

The Ravine   This was created along the terminal moraine of the glacier that retreated ten thousand years ago. Cut through by a gorge, the Ambergill Stream, and waterfalls, the Ravine is thick with oaks, black cherry, and sweet gum trees. Native shrubs such as elderberry and dogwood have been planted, providing food and shelter for wildlife. Year-round look for downy, hairy, and red-bellied woodpeckers and white-breasted nuthatches. In spring and summer vireos, thrushes, and warblers can be found here. No buildings or roads can be seen from the Ravine, which is located

The newly renovated Audubon Center at the Boathouse. Housed inside this historic New York City landmark is the Prospect Park's Visitor Center, a nature education center with interactive exhibits on birds and wildlife, and during summer, a starting point for boat trips down the Lullwater.

between the Long Meadow and the Nethermead. The closest park entrances are at 15th Street, 9th Street, and 3rd Street along Prospect Park West.

Wildflower Meadow at the Pools Park naturalists created this grassland habitat by planting native switchgrass, little bluestem, and Indian grass, along with wildflowers such as black-eyed Susan, beardtongue, goldenrod, and milkweed. This small, half-acre native garden attracts grassland birds, including song sparrows, white-crowned sparrows, field sparrows, Lincoln's sparrows, and indigo buntings. The wildflowers attract butterflies and other pollinating animals.

The Pools Thousands of native aquatic plants make the Pools a thriving ecosystem attracting wading birds such as great blue herons, and great egrets. Look for red-winged blackbirds in the summer, and many species of ducks, including the hooded merganser and ring-necked duck, in the winter. To get to the Pools and the Ravine, enter the park at the 3rd Street, 15th Street, or 9th Street / Prospect Park West entrances or the 16th Street / Prospect Park Southwest entrance.

The Nethermead Surrounding this rolling meadow located near the center of Prospect Park are some of the oldest trees in the park and mature lindens, sweetgums, and young cherry trees. Birders spot year-round and migratory birds, and the open sky makes this a good place to look for red-tails and other hawks. These raptors soar on thermals (warm updrafts of air) from nearby hills and hunt for pigeons and squirrels. Birds that forage in open areas on the edges of woods, such as robins, flickers, eastern phoebes, flycatchers, tree swallows, and occasionally an eastern bluebird, can be seen here. A dead branch in a pagoda tree just past the water fountain is a perch for falcons, including the American kestrel and the merlin. The Nethermead is accessible from the 16th Street / Prospect Park Southwest entrance, the Bartel-Pritchard entrance, the 9th Street entrance, the 3rd Street entrance, or the Willink entrance at Ocean and Flatbush avenues.

Long Meadow Nearly one mile in length, the Long Meadow is thought to be the longest meadow in any American park. The Long Meadow stretches from the park's northern end at Grand Army Plaza, to its western end at Prospect Park Southwest. The large oaks and American elm trees are filled with migrating warblers in the spring. Look under the trees where abundant leaf litter and the invertebrates that decompose the dead leaves attract white-throated sparrows, wood thrushes, and hermit thrushes. The Long Meadow is accessible from almost anywhere in the park, with the main entrances being Grand Army Plaza, Bartel-Pritchard Circle, and any entrance along Prospect Park West, such as 3rd Street or 9th Street.

The Audubon Center at the Boathouse A newly built facility dedicated to environmental preservation and nature education, the Audubon Center houses hands-on exhibits and programs for children and adults. Using interactive technology, the exhibits help visitors explore the natural world. The Center supplies maps and other materials you will need for a self-guided tour of the three major interpretive nature trails surrounding it, including printed and audio guides detailing the area's natural features, design, and history. On the weekends, large gondola-style boat rides with a tour guide are available from the "porch" of the Audubon Center and follow the watercourse all the way to the Lake. The park's visitor center is also located at the Audubon Center, with an information desk, café, and gift shop. The Brooklyn Bird Club holds its meetings there as well. The center is a result of a partnership between the Prospect Park Alliance and Audubon New York, the state office of the National Audubon Society. The Boathouse is located just inside the Lincoln Road / Ocean Avenue entrance to the park.

The Lullwater Nature Trail　The trail begins at the Audubon Center and follows the banks of the Lullwater, a peaceful waterway that is home to a variety of wildlife including ducks, herons, frogs, and turtles. The plants along the banks provide perching areas for songbirds, herons, and belted kingfishers. In summer, the calm Lullwater is covered with duckweed, which is eaten by mallard ducks and their ducklings. A rustic arbor recreated to resemble an original shelter by park designer Calvert Vaux serves as an outdoor classroom for the Audubon Center.

The Watercourse　Composed of bodies of water connected through a system of pools, streams, and waterfalls, the Watercourse terminates in the sixty-acre Prospect Lake. All the water in the park flows from one source, beginning at Fallkill Falls, then feeds into the Pools, which flow into the Ravine. The Ravine carries the water into the Lullwater, which then meanders gently downstream until it reaches the Lake.

The peaceful Lullwater drifts by the Rustic Shelter.

Prospect Lake　This feature of Prospect Park attracts a wide diversity of waterfowl. Year-round species include mallards, Canada geese, and herring gulls. Wood ducks and spotted sandpipers visit the Lake's islands, and in winter, more than ten species of ducks can be seen, including ruddy ducks and northern shovelers.

The Peninsula juts out into Prospect Lake, attracting a variety of waterfowl, including Canada geese, double-crested cormorants, and mallards. It is located on the northern edge of the lake, near the Lullwater and pedal boat rentals at Wollman Rink. To reach the Peninsula, enter the park through the Vanderbilt Street / Prospect Park Southwest entrance or the Lincoln Road / Ocean Avenue entrance and walk toward the interior of the park.

Lamppost No. 249　During the spring and fall migrations, bird watchers gather on Well House Drive next to lamppost no. 249. From here there is an unobstructed view of migrating birds over the southern slope of Lookout Hill. During migration, songbirds stop here to consume insects.

Prospect Park designers Frederick Law Olmsted and Charles Vaux created the Watercourse to resemble mountain streams and pools. After more than a century of use by parkgoers, the Prospect Park Alliance's massive restoration project has restored the Watercourse's beauty using native aquatic plants.

GETTING THERE

By Car In Brooklyn, take Flatbush Avenue to Grand Army Plaza. Go partway around the circle to Prospect Park West. There is free public parking at Prospect Park West and 5th Street at the Litchfield Villa. Or continue to Prospect Park Southwest and Parkside Avenue. Take Parkside Avenue to Ocean Avenue. Turn into the park entrance on the left, which leads to a free parking lot near the Wollman Rink.

By Subway From the Bronx, Brooklyn, and Manhattan, take the IRT #2 or #3 to Brooklyn's Grand Army Plaza stop. The park's main entrance is three hundred yards from this stop. Or take the IND Brooklyn-bound F train to the 15th Street Prospect Park stop. Enter the park and follow Center Drive to Lookout Hill. Or take the IND Brooklyn-bound D or Q train to the 7th Avenue stop near Grand Army Plaza; or the Prospect Park stop near the Zoo, or the Parkside Avenue stop near the Lake.

By Bus In Brooklyn take the B41, which runs on Flatbush Avenue to the park. Or take the B68 bus that runs along Prospect Park Southwest, the B69 that runs south along Prospect Park West, or the B165 that runs along Ocean Avenue.

MANHATTAN

Central Park

LOCATION
Central Park South (59th Street) to 110th Street;
5th Avenue to Central Park West
TELEPHONE
Central Park Conservancy: (212) 310-6600
SIZE
843 acres
HABITATS
meadows, grassy hills, woodlands, lakes, ponds, ravines, streams,
rocky outcroppings and crags, a reservoir, wildflower gardens and
formal French, Italian, and English gardens, a zoo

Natural History   Over the last million years a succession of
glaciers eroded the land of Manhattan Island, polishing its bedrock
and leaving grooves in the exposed outcrops of Manhattan schist.
Glaciers flowing from the north-northwest and north-northeast and
then from the northwest to the southeast, carried large boulders,
some from great distances and some from as close as the Palisades,
and left them perched on the landscape that is now Central Park.
Many of the park's exposed outcrops of rock show glacial polishing
as well as grooves carved from the rocks and debris carried by the ice
sheets as they moved south over the land.

Human History   Before 1858, the area that is now Central Park
was a swamp. Frederick Law Olmsted and Calvert Vaux transformed
this swampy, rocky area into America's first "people's park." In
doing so, however, Seneca Village, New York City's first major
community of African American property holders, which thrived
between 82nd and 89th streets from 1825 to 1857, in what is now
Central Park, was demolished to make way for Central Park. The city
had been developed only to 38th Street when construction began on
Central Park at 59th Street. The designers believed in the power of
nature to lift the people's spirit from the dreariness of city life, creating the first significant park in the United States designed for public use. Central Park was considered a rural getaway for the masses
crammed into the tenements of lower Manhattan. Olmsted called
the dream of Central Park "a democratic development of the highest
significance." In 1965 Central Park was designated a National Historic Landmark, and in 1998 the National Audubon Society designated it an Important Bird Area in New York State. Two hundred and

seventy-five bird species have been identified in the park; 192 species live in the park year-round or are frequently observed in the park. Birders too, are frequent visitors to the park: during spring migration, more than five hundred people at a time sometimes bird in the Ramble, an internationally renowned sanctuary for birds in the middle of the park.

Central Park is a masterpiece. It took twenty thousand workers sixteen years to complete this marvel of landscape architecture. More than five million cubic yards of stone and soil were moved and millions of trees, shrubs, vines, and wildflowers were planted. Ponds, lakes, and streams were created, as were thirty beautiful bridges and arches and eleven overpasses that cross the sunken transverses, allowing traffic to cross the park east to west without interfering with the more than fifty-eight miles of pedestrian paths. The park fell into a state of disrepair during the city's fiscal crisis of the 1970s. In 1980 the Central Park Conservancy, a nonprofit organization formed by Betsey Barlow Rogers and other concerned citizens, was created to save the park. They are presently responsible for two-thirds of the park's budget. The Conservancy has restored Central Park and made it, once again, a masterpiece. More than twenty-five million people visit the park each year. Many birdwatchers bird in the park on their way to work or join guided walks with leaders from one of the many organizations offering nature walks. Among these groups are the New York City Audubon Society, the Brooklyn Bird Club, the American Museum of Natural History, the Linnean Society of New York, the Torrey Botanical Society, the New York Mycological Society, the Central Park Conservancy, the Urban Park Rangers, and the Natural Resources Group of the New York City Parks Department.

Bethesda Fountain, Central Park Lake (also known as Rowboat Lake), and the shoreline of the Ramble in early spring.

Standing across the park from each other are two of the city's and the world's greatest museums: the American Museum of Natural History on Central Park West between 77th Street and 81st

Bow Bridge, considered one of the most beautiful cast-iron bridges in the world, spans Central Park Lake midpark. Ducks, geese, swans, and cormorants swim beneath it year-round. Turtles bask on emergent rocks along the shore as rowboats glide beneath during spring, summer, and fall.

Street, and the Metropolitan Museum of Art, which is inside the park on 5th Avenue between 80th and 84th streets.

LOWER PARK: 59TH STREET TO 72ND STREET

The 59th Street Pond In 2001, the Central Park Conservancy completed a $4 million reconstruction of the pond at 59th Street and 5th Avenue. The 11.5-acre restoration included shoreline and upland plantings, a new island habitat for birds and turtles, a waterfall, and a series of cascades on the west side of the pond.

Hallett Nature Sanctuary In 1934, Parks Commissioner Robert Moses created a 3.4-acre nature sanctuary known as the Promontory because of its rocky outcrop projecting into the pond. In 1986 it was renamed the Hallett Nature Sanctuary by Parks Commissioner Henry J. Stern, in honor of George Hervey Hallett, Jr. (1895–1985), an avid birdwatcher and city nature lover, but it is often informally known as the Bird Sanctuary. Surrounded by a fence, the sanctuary is open for special tours.

The Central Park Lake   Often called the Rowboat Lake, the lake stretches from 72nd Street to 79th Street and sits in the middle of the park. You can rent a rowboat at the Loeb Boathouse and row alongside swans, ducks, geese, cormorants, and gulls. Egrets and herons fish the shores, and carp, pumpkinseed, largemouth bass, and bluegill sunfish swim below. At twenty-two acres, the lake is Central Park's largest body of water excluding the reservoir. Olmsted and Vaux created the lake to provide boating in the summer and ice skating in the winter. In December 1858, while the rest of Central Park was under construction, the lake was opened for ice skating. The opening sparked an instant ice skating craze. According to an account in the park's annual report, as many as forty thousand people skated on the lake in one day. To let New Yorkers know that the lake's ice was frozen, a ball was raised to the top of a pole near the bell tower of what is now Belvedere Castle, and the downtown trolleys would fly red flags, signaling that the ice in Central Park was ready. The Wollman Rink opened in 1951, and ice skating was no longer allowed on the lake.

In winter, wood ducks, red-breasted mergansers, and hooded mergansers can be seen on the lake, along with the year-round mallards, black ducks, Canada geese, and mute swans. A peninsula called Hernshead juts out into the western shore of the lake near 77th Street. Olmsted and Vaux named it Hernshead because it resembled the head of a heron, or "hern" in Old Eng-

The Lake in Central Park with views of cherry trees in bloom, new spring leaves, and midtown Manhattan.

lish. Granite and Manhattan schist outcrops rise from the edge of this peninsula, and the views of the lake and midtown Manhattan from atop these outcrops are gorgeous. Perennials like cardinal flowers, New York ironweed, joe-pye weed, and blue vervain have been planted on the shores of Hernshead, and in summer, pollinating butterflies and bees work the flowers, while dragonflies and damselflies hunt smaller insects. In spring, flowers such as crocuses, bluebells, irises, and daffodils bloom throughout the area. The Ladies Pavilion, a Victorian wrought-iron structure designed in 1871

CENTRAL PARK

63

as a shelter for people waiting for horse-drawn carriages near Columbus Circle, was moved to this site in 1912.

Turtle Pond, which sits beneath the Manhattan schist outcrop known as Vista Rock and Belvedere Castle at the southern end of the Great Lawn, was, before the 1930s, part of the Croton Reservoir in the park. In the 1930s the reservoir was filled in, and the Great Lawn and Belvedere Lake were created. In 1987 this small lake was renamed Turtle Pond. In 1997 the Parks Department restored the Great Lawn and Turtle Pond, which they dredged, reshaped, and landscaped. Plants such as lizard's tail, bullrush, turtlehead, and blueflag iris, providing habitat for birds, insects, amphibians, and reptiles, were planted along the shore. Turtle Island was added, providing wildlife habitat such as sand for turtles to lay their eggs and nesting and foraging sites for birds. A dock and bird blind extends out to the pond, affording a view of basking red-eared sliders and painted turtles, foraging herons, and other waterfowl. During winter, when the water is not frozen, many overwintering birds can be seen in Turtle Pond, including bufflehead ducks, and hooded mergansers.

Vista Rock and Belvedere Castle   Sitting 130 feet high over Turtle Pond, Vista Rock is the second highest Manhattan schist outcrop in Central Park (the highest being the 137 1/2- foot Summit Rock at Central Park West and 83rd Street). Belvedere Castle sits on top of these massive outcrops. Designed as a Victorian fantasy, the castle is now home to the Henry Luce Nature Observatory and is operated by the Central Park Conservancy. In the nature room on the first floor, children can observe resident turtles. Visitors can borrow a nature backpack, which contains a map of the Ramble, the *Peterson Field Guide to Birds*, and a pair of binoculars. On the second floor, sculptures of birds seen in Central Park hang from the ceiling and roost in the branches of a tree. By pushing a button on a recording box, you can listen to the songs belonging to the birds in the tree.

The Ramble   The thirty-eight-acre Ramble, called a "wild garden" by Olmsted, features rocky outcrops, wooded hills, rambling paths, peaceful coves around the lake, a pond, and a stream called the Gill. The Ramble is an internationally renowned site for seeing birds. Over two hundred species have been identified, particularly during spring and fall migrations. Woodland species of butterflies, such as the mourning cloak, can be seen in the Ramble. Another good spot for viewing butterflies is the Shakespeare Garden, just west of Belvedere Castle. Every plant mentioned in Shake-

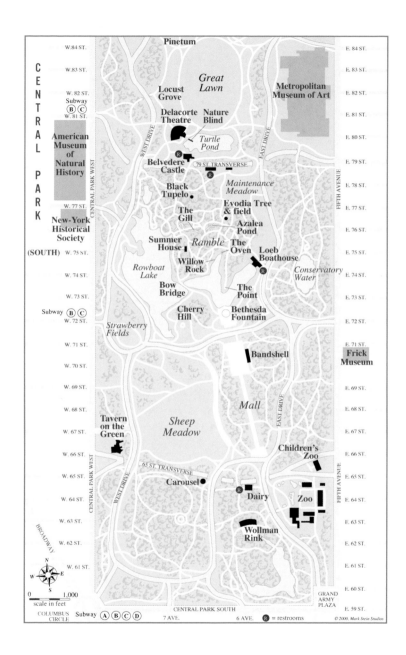

CENTRAL PARK

Pinetum

W. 84 ST.   E. 84 ST.

W. 83 ST.   E. 83 ST.

Great Lawn

W. 82 ST.   Locust Grove   Metropolitan Museum of Art   E. 82 ST.

Subway **B C**

W. 81 ST.   Delacorte Theatre   Nature Blind   E. 81 ST.

American Museum of Natural History   Turtle Pond   E. 80 ST.

Belvedere Castle   79 ST. TRANSVERSE   E. 79 ST.

Black Tupelo   *Maintenance Meadow*   E. 78 ST.

W. 77 ST.   Evodia Tree & field   E. 77 ST.

New-York Historical Society   The Gill   Azalea Pond   E. 76 ST.

Summer House   *Ramble*   The Oven   Loeb Boathouse   E. 75 ST.

(SOUTH) W. 75 ST.

Rowboat Lake   Willow Rock   *Conservatory Water*   E. 74 ST.

W. 74 ST.

Bow Bridge   The Point   E. 73 ST.

W. 73 ST.

Subway **B C**   Cherry Hill   Bethesda Fountain   E. 72 ST.

W. 72 ST.

Strawberry Fields   E. 71 ST.

W. 71 ST.   Bandshell   Frick Museum

W. 70 ST.   E. 70 ST.

W. 69 ST.   E. 69 ST.

W. 68 ST.   *Mall*   E. 68 ST.

Tavern on the Green   *Sheep Meadow*   E. 67 ST.

W. 67 ST.   Children's Zoo   E. 66 ST.

W. 66 ST.

W. 65 ST.   65 ST. TRANSVERSE   E. 65 ST.

Carousel   Dairy   Zoo   E. 64 ST.

W. 64 ST.

W. 63 ST.   E. 63 ST.

Wollman Rink   E. 62 ST.

W. 62 ST.

W. 61 ST.   E. 61 ST.

N W E S

0   1,000
scale in feet   E. 60 ST.

GRAND ARMY PLAZA   E. 59 ST.

COLUMBUS CIRCLE   Subway **A B C D**   CENTRAL PARK SOUTH

7 AVE.   6 AVE.   **R** = restrooms   © 2000. Mark Stein Studios

CENTRAL PARK WEST   WEST DRIVE   EAST DRIVE   FIFTH AVENUE   BROADWAY

CENTRAL PARK

65

Beautifully serene in every season, the Pool is an idyllic pond at 100th Street and Central Park West.

speare's works can be found in this garden. Within the heart of the Ramble, it is hard to believe you are in Manhattan, and you can easily become lost in the maze of paths. As you get closer to 5th Avenue or Central Park West, you can see buildings. Maps of the Ramble are available at Belvedere Castle.

The Gill Named after the Scottish word for "stream," the Gill starts in the middle of the Ramble, widens to form Azalea Pond, and then winds downstream and empties into the lake. Many birds can be seen bathing in the shallow Gill. Large and mature azalea bushes flower each May near the pond, and perennial herbs and shrubs have been planted along the shore. Bird feeders hang from trees nearby and are filled with seed throughout the winter by local birders.

Jacqueline Kennedy Onassis Reservoir This 106-acre body of water is 40 feet deep and holds over a billion gallons. Under the jurisdiction of the New York City Department of Environmental Protection, it is no longer used as a reservoir. It does provide fresh water to the Pool, the Loch, and the Harlem Meer, connecting bodies of water in the northern park. There is a running track around the reservoir, which is a good place to view many species of waterfowl, including loons and grebes, particularly during the winter.

UPPER PARK: 96TH STREET TO 110TH STREET

The Wildflower Meadow The meadow was created as a perennial garden with native species of wildflowers such as common milkweed and goldenrods to attract butterflies, hummingbirds, and other pollinating animals.

The Pool A freshwater pond stretching from 100th to 103rd Street, from Central Park West toward the middle of the park, the pool is one of the most beautiful sites in the park. With weeping willow trees along its shoreline, it invokes a feeling of serenity. A stand of cattails grows along the southern edge of the Pool, and green frogs and bullfrogs live in the water. Herons and egrets fish along the shores, and mallards and wood ducks can also be observed. There are some notable trees along its banks, including a large, bald cypress tree with knobby "knees" emerging from the soil at the far western edge near Central Park West, and several gorgeous red maples whose leaves are aflame in fall.

The Loch   At the eastern end of the Pool, a cascading waterfall spills into a stream known as the Loch. Follow the path alongside the Loch under Glenspan Arch and east through the North Woods. Glossy ibis forage in the Loch and you can see many birds bathing in this oftentimes shallow stream. The Ravine is the name of the wooded valley at the north end of the park through which the Loch winds as it heads east before spilling into the lake known as the Harlem Meer. The Ravine includes the North Woods, which is filled with birds and other wildlife.

The Meer   Named after the Dutch word for "small sea," the Meer is an eleven-acre lake stretching from 110th Street to 106th Street and 5th Avenue to

Cascading waterfalls grace the Loch, a stream that starts at the eastern edge of the Pool, flows through the wooded valley known as the Ravine, and ends at the Harlem Meer.

The Dana Discovery Center, a Victorian-style jewel built in 1993 sits on the northern shore of the Harlem Meer near 110th Street and Fifth Avenue and offers free environmental education programs through the Central Park Conservancy.

Lenox Avenue. At its southeastern corner, just across the path from the Conservatory Garden, you'll find a cove with steps leading to the water.

A variety of specimen trees grow on the eastern shore of the Meer, including massive European beeches, bald cypresses, turkey oaks, and black locusts. Native wildflowers such as joe-pye weed and New York ironweed bloom along the southern shore. Native aquatic plants such as arrow arum and pickerelweed emerge from the water, and buffleheads, ruddy ducks, and mergansers winter on the Meer.

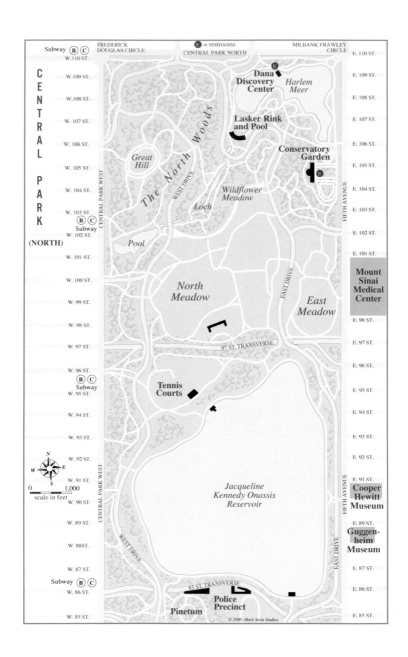

Subway Ⓑ Ⓒ

FREDERICK
DOUGLAS CIRCLE

Ⓡ = restrooms
CENTRAL PARK NORTH

MILBANK FRAWLEY
CIRCLE

E. 110 ST.

W. 110 ST.

C
E
N
T
R
A
L

P
A
R
K

(NORTH)

W. 109 ST.

W. 108 ST.

W. 107 ST.

W. 106 ST.

W. 105 ST.

W. 104 ST.

W. 103 ST.
Ⓑ Ⓒ
Subway
W. 102 ST.

W. 101 ST.

W. 100 ST.

W. 99 ST.

W. 98 ST.

W. 97 ST.

W. 96 ST.
Ⓑ Ⓒ
Subway
W. 95 ST.

W. 94 ST.

W. 93 ST.

W. 92 ST.

W. 91 ST.

W. 90 ST.

W. 89 ST.

W. 88 ST.

W. 87 ST.

Subway Ⓑ Ⓒ
W. 86 ST.

W. 85 ST.

Dana
Discovery
Center

Harlem
Meer

E. 109 ST.

E. 108 ST.

Lasker Rink
and Pool

E. 107 ST.

E. 106 ST.

Conservatory
Garden

E. 105 ST.

Great
Hill

The North Woods

WEST DRIVE

Wildflower
Meadow

E. 104 ST.

FIFTH AVENUE

Loch

E. 103 ST.

E. 102 ST.

Pool

E. 101 ST.

North
Meadow

EAST DRIVE

East
Meadow

Mount
Sinai
Medical
Center

E. 98 ST.

97 ST. TRANSVERSE

E. 97 ST.

E. 96 ST.

Tennis
Courts

E. 95 ST.

E. 94 ST.

E. 93 ST.

E. 92 ST.

N
W   E
S

0   1,000
scale in feet

CENTRAL PARK WEST

E. 91 ST.

Jacqueline
Kennedy Onassis
Reservoir

FIFTH AVENUE

Cooper
Hewitt
Museum

E. 89 ST.

Guggen-
heim
Museum

E. 87 ST.

WEST DRIVE

EAST DRIVE

85 ST. TRANSVERSE

E. 86 ST.

Pinetum

Police
Precinct

© 2000, Mark Stein Studios

E. 85 ST.

In summer egrets and herons fish from Duck Island, a small island in the southwestern part of the lake. The Meer has been stocked with sunfish, including largemouth bass, pumpkinseed, and bluegill.

The Charles A. Dana Discovery Center sits on the northeastern shore of the Meer at 110th Street and Fifth Avenue. Modeled in the Victorian style, this visitor's center houses a classroom for children's programs upstairs, and downstairs the Great Hall displays nature exhibits of the local flora and fauna.

House sparrows bathe in the Secret Garden fountain on a hot August afternoon in the English Garden, part of the six-acre Conservatory Garden along upper Fifth Avenue.

The Center offers free family and community programs year round.

The Conservatory Garden encompasses six acres of formal French, Italian, and English gardens along 5th Avenue south of the Meer from 106th Street to 103rd Street.

GETTING THERE

By Car   If you are lucky enough to find a spot, park on the East Side or West Side, from 50th to 110th streets.

By Bus   The #10 bus goes up and down Central Park West. The #1, #2, #3, and #4 go down 5th Avenue and up Madison Avenue.

By Subway   The IRT #1 train stops along Broadway from Columbus Circle at West 59th Street, which is across the street from Central Park and upstairs from the A, B, C, and D lines, up to West 110th Street. The express #2 and #3 stop at West 72nd Street and West 96th Street. The Lexington Line IRT local #6 stops along Lexington Avenue from East 59th Street to East 110th Street. The express #4 and #5 stop at East 59th Street and East 96th Street. The IND Line B train stops along Central Park West at 59th Street, 72nd Street, 81st Street, 86th Street, 96th Street, 103rd Street, and 110th Street.

Inwood Hill Park

LOCATION
Bordered by the Henry Hudson Parkway on the west; the Harlem River on the north; Seaman Avenue, 214th and 218th streets, and Indian Road on the east; and Dyckman Street on the south

TELEPHONE
Urban Nature Center: (212) 304-2365

SIZE
196 acres

HABITATS
saltwater marsh, native flowers, meadows, forest, boulders, caves

Inwood Hill Park's caves were used as gathering sites for local native people.

Natural History   Glacial activity sculpted Inwood Hill Park's distinctive caves, valleys, and rocky ridges. Schist, gneiss, and marble can be seen here. White Inwood marble, visible on the northeast corner of Seaman Avenue and Isham Street, was named for the neighborhood of Inwood Hill Park. Veins of marble once connected Manhattan to the Bronx. Inwood marble, softer than schist and gneiss, eroded over time and was washed away by local rivers. As a result, the Hudson, Harlem, and East rivers eventually surrounded Manhattan Island. As glacial ice melted, boulders toppled, forming caves in the park where local Native Americans gathered. Artifacts and shell middens have been found here, and many of these artifacts can be seen at the Museum of the American Indian in lower Manhattan. Glacial meltwater also carved holes in the boulders. The largest glacial pothole in the city can be found in Inwood Hill Park.

Human History   Human activity in Inwood Hill Park can be traced from prehistoric times. The Lenape inhabited the area and fished the Hudson and Harlem rivers. Historic activities took place here, such as the planting of a tulip tree at the site where the Lenape Indians reportedly first met with Henry Hudson. It is thought that Dutch governor Peter Minuit, purchased Manhattan Island from the Indians at this site in 1626. This tulip tree was revered by the

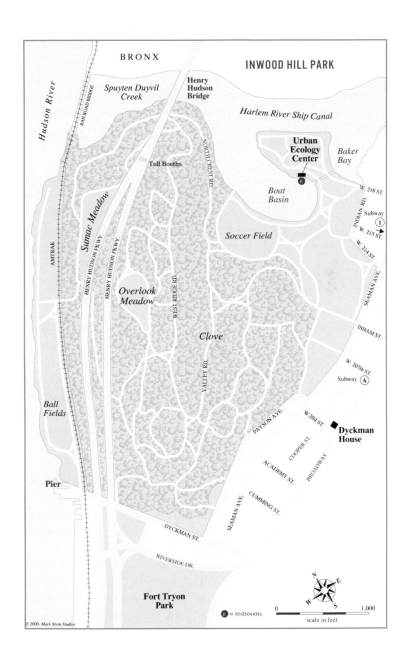

INWOOD HILL PARK

BRONX

Hudson River

Spuyten Duyvil Creek

Henry Hudson Bridge

Harlem River Ship Canal

RAILROAD BRIDGE

NORTH CREST RD.

Toll Booths

Urban Ecology Center

Baker Bay

Boat Basin

W. 218 ST.

Sumac Meadow

AMTRAK

HENRY HUDSON PKWY.

HENRY HUDSON PKWY.

Soccer Field

INDIAN RD.

Subway ①

W. 215 ST.

W. 214 ST.

Overlook Meadow

WEST RIDGE RD.

Clove

SEAMAN AVE.

ISHAM ST.

W. 207th ST.

Subway Ⓐ

VALLEY RD.

Ball Fields

W. 204 ST.

PAYSON AVE.

Dyckman House

COOPER ST.

BROADWAY

ACADEMY ST.

Pier

SEAMAN AVE.

CUMMING ST.

DYCKMAN ST.

RIVERSIDE DR.

Fort Tryon Park

Ⓡ = restrooms

N
W E
S

0   1,000
scale in feet

© 2000, Mark Stein Studios

Inwood Hill Park's large glacial pothole can be found along the Eastern Ridge Walk in the Clove.

Wiechquaeskeck, the local native people. The tree lived for almost three hundred years until it was destroyed by the hurricane of 1938. A boulder at the site of the tree now bears a plaque attesting to the site's natural and human history. Inwood Hill became a city park in 1916.

Urban Nature Center Be sure to spend some time inside this educational nature center. Well-maintained tanks with local animals, including blue crabs, sheepshead minnows, shore shrimp, and a beautiful eastern box turtle, can be found here. The staff are caring and helpful.

Salt Marsh Walk Walk along the saltwater marsh where you'll find both saltmarsh cordgrass and saltwater cordgrass and two species of bulrush. Between the low marsh and the park path are a number of marsh plants rarely found in the city, including water hemp and salt marsh bulrush. At low tide, mudflats run from the marsh to the channel of the Harlem River. Great blue herons and great and snowy egrets can be observed here from spring through fall.

Eastern Ridge Walk At the southwest corner of the soccer field take the path on the left up into the Clove. You will pass the boulder holding the plaque at the site of the ancient tulip tree. As you walk up the Valley Road you will pass beneath the Native American cave outcroppings. Stay to your right and you will walk through Manhattan's most ancient forest. Throughout spring the ground is carpeted with native wildflowers such as Dutchman's breeches, trillium, and bloodroot. Flowering plants attract unusually high numbers and diverse species of butterflies, including tiger swallowtails, parsnip swallowtails, blue sulphur, skippers, and other pollinating invertebrates. These support insect-eating birds such as indigo buntings, warblers, woodpeckers, and thrushes.

Western Ridge Walk Enormous copper and European beeches, tulip trees, red, chestnut, white oaks, and a huge ginkgo tree can be found here. Walk to the Overlook Meadow and look west at spectacular views of the Hudson River and the Palisades.

Early spring in the Clove. The ecologically important spicebush trees bear tiny yellow flowers. Many birds consume their red berries, and the caterpillar of the spicebush swallowtail butterfly feeds on their leaves.

GETTING THERE

By Subway Take the A train to 207th Street and Broadway (the last stop). Walk west two blocks to Seaman Avenue. You have a choice of walking one block north to Isham Street and entering the park, or walking north on Seaman another long block to Indian Road, then walking west on Indian Road to enter the park at 218th Street. You can also take the IRT #1 train to 215th Street and Broadway. Walk to 218th Street and then west four blocks to Indian Road and the park entrance at 218th Street.

By Bus Take the M100 to Dyckman Street from 124th Street and 3rd Avenue.

By Car Take Henry Hudson Parkway to Dyckman Street. Take Dyckman Street five blocks east to Broadway and turn left. Follow Broadway north to 218th Street and turn left. Then take 218th Street west four blocks. Parking spots can usually be found near the park.

Riverside Park South

LOCATION
West 59th Street to West 72nd Street along the Hudson River
SIZE
27.5 acres
HABITATS
ornamental grasses; manicured lawns; willow, birch, red maple, and linden trees; meandering wooden boardwalks surrounded by marsh grasses; river coves; the Hudson River

Human History Designed by landscape architect Thomas Balsley, Riverside Park South was first created in 2000 as part of the development of Trump Place. The park continues to be funded and maintained by the developer. A con-

Riverside Park South and its winding boardwalk and ornamental grasses.

tinuation of Riverside Park, this lovely park stretches from 72nd Street to 59th Street. All along the river are little piers and park benches, offering many places to sit and contemplate the river, waterfowl, beautiful trees, ornamental grasses, and wildflowers. A 715-foot pier with spectacular views and an undulating, wave-like edge extends out into the Hudson River. Celebrating the maritime and railroad history of New York City, piers and metal structures that once connected cargo ships to the New York Central Railroad's West 60th Street Yard have been preserved, marked by historical plaques. A restored 1946 locomotive train sits in the park. Resting on a grassy promontory along the river at about 62nd Street sits a large sundial crossed with shadow lines that mark the spring, summer, autumnal, and winter equinoxes.

GETTING THERE
By Subway Take the IRT subway #1, #2, or #3 to 72nd Street. Walk west down 72nd Street and enter park. Walk through tunnel then down steps. Turn left at the river.

By Bus The #5 bus runs along Riverside Drive in both directions. Get off at 72nd Street and Riverside Drive.

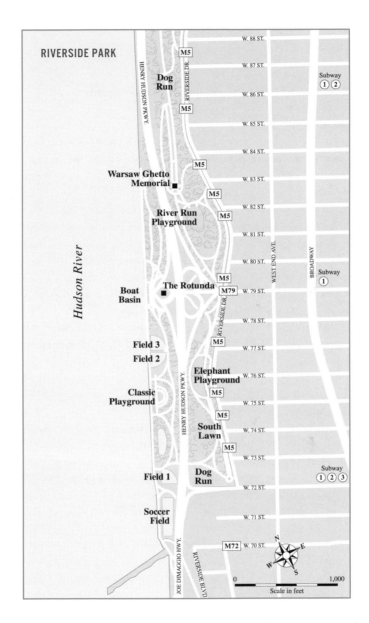

RIVERSIDE PARK

Dog Run
M5
M5
HENRY HUDSON PKWY.
RIVERSIDE DR.
Warsaw Ghetto Memorial ■
M5
River Run Playground
M5
M5
Hudson River
Boat Basin
The Rotunda ■
M5
M79
RIVERSIDE DR.
Field 3
Field 2
M5
Elephant Playground
M5
Classic Playground
HENRY HUDSON PKWY.
South Lawn
M5
M5
Field 1
Dog Run
Soccer Field
JOE DIMAGGIO HWY.
RIVERSIDE BLVD.
M72

W. 88 ST.
W. 87 ST.
W. 86 ST.
W. 85 ST.
W. 84 ST.
W. 83 ST.
W. 82 ST.
W. 81 ST.
W. 80 ST.
W. 79 ST.
W. 78 ST.
W. 77 ST.
W. 76 ST.
W. 75 ST.
W. 74 ST.
W. 73 ST.
W. 72 ST.
W. 71 ST.
W. 70 ST.

WEST END AVE.
BROADWAY

Subway ① ②
Subway ①
Subway ① ② ③

N
E
W
S

0   1,000
Scale in feet

By Car   Driving south on the West Side Highway, exit at the 79th Street Boat Basin. Driving north on the West Side Highway, exit at 72nd Street.

By Foot or Bicycle   Enter the park at 59th Street along the river.

Riverside Park

LOCATION
Hudson River to Riverside Drive; West 72nd Street to
West 158th Street

TELEPHONE
Riverside Park Administrator: (212) 408-0264; Riverside Park Fund:
(212) 870-3070; 79th Street Boat Basin: (212) 496-2105

SIZE
323 acres

HABITATS
deciduous trees; the brackish estuary and tidal Hudson River, which
runs along the park's entire western edge; a large stand of mature
American elm trees along Riverside Drive; gardens: 91st Street;
138th Street; Warsaw Ghetto Memorial and garden along West-side
Highway 79th–83rd streets; native perennial wildflowers; bird
sanctuary from 116th Street to 124th Street

Natural History   During the thousands of years that Native
Americans lived, fished, and farmed on the island of Manhattan, the
area now known as the Upper West Side, with the Hudson River
running along its western shores, was a heavily forested and rocky
landscape with streams spilling over the rocky ledges into the Hudson River below.

Human History   In 1873 Frederick Law Olmsted, the designer
and builder of Central Park, began building the first stage of Riverside Park, which stretched from 72nd Street to 125th Street. Olmsted
designed the upper terrace and the lovely, winding Riverside Drive
with beautiful views of the Hudson River hundreds of feet below. In
1937 designers Gilmore Clarke and Clinton Lloyd, working under
Parks Commissioner Robert Moses, added 134 acres to Riverside
Park, which now stretched to 158th Street. By creating a new shoreline, a six-lane West Side Highway separating the upper and lower
parks, a marina (the 79th Street Boat Basin), ball fields, monuments,
and playgrounds, Moses gave the users of the park recreational
facilities. In 1986 grassroots neighborhood activists formed the
Friends of Riverside Park (since renamed The Riverside Park Fund)
to work in cooperation with the New York City Department of Parks
and Recreation to restore and maintain Riverside Park.

River Esplanade Walk (West 72nd Street to West 83rd Street) Come into the park at 72nd Street and Riverside Drive. Walk past the Eleanor Roosevelt statue, head west under the West Side Highway bridge, and walk down the ramp past the running track to the Hudson River. Looking north you will see the 79th Street Boat Basin marina. Looking west you'll see the Hudson River, almost a mile wide at this point. Year-round on the river you may see Canada geese, mallards, and black ducks. The summer brings diving double-crested cormorants, common terns, and great black-backed gulls. Summer is the time to look at the surface of the river for lion's mane jellyfish that drift up and down

Manhattan's Riverside Park runs alongside the mighty and historic Hudson River. Because of the Clean Water Act, all of the native fishes, including striped bass, American shad, white perch, menhaden, and northern pipefish, have returned to the Hudson.

with the currents. You may see a cormorant surface with an American eel in its bill. Winter waterfowl include canvasback ducks, gadwalls, bufflehead ducks, and red-breasted mergansers. During extremely cold winters, you may see a harbor seal or harp seal haul out onto the Hudson's floating ice.

Land birds that can be seen year-round are red-tailed hawks, mockingbirds, blue jays, northern cardinals, house sparrows, and house finches.

When you first walk into the park at 72nd Street, and again at 79th Street, you will see a number of American linden trees. In

A young harp seal on river ice at the 79th Street Boat Basin.

late June their fragrant blossoms permeate the air with a heady, sweet perfume. Coming down to the lower park you will find a stand of American sycamores and London plane trees by the river, just south of a long line of crabapple trees. These bloom in late April and early May from the ballfield north to just before the 83rd Street tunnel that leads you to the upper promenade.

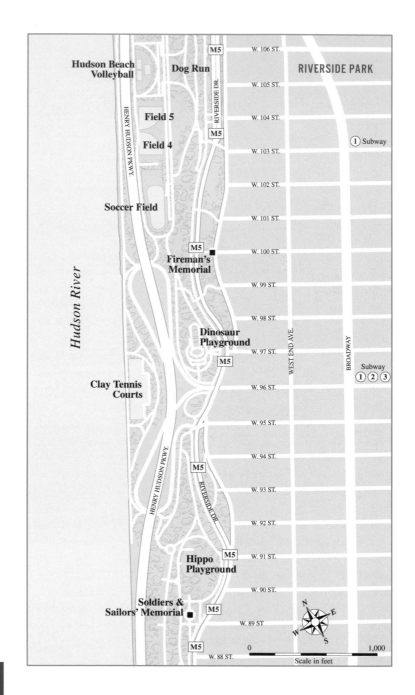

Hudson Beach Volleyball

Dog Run

M5

W. 106 ST.

RIVERSIDE PARK

W. 105 ST.

RIVERSIDE DR.

Field 5

W. 104 ST.

M5

Field 4

W. 103 ST.

1 Subway

HENRY HUDSON PKWY.

W. 102 ST.

W. 101 ST.

Soccer Field

W. 100 ST.

M5

Fireman's Memorial

W. 99 ST.

W. 98 ST.

Hudson River

Dinosaur Playground

WEST END AVE.

BROADWAY

W. 97 ST.

M5

Subway
1 2 3

Clay Tennis Courts

W. 96 ST.

W. 95 ST.

W. 94 ST.

HENRY HUDSON PKWY.

M5

W. 93 ST.

RIVERSIDE DR.

W. 92 ST.

W. 91 ST.

M5

Hippo Playground

W. 90 ST.

N
E
W
S

Soldiers & Sailors' Memorial

M5

W. 89 ST

M5

W. 88 ST.

0

1,000

Scale in feet

This trumpet creeper vine covers the lamppost at the southeastern edge of the octagonal community garden plot in Riverside Park around W. 91st Street. The trumpet-shaped red-orange flowers attract ruby-throated hummingbirds.

Promenade Walk To get from the River Esplanade to the upper promenade, go through the 83rd Street tunnel, turn left, and head north up the ramp to the promenade. Along the promenade you will see steep, tree-filled slopes coming down from Riverside Drive to the upper Promenade. At about 91st Street you will pass by an extremely well-maintained community garden. In 1981 a group of individuals formed the Garden People, an association devoted to planting and tending this garden. The rectangle is made up of twenty-six gardens that are cared for individually. The octagon is tended communally. Just east of the gardens, you will see Japanese kerria, the lovely yellow flowering shrubs that bloom from spring through summer. From 91st to 95th streets you will see a grassy area filled with ornamental cherry and crabapple trees. In April and May the cherry and apple blossoms are exquisite.

100th to 116th streets The middle level, or promenade, is broad and tree-lined, a wonderful habitat for year-round birds, particularly along the path near the wall. At 107th Street you will see the Peter J. Sharp Volunteer House, which serves as an educational meeting place above and a gardening shed below.

Bird Sanctuary The forested and meadow areas between 116th and 124th streets have been designated the Riverside Park Bird Sanctuary. Invasive trees and shrubs, such as Japanese knotweed, Norway maple, and ailanthus are being removed, and bird-friendly trees, shrubs, and ground cover have been planted, including chokeberry, shadblow, viburnum, dogwood, sumac, and witch hazel trees. More than one hundred species of birds have been recorded each year, including thrushes, scarlet tanagers, warblers, and peregrine falcons. When the wildflower meadow northeast of the 119th Street tennis courts is in full bloom, it is one of the best butterfly gardens in New York City, with monarchs, red admirals, painted ladies, cabbage whites, clouded sulphurs, question marks, tiger swallowtails, black swallowtails and others. Raccoons, cottontail rabbits, chipmunks, woodchucks, opossums, and occasionally a coyote have been observed here.

Bird Sanctuary Walk Start at the 116th Street entrance near the fenced-in Women's Grove. In 1926, the Women's League for the Protection of Riverside Park planted sixty-five trees as a war memorial. Walk the wood-chip trail through this grove in summer, looking up in the trees for warblers, tanagers, rose-breasted grosbeaks, and Baltimore orioles. Be sure to gaze up at Riverside Church at 120th and Riverside Drive to look for the pair of nesting peregrine falcons that feed on nearby pigeons.

GETTING THERE

By Subway Take the IRT Subway #1, #2, #3 to 72nd Street or 96th Street or the #1 (local) to 72nd, 86th, 96th, 103rd, 110th, or 116th Streets. Get out and walk west from Broadway to Riverside Park.

By Bus The #5 bus runs along Riverside Drive in both directions. Get off anywhere along the Drive between 72nd Street and 120th Street.

By Car Driving south on the West Side Highway, exit at 95th Street or the 79th Street Boat Basin. Driving north on the West Side Highway, exit at 72nd, 79th, 96th, or 125th Street.

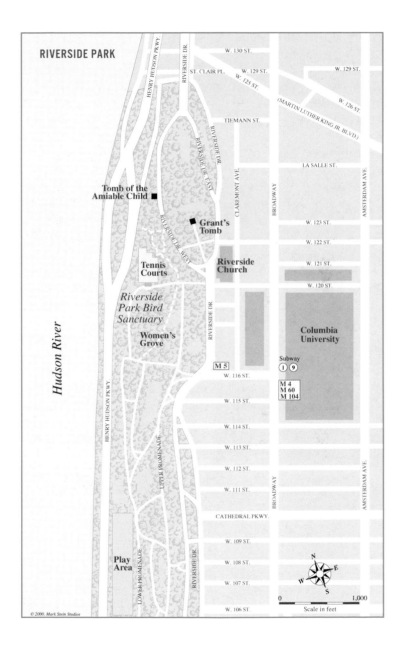

RIVERSIDE PARK

W. 130 ST.

HENRY HUDSON PKWY

RIVERSIDE DR.

ST. CLAIR PL.

W. 129 ST.

W. 125 ST.

W. 129 ST.

(MARTIN LUTHER KING JR. BLVD.)

W. 126 ST.

TIEMANN ST.

RIVERSIDE DR. EAST

LA SALLE ST.

CLAREMONT AVE.

BROADWAY

AMSTERDAM AVE.

Tomb of the Amiable Child ■

RIVERSIDE DR. WEST

■ **Grant's Tomb**

W. 123 ST.

W. 122 ST.

Tennis Courts

Riverside Church

W. 121 ST.

W. 120 ST.

Riverside Park Bird Sanctuary

RIVERSIDE DR.

Columbia University

Women's Grove

Hudson River

M 5

Subway
① ⑨

W. 116 ST.

M 4
M 60
M 104

W. 115 ST.

W. 114 ST.

HENRY HUDSON PKWY

W. 113 ST.

UPPER PROMENADE

W. 112 ST.

W. 111 ST.

BROADWAY

AMSTERDAM AVE.

CATHEDRAL PKWY.

W. 109 ST.

Play Area

LOWER PROMENADE

RIVERSIDE DR.

W. 108 ST.

N
W   E
S

0   1,000

W. 107 ST.

W. 106 ST.

Scale in feet

© 2000, Mark Stein Studios

QUEENS

Alley Pond Park

LOCATION
228–06 Northern Boulevard, Douglaston, NY 11363

TELEPHONE
Alley Pond Environmental Center: (718) 229-4000

WEBSITE
www.alleypond.com

SIZE
655 acres

HABITATS
tidal salt marsh, freshwater wetlands, spring-fed glacial kettle ponds, streams, meadows, 221-acre native hardwood forest, 23-acre bird sanctuary

Natural History   Alley Pond Park's terrain is the result of glacial activity that took place more than ten thousand years ago.

The salt marsh of Alley Pond Park is formed by a saltwater creek coming in from Little Neck Bay.

The retreating glacier deposited debris across what is now Queens and Long Island. At the glacier's southernmost point, where it melted more quickly, the debris formed a range of hills known as the terminal moraine. These ridges formed the forested hills of the park and the hills of what are now Bayside and Douglaston, the towns surrounding Alley Pond Park. The retreating glacier left behind kettle ponds and high ridges surrounding a wide valley (known as the "Alley") scoured out by the glacier. The kettle ponds emptied into a ravine created by the glacier's meltwaters. The ravine flowed into Alley Creek, which emptied into Little Neck Bay.

Human History   The Native Americans living along Little Neck Bay and the nearby countryside were the Mattinecock. They caught oysters, clams, and fish, and hunted forest game. The early English settlers built a dam across Alley Creek in order to use the tidal current to turn a grist mill. Water flooded the nearby meadow, creating a three-acre pond known as Alley Pond. Colonists walked the Alley from Little Neck Bay to Brooklyn to take the ferries into Manhattan.

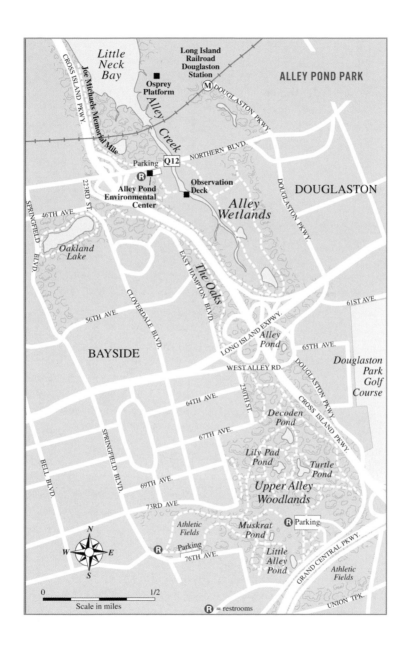

It is reported that George Washington stopped at the Alley to rest during his tour of Long Island in 1790. In the nineteenth century the area was a favorite summer destination for nature lovers and artists who swam and fished in the bay. However, during the twentieth century major roads were built from Queens to Long Island, which carved up the park. These roads include the Long Island Expressway, the Cross Island Parkway, and the Grand Central Parkway.

Parks Commissioner Robert Moses created the first city park nature trail at Alley Pond Park in 1935. In 1974, the New York City Department of Parks and Recreation created the Wetlands Reclamation Project and began rehabilitating the natural wetlands of the park. The Parks Department's Natural Resources Group has been monitoring the plant and animal diversity of the park for years and is involved in ongoing restoration projects.

Alley Pond Environmental Center   During the 1970s citizens' groups worked to restore and protect Alley Pond Park. The Alley Pond Environmental Center (APEC), founded in 1972, educates the

The "Alley" cuts through Alley Pond Park with its ribbonlike saltwater creek.

public about the park's history and ecology. APEC provides children, teachers, and families with environmental education programs, which include nature hikes, and bird walks. The Queens County Bird Club meets the third Wednesday of each month (except during July and August) at APEC. Inside the center, aquatic tanks house turtles such as the diamondback terrapin, red-eared sliders, wood turtles, and painted turtles.

Cattail Pond Trail   This trail is a quarter-mile walk along Alley Creek and the marsh. A platform allows you to observe the freshwater pond. The deck leads out onto the creek for closer observation.

Joe Michaels Memorial Mile and Cross Island Bike Path   2 3/4 miles long, this is a bike and pedestrian path between the parkway and Little Neck Bay. Search for nesting saltmarsh sharp-tailed sparrows and swamp sparrows. Look for the osprey platform. During winter, Little Neck Bay is home to red-throated loons, common loons, horned grebes, and northern pintail, canvasback, greater scaup, bufflehead, common goldeneye, and ruddy ducks.

Mergansers, green-winged teals, and great cormorants can also be found here.

Oakland Lake   Follow the trail for a one-mile long hike around this twenty-foot-deep glacial pond, which has the only black bass fish population in Queens.

Pitobick Trail   This almost two-mile-long trail is an easy walk along the saltwater marsh. It begins at APEC, circles around the Alley, and takes you through most of the park's habitats. Muskrat, ring-necked pheasants, saltwater cordgrass, and saltmeadow cordgrass can be seen here. All along the creek, phragmites reed grass is home to muskrats, and red-winged blackbirds. Black-crowned night herons fish along the shore of the creek. Look for diamondback terrapins in the creek.

Oakland Lake is a 20-foot-deep glacial pond located just north of the entrance to Alley Pond Park.

Yellow Nature Trail and Turtle Pond Trail   1 1/2 miles long, these connected trails will take you around the three major kettle ponds, Turtle, Decodon, and Lily Pond, where the forest meets freshwater wetlands. Eastern box turtles forage on the forest floor. In summer, look for American ginseng flowers and wineberries. Painted turtles, wood ducks, and mallards consume the floating duckweed. Decodon Pond is named for the *Decodon verticulum*, commonly known as waterwillow, that emerges from the pond.

The forest of Alley Pond Park in autumn.

Bladderwort, a submerged carnivorous plant, is commonly seen in Turtle Pond. Its minute underwater leaves have bladders that trap aquatic insects, their larvae, and tiny crustaceans. Red maple and black tupelo trees grow from Lily Pond, and white water-lily pads float on its surface. Spotted salamanders deposit their eggs in these ponds, and bullfrogs and spring peepers can be seen along their edges in the spring and summer.

The female yellow-spotted salamander returns to its natal pond each spring to lay her eggs. Wooded wetlands offer protected habitat for this and other amphibians.

Red Oak Trail Half a mile long, this trail will take you to Little Alley Pond and back. The forest floor is home to shade-tolerant plants such as mapleleaf viburnum, Canada mayflower, jewelweed, Virginia knotweed and white wood aster. During spring, ephemeral plants such as nodding trillium, bloodroot, and Solomon's seal bloom briefly before the trees leaf out and the forest floor is shaded by the canopy.

Tulip Tree Trail One mile long, this hike winds through the forested hillside of mature native trees, including one of the largest tulip trees in New York City or Long Island. Many of the trees here are two hundred years old. This is the place to look for spring and fall migrants such as warblers, thrushes, and vireos. Keep an eye out for nesting wood ducks, eastern wood pewees, red-eyed vireos, the Carolina wren, wood thrushes, American redstarts, and Baltimore orioles in summer.

GETTING THERE

By Subway and Bus Take the IRT Flushing Line #7 subway to Main Street, Flushing. Then take the #12 bus toward Northern Boulevard, getting off at the APEC bus stop at 228th Street (a 20-minute ride). Directions by Long Island Railroad: Call (718) 217-5477 for train schedules. Take the LIRR to Douglaston station. Walk south along Douglaston Parkway to Northern Boulevard. Go right (west) on Northern for about ¼ mile to APEC.

By Car Grand Central Parkway to Cross Island Parkway, north. Exit at Northern Boulevard east and turn right into the APECparking lot. Parking is free and the lot is open from 9 a.m.–4:30 p.m. daily, except for the major holidays.

Jamaica Bay Wildlife Refuge

LOCATION

Cross Bay Boulevard north of Broad Channel

TELEPHONE

(718) 318-4340

SIZE

9,155 acres

VISITOR CENTER

open year-round except Thanksgiving, Christmas, and New Year's Day, 8:30 a.m.–5 p.m. Before hiking you need to stop by the Visitor Center to check in and receive a free hiking permit. There are no entrance or parking fees. The center has a parking lot, bookstore, and bathroom. There are a few displays on local flora and fauna and bird migration and an excellent history of the Bay. Contact the center for information on tours and special programs.

Double-crested cormorants, terns, and gulls on the West Pond.

HABITATS

salt marshes, fields and woods, freshwater pond, brackish pond, five miles of trails, gardens, open expanse of bay and islands. The refuge is an internationally renowned birding spot where thousands of water, land, and shorebirds stop during migration. Over the past 30 years more than 330 species have been recorded here.

Natural History   For thousands of years after the last ice age, wave action carried glacial debris along the shores of Long Island and deposited it in new locations, forming beaches and eroding inlets. The Rockaway Peninsula was formed from these shifting glacial deposits, and behind it were the waters of Jamaica Bay. As the peninsula grew, Jamaica Bay became more and more sheltered from the Atlantic Ocean, and over centuries, saltwater marshes were built up from sediment accumulation and eroded away by storms and wave action. The waters were calm enough for saltwater-tolerant plant life to take hold. Saltmarsh cordgrass was able to colonize the sand and silt, inundated twice each day by the ocean's tides. In the fall and early winter the cordgrass dies back, creating a spongy layer of peat that raises the surface of the marsh. New plants, colonizing the peat and high enough to be almost free of the salty tides, form salt meadows. Along with these, two separate plant communities—the intertidal marsh and the salt meadow mudflats—are formed. Each of these communities has its own distinctive plant growth, and invertebrates, fish, reptiles, birds, and mammals that have adapted to survive in a saltwater marsh. From the late 1800s until the early

Sunset over a wintry Jamaica Bay covered in snow and ice.

1950s, the saltmarsh islands in Jamaica Bay were covered, in part, with sand and mud dredged from the bay, creating the uplands on Canarsie Pol, Ruffle Bar, Big Egg Marsh, Elder's Point Marsh, and Subway Island. Ruler's Bar Hassock, the land on which Jamaica Bay Wildlife Refuge Center is located, and once part of a group of small islands that included Broad Channel Island, was also filled in with dredge spoil. This filling in of the islands of Jamaica Bay has disrupted the pattern of marsh accretion and erosion. As a result of this and the sea level rise, the salt marshes are being flooded for longer periods and close to 50 percent have disappeared. Some believe that the treated sewage pouring into the bay is also killing the marshes. While recent conservation efforts have improved the condition of the salt marshes, this rich ecosystem continues to decline. Scientists believe that the salt marshes of Jamaica Bay may soon vanish. Research is being conducted and work is being done to preserve this valuable ecosystem.

Human History   The Canarsie and Rockawanie Indians inhabited the bay, living on shellfish, fish, and other wildlife, as did the early Dutch settlers who farmed the area. Starting in the late seventeenth century and well into the twentieth century, the area became more developed and raw sewage poured into the bay, destroying the renowned oyster fields. In 1921, shell fishing was banned after an outbreak of typhoid. Broad Channel Island, which is about 1,200 acres, is divided between the Broad Channel community in the south and the Jamaica Bay Wildlife Refuge in the north.

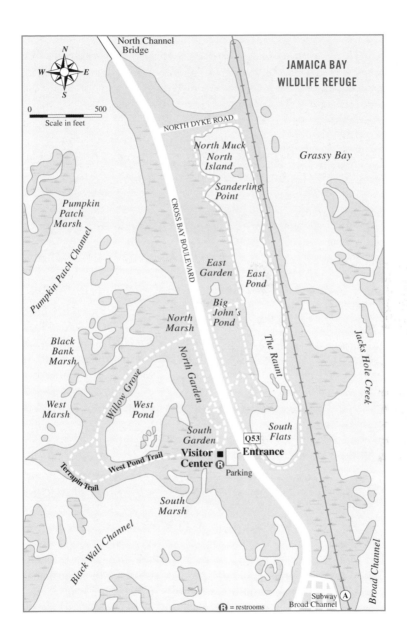

North Channel
Bridge

JAMAICA BAY
WILDLIFE REFUGE

N
W E
S

0   500
Scale in feet

NORTH DYKE ROAD

North Muck
North
Island

Grassy Bay

Sanderling
Point

Pumpkin
Patch
Marsh

Pumpkin Patch Channel

CROSS BAY BOULEVARD

East
Garden

East
Pond

Big
John's
Pond

North
Marsh

North Garden

Black
Bank
Marsh

The Raunt

Jacks Hole Creek

Willow Grove

West
Marsh

West
Pond

South
Garden

South
Flats

Q53

Entrance

Visitor
Center ℝ

Parking

Terrapin Trail

West Pond Trail

South
Marsh

Black Wall Channel

Broad Channel

ℝ = restrooms

Subway Ⓐ
Broad Channel

Aerial view of Jamaica Bay marshes.

By 1953, at the urging of urban planner and New York City Parks Commissioner Robert Moses, a wildlife refuge was established in Jamaica Bay. The refuge was first developed by Herbert Johnson, the dedicated manager who transformed the barren landscape into a sanctuary for birds and wildlife through the planting of grasses, wildflowers, shrubs, and trees. Under Johnson's direction, park workers planted 1.5 million beach grass plants. Dredge spoil deposits created uplands on the salt marsh islands, or "hummocks," of Jamaica Bay. In 1972 Johnson retired, and the refuge was taken over by the newly created Gateway National Recreation Area. The first national park system for urban areas, Gateway's units also include Floyd Bennett Field in Brooklyn; Jacob Riis Park, Fort Tilden, and Breezy Point in Queens; Great Kills Park in Staten Island; and Sandy Hook in New Jersey. Jamaica Bay Wildlife Refuge is the U.S. Department of the Interior's only wildlife refuge run by the National Park Service. In 1972 the Clean Water Act made dumping in Jamaica Bay, and every other body of water in the United States, illegal. Today, Jamaica Bay Wildlife Refuge is internationally renowned as one of the most important urban wildlife preserves in the country. Don Riepe, appointed Jamaica Bay Guardian by the New York State Department of Conservation, leads tours through the Littoral Society and the New York City Audubon Society. The New York City Audubon Society and the National Audubon Society have designated the Jamaica Bay district an "Important Bird Area of Global Significance."

Butterflies and Flowering Plants   Close to seventy species of butterflies have been identified at Jamaica Bay. To attract anglewings and emperors, park managers place a blend of fermenting fruit and beer—or mung—on the trees. The open field to the left of the Visitor Center has camphorweed, milkweed, and bouncing Bets among other flowers upon which black swallowtail, question mark, eastern tailed-blue, pearl crescent, swarthy skipper, and clouded and orange sulphur butterflies may be observed. Other butterflies on the refuge include the American snout and tawny emperor, both of which breed on the hackberry trees. Saltmarsh

Glossy ibises, Jamaica Bay Wildlife Refuge.

skipper caterpillars use the saltmarsh spike grass as a host plant, and the adults nectar on camphorweed. The broad-winged skipper can be found at the reserve because it uses phragmites as a foodplant for its caterpillar. The cloudless sulphur, fiery skipper, variegated fritillary, and common buckeye, not usually found this far north, share the Atlantic flyway with migrating birds and usually can be seen at the Jamaica Bay Wildlife Refuge in late summer.

Birds   "All the trails and gardens are designed and maintained for the purpose of breeding, feeding, and caring for the hundreds of bird species that stop here to nest and rest until they move on," says Don Riepe, former Park Manager, Gateway National Recreation Area, and presently the guardian of the Jamaica Bay Wildlife Refuge.

More than eighty species of birds nest at the refuge. These include:

Mute swans	Clapper rail
Laughing gull	American oystercatcher
Forster's tern	American woodcock
Great egret	Willet
Snowy egret	Osprey
Little blue heron	Barn owl
Tricolored heron	Willow flycatcher
Cattle egret	American redstart
Black-crowned night heron	Boat-tailed grackle
Yellow-crowned night heron	Saltmarsh sharp-tailed sparrow
Green heron	Seaside sparrow
Glossy ibis	

In the fall, thousands of waterfowl arrive at the refuge, including Brant geese, snow geese, hooded mergansers, Eurasian widgeons, and lesser and greater scaup. Waterfowl arrive beginning in late September, and their numbers grow through November. They remain at the refuge into spring. Raptors, such as rough-legged hawks, and snowy, long-eared, short-eared, and northern saw-whet owls also winter at the refuge. During fall and spring migrations, waves of shorebirds alight on the bay's mudflats to feed. In late spring, breeding horseshoe crabs return to this area, as they have been doing since prehistoric times, each female to lay thousands of eggs on the beach. These eggs are consumed by hungry migrating shorebirds who depend upon this source of energy to complete their spring migration north. Autumn also brings great numbers of migrating swallows, songbirds, warblers, monarch butterflies, and dragonflies to the refuge.

Breeding horseshoe crabs converge on Jamaica Bay Wildlife Refuge in late spring. Each female lays up to twenty thousand eggs on the beach, providing food for scores of hungry migrating birds.

Amphibians and Reptiles Except for the Fowler's toad, the eastern garter snake, and the northern diamondback terrapin, which have all maintained breeding populations in the Jamaica Bay area, the following native amphibian and reptile species were introduced by Dr. Robert Cook of the National Park Service in the 1980s and are now established breeders: spring peepers, gray treefrogs, eastern spotted newts, red-backed salamanders, eastern milk snakes, black racer snakes, northern brown snakes, smooth green snakes, snapping turtles, eastern painted turtles, and eastern box turtles. Diamondback terrapins nest in June, July, and early August.

Mammals Mammals at the Jamaica Bay Wildlife Refuge include the little brown bat, red bat, hoary bat, silver-haired bat, meadow vole, white-footed mouse, opossum, Norway rat, raccoon, muskrat, eastern chipmunk, eastern cottontail rabbit, and the black-tailed jackrabbit (which is found at JFK Airport).

West Pond Trail Beginning through the back door of the Visitor Center, this trail is about 1.5 miles long and first takes you through a section of wildflowers, shrubs, trees, and New York City's only native cactus, the prickly pear. You will pass camphorweed, sweet everlasting aster, winged sumac, rugosa rose, and bayberry. As you come out into the open you will look out at the saltwater marshes along the shore of Jamaica Bay. On your left you will view the nesting platform used each spring and sum-mer by a breeding pair of osprey. On the saltwater side of the trail are the mudflats. Particularly at low tide, you will see shorebirds such as sandpipers and plovers probing the mud for crabs, snails, worms, and other aquatic invertebrates. A short distance ahead and on your right you will find the forty-five-acre freshwater West Pond. During fall, winter, and early spring, thousands of snow geese, Brant geese and other wintering waterfowl fly back and forth between the pond and the bay. A side trail between benches nine and ten leads through the Diamondback Terrapin Nesting Area, which is closed during the June, July, and August breeding season. All along the side trail, you will see metal grates, which are there to protect the buried terrapin eggs from foraging raccoons.

Yellowlegs, Jamaica Bay Wildlife Refuge.

The West Pond is an excellent habitat for coastal shorebirds and waterfowl. In summer and fall trees and shrubs around the pond often fill with roosting egrets and herons. In the winter, large flocks of snow geese can be found on West Pond, along with other waterfowl such as lesser and greater scaup, ruddy duck, ring-necked duck, green-winged teal, northern pintail, American widgeon, and gadwall.

North and South Gardens As you walk on the east side of West Pond heading back to the Visitor Center, you will eventually pass through North and South gardens, which contain a wide variety of trees and shrubs, including autumn olive, bayberry, gray birch, red maple, willow oak, and Japanese black pine. In autumn, native vines such as poison ivy and Virginia creeper bear berries consumed by wildlife. These gardens are a haven for warblers, vireos, and other songbirds, and, in the summer, butterflies.

East Pond Trail   Cross over Cross Bay Boulevard at the traffic light and walk south (right) about two hundred yards, entering the pond trail through a narrow path. The trail around this hundred-acre pond is accessible in summer when the water level is artificially lowered so that shorebirds can forage for food in the muck. Wear shoes or boots that you don't mind getting muddy as you circum-navigate the pond. The trail circles around the southern tip to the east side of the pond and then to the northern tip where the trail takes you back to Cross Bay Boulevard. Big John's Pond, roughly one-quarter acre in size and 3 feet deep when full, is a freshwater pond excavated, at the request of a ranger, by "Big John," a helpful bulldozer operator. This vernal pond is the home of spring peepers, gray treefrogs, and eastern painted turtles. Big John's Pond often dries up in summer. If you want to go directly to Big John's Pond at the northern end of East Pond, walk left after you have crossed Cross Bay Boulevard. The entrance is about eight hundred yards away.

GETTING THERE

By Car   From Brooklyn-Belt Parkway (east) to exit 17 (Cross Bay Boulevard) go over North Channel Bridge and continue 1 1/2 miles to the traffic light. Turn right, into the the refuge.

From Rockaway, take Cross Bay Bridge (94th Street) and go through the Broad Channel community. The refuge visitor center is about half a mile on the left.

From Manhattan, take the Midtown Tunnel to the Long Island Expressway. Get off at the Woodhaven Boulevard exit. Take Wood-haven Boulevard, which becomes Cross Bay Boulevard, all the way to Howard Beach. Continue through Howard Beach, over the North Channel Bridge, and 1 ½ miles to the traffic light. Turn right, into the refuge.

By Subway   Take the A train going toward the Rockaways. Exit at Broad Channel Station. Walk west to Cross Bay Boulevard, then north, (right), about half a mile. Cross Cross Bay Boulevard at the light to the visitor center of the refuge.

By Bus   Take the Q53 bus from Roosevelt Avenue / Jackson Heights. Exit at the refuge stop. You can also take the Q21 from the intersection of Woodhaven and Liberty Avenue. Exit at refuge entrance.

STATEN ISLAND

Mount Loretto Unique Area Nature Preserve

LOCATION
6450 Hylan Boulevard,
Staten Island, NY 10312

TELEPHONE
New York State Department of
Environmental Conservation
Educator: (718) 482-7287

SIZE
194 acres

HABITATS
grassland, woodland, freshwater
and tidal wetlands, red clay
coastal bluffs, shoreline beach,
open water, Prince's Bay

The Church of St. Joaquim and St. Ann is a visual landmark as you approach Mount Loretto. Grasslands filled with wildflowers attract butterflies.

Natural History Mount Loretto features vast rolling grassland meadows, freshwater and brackish water wetlands, and woodlands. The Mount Loretto property includes the only natural red clay cliff bluffs in New York City, which stand seventy-five feet above Prince's Bay (an arm of Raritan Bay off the Atlantic Ocean). These are part of the terminal moraine, the sand, gravel, and rocks deposited by the glacier at its southernmost point before it retreated approximately fifteen thousand years ago. From the top of the cliffs there is a spectacular view of New York's Raritan Bay and Sandy Hook, New Jersey, as well as the mile-long beach below the bluff. The water of Prince's Bay is home to many species of fish and shellfish. It is an overwintering area for waterfowl, which can be seen in large numbers from the bluffs. Waterfowl can be observed year round in the freshwater and brackish ponds of Mount Loretto.

Human History Formerly owned by the Archdiocese of New York, and once the site of the St. Elisabeth's Home for Girls, Mount Loretto had orphanages for both boys and girls throughout the late nineteenth and much of the twentieth centuries. Mount Loretto was purchased by New York State and the Trust for Public Land in 1999. Now a state natural area owned and managed by the New York State Department of Environmental Conservation, it is one of the last remaining natural areas in the city, with woods, meadows, freshwater and tidal wetlands, and shoreline. Across Hylan Boulevard stands the Church of St. Joachim and St. Ann, site of the baptism scene in

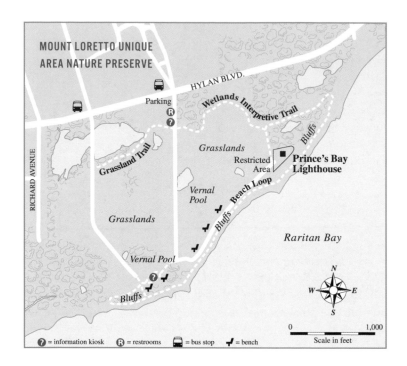

MOUNT LORETTO UNIQUE
AREA NATURE PRESERVE

HYLAN BLVD.

Parking

Wetlands Interpretive Trail

Grassland Trail

RICHARD AVENUE

Grasslands

Restricted
Area

Prince's Bay
Lighthouse

Bluffs

Vernal
Pool

Beach Loop

Bluffs

Grasslands

Raritan Bay

Vernal Pool

Bluffs

N
W   E
S

0   1,000

Scale in feet

= information kiosk   = restrooms   = bus stop   = bench

The Godfather. The archdiocese still owns the acreage the church stands on.

Grasslands Trail Walking up the paved road from your car, turn right at the post marked "Grassland Trail." You will walk with grasslands on your left and a hidden vernal pool on your right and come out onto another paved road. Turn right until you reach a pair of ponds, one on your left and another on your right. More than half of Mount Loretto is its grasslands. The managers of Mount Loretto have made it their goal to improve and maintain nesting habitats for grassland birds. Grassland habitat has disappeared from most of the New York City area, resulting in the decline of several species of birds, including the bobolink, the meadowlark, and the savannah sparrow. All three species prefer the kind of fields prevalent in Mount Loretto, which also support numerous species of wildflowers and nectaring butterflies during late spring, summer, and early fall. In the spring look for sora, cliff swallows, white-crowned sparrows, bobolinks, and orchard orioles. Falcons such as the merlin and American kestrel hunt smaller birds in these fields. During fall and spring migration wood ducks and green-winged teals may be seen on the ponds. From August to October, osprey can be seen hunting near the ponds.

Wetlands Interpretive Trail Directly across from the Grasslands Trail post is the post marking the Wetlands Trail. Turn left and head east on this trail. At post #2, a tidal inlet from Prince's Bay washes into this wetland so that the water is brackish (a mix of fresh water and salt water). At post #3 you will find a freshwater pond on your right that is home to frogs, salamanders, and turtles.

Red clay bluffs along the coast of Mount Loretto rise to 75 feet in some places with dramatic views of Raritan Bay and Sandy Hook, New Jersey.

You may see mallard ducks and other birds visiting the pond. At post #4 you have a panoramic view of the tidal wetland system of Mount Loretto. Phragmites is prevalent here. At post #5 follow the path and you will cross a stream that connects the tidal wetland to Prince's Bay. The tidal wetland habitat serves as a nursery for fish and crabs, and a place for wading birds such as herons and egrets to forage for fish, frogs, and aquatic invertebrates.

Prince's Bay Lighthouse On the Wetlands Interpretive Trail, walk along the right side of the stream until you are on the beach and follow the Beach Trail west (see map). Or, double back the way you came to post #3 and head up the hill to post #6. At the top of the hill turn around and see the spectacular views of Mount Loretto. This is the highest point on the property and the view is glorious. Built in 1828, the lighthouse guided ships sailing along the coast of Staten Island. The original wooden structure served until the Civil War. In 1864, a new brownstone and brick structure was built. In 1922, the lighthouse was deactivated. Although you cannot enter the building, you may view the lighthouse from the gate around the keeper's house.

Turn right and walk down the road. On your left will be Prince's Bay, and at post #7 you will have a scenic view of the bay. The green and red buoys mark shipping channels and guide ships through deep water. When you reach the paved road turn right and head back to the parking area and main road. At post #8 you will pass another vernal pool on your right that is usually filled with dabbling

A double-crested cormorant dries its wings atop a rock in Prince's Bay off the coast of Mount Loretto.

waterfowl such as mallards and black ducks that forage in the muddy pond bottom.

Beach Trail The coastal and marine habitat is the second largest habitat zone (25 percent) at Mount Loretto. For a mile or so, a narrow red sand and rocky beach makes up the coastline, banked by tall red clay bluffs. The property also includes forty-nine acres of underwater lands. On the beach, toward the eastern end of the property is the tidal inlet that links Prince's Bay to the tidal wetlands. This inlet brings salt water into the tidal wetlands. The course of the inlet changes with the tide, the wind, and the waves. Fish and shellfish of Prince's Bay include striped bass, winter flounder, bluefish, quahogs or hard clams, mussels, and horseshoe crabs. The sand is covered by broken seashells. At low tide during the warm months, large, transparent moon jellies are stranded on the sand. Remnants of redbeard sponge can also be found on the beach. Osprey soar overhead, as do turkey vultures and several species of hawks. The coastline is on the Atlantic flyway for migrating birds. Overwintering waterfowl such as long-tailed ducks (oldsquaw), double-crested cormorants, greater scaup, and common goldeneye can be observed in large numbers on Prince's Bay. Occasionally you may see harbor seals in the bay during winter.

Local artists created stone sculptures from the crumbling seawall along Mount Loretto's beach.

The Bluffs The red clay bluffs rise seventy-five to eighty feet above the coast and offer spectacular views of Raritan Bay and Sandy Hook, New Jersey. You will see sculptures all along the beach created by a Staten Island zookeeper and other local artists using stones that were once part of the crumbling seawall.

GETTING THERE

By Car From the Goethals Bridge take 1-278 to the exit for 440 South (West Shore Expressway). Take the last exit (exit 1) on 440 South (just before the Outerbridge Crossing). At the end of the ramp make a right at the light. At the next light, take another right. Turn right again at the third traffic light. This puts you on Boxcombe Avenue, which turns into Page Avenue. Follow Page Avenue to its end at Hylan Boulevard and take a left onto Hylan. After about three-quarters of a mile, the parking lot for Mount Loretto will be on your right-hand side, across the street from the Church of St. Joaquim and St. Ann. Pull in and you will see the welcome kiosk.

From the Verrazano Bridge: take the exit for Hylan Boulevard and follow that south until you come to Mount Loretto. Turn left into the small parking lot.

By Ferry to the Bus From the southern tip of Manhattan take the Staten Island Ferry (last stop on the IRT #1 train) to the St. George Terminal in Staten Island. On the D-ramp, board the S78 Bus bound for Tottenville, which goes south along Hylan Boulevard. Tell the driver you want to stop near the Mount Loretto Unique Area.

MOUNT LORETTO UNIQUE AREA NATURE PRESERVE

Wolfe's Pond Park

LOCATION

Cornelia Avenue and Hylan Boulevard, Staten Island, NY 10312

PHONE

(718) 984-8266

SIZE

341 acres

HABITATS

shoreline beach, dunes, open water, Raritan Bay, freshwater pond, deciduous forest, freshwater stream

Natural History　Once a tidal inlet, the sixteen-acre Wolfe's Pond sits above the water table just yards from the beach. Over the years, wind and ocean waves dammed up the inlet with clay and the freshwater pond was formed. The five-acre Acme Pond, connected to Wolfe's Pond by a ravine, is a kettle pond, created when a chunk of glacial ice melted in a depression.

Human History　Six thousand years ago, ancestors of the Lenape settled on bluffs overlooking Raritan Bay, where they collected fish and shellfish, hunted deer and turkey, and grew squash and corn. In the 1700s, European colonists arrived and developed a thriving oyster industry. Joel Wolfe farmed this area in the early 1800s. In 1857 New York State purchased Wolfe's farm to be used as a quarantine station for diseased immigrants. However, local fishermen believed that the facility contaminated the pond water, which they used to clean their catch, and burned down the buildings. The state then used the land as a cemetery. In 1929 and 1930, New York City procured the land for a city park. In 1933 a dam was built to protect the pond from incoming seawater. Since the 1990s, the city has constructed a pond embankment, picnic areas, benches, paths, lawns, trees, shrubs, playground equipment, picnic areas, tot lot, tennis courts, basketball courts, roller hockey rink, paths, and beach and shoreline protection.

Pond Walk　Head from the parking lot across the lawn to the pond. Walk around the pond looking for ducks, geese, egrets, and herons. Follow the old roadbed into the woods to the five-acre Acme Pond on the north side of Hylan Boulevard. Sweet pepperbush, highbush blueberry, and serviceberry provide food and shelter for birds. Along the shore of the pond and between the beach and the pond you will find asiatic bittersweet and Japanese honeysuckle.

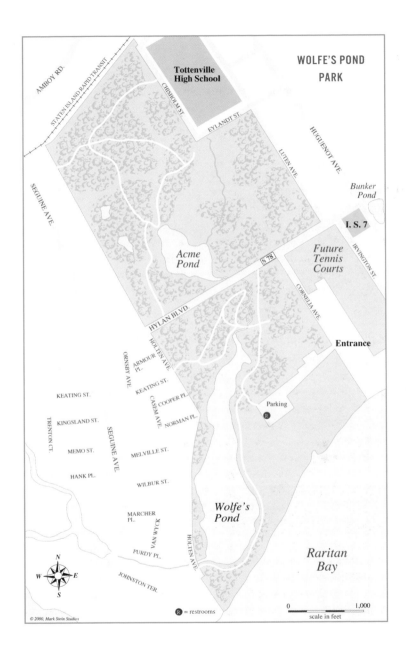

WOLFE'S POND
PARK

Tottenville
High School

Bunker
Pond

I. S. 7

Acme
Pond

Future
Tennis
Courts

Entrance

HYLAN BLVD.

Parking

KEATING ST.

KINGSLAND ST.

MEMO ST.

HANK PL.

MELVILLE ST.

WILBUR ST.

MARCHER
PL.

PURDY PL.

JOHNSTON TER.

Wolfe's
Pond

Raritan
Bay

AMBOY RD.

STATEN ISLAND RAPID TRANSIT

CHISHOLM ST.

EYLANDT ST.

LUTEN AVE.

HUGUENOT AVE.

IRVINGTON ST.

S 78

CORNELIA AVE.

SEGUINE AVE.

HOLTEN AVE.

ORMSBY AVE.

ARMOUR PL.

KEATING ST.

CASIM AVE.

COOPER PL.

NORMAN PL.

TRENTON CT.

SEGUINE AVE.

VAN WYCK

HOLTEN AVE.

N
W E
S

Ⓡ = restrooms

© 2000, Mark Stein Studios

0   1,000
scale in feet

Emergent marsh grasses, foraging Canada geese, and a sailboat in the distance seen from the beach at Wolfe's Pond Park.

The freshwater Wolfe's Pond is only yards from Raritan Bay on the coast of Staten Island.

Beach Walk Walking along the beach, look out at Raritan Bay for sea ducks, brant geese, cormorants, loons, grebes, and the occasional harbor seal. You will find redbeard sponge washed up on the beach and a number of seashells, including whelks.

Forest Walk   Look for a giant black oak tree as you walk through the forest toward Hylan Boulevard. This mature forest has not been logged since colonial days. A stream meanders along the forest's valley.

GETTING THERE

By Public Transportation   From Manhattan take the IRT #1 train to South Ferry (last stop in Manhattan), and then take the Staten Island Ferry to the St. George Terminal. Take the Tottenville-bound S78 NYC transit bus (D ramp), which runs along Hylan Boulevard. Disembark at the Luten Avenue stop, cross Hyland Boulevard, go one block west to Cornelia Avenue. Turn left on Cornelia Avenue to the park entrance on your right.

By Car   Take the Verrazano Bridge and follow signs to Route 278 (Staten Island Expressway). Take the Hylan Boulevard exit (left). Drive south on Hylan Boulevard for six miles and turn left on Cornelia Avenue. Wolfe's Pond Park is on the right.

Wolfe's Pond Park forest contains many mature trees and a lovely stream meandering through the valley floor.

CHAPTER 3

forever wild

THE NEW YORK CITY DEPARTMENT OF PARKS AND RECREATION created the Forever Wild Program to protect animals, plants, and their habitat through restoration and land acquisition. These fragile sites are preserved and kept "forever wild." Forty-eight Forever Wild nature preserves encompass nearly nine thousand acres of forests, freshwater and saltwater wetlands, shorelines, and meadows within the five boroughs of New York City. Most sites are accessible by subway or bus. Many Forever Wild sites have trails and nature centers.

Let's look closely at several Forever Wild sites.

North Brother Island, the Bronx, 20 acres of forest

North Brother Island is part of a group of uninhabited islands in the Harbor Herons Region. Gulls, herons, cormorants, and egrets favor the isolation of these islands for nesting and raising their young. Each spring they flock to North Brother, nearby South Brother Island in the East River, and several islands in Staten Island. During the 1890s and early 1900s, North Brother was the site of the Riverside Hospital for Communicable Diseases, a quarantine hospital for people, such as Typhoid Mary, with contagious diseases. These buildings now lie in decay, and climbing vines, trees, and shrubs have reclaimed the island.

The decline in numbers of birds in the New York Harbor has concerned local conservation biologists. Each spring the New York City Audubon Society, New York City Parks Natural Resources Group, and many volunteers visit and count the nests, eggs, and baby birds at North Brother and the other Harbor Heron Islands.

Although no visitors are allowed on the island during nesting season, contact the New York City Audubon Society at www.nycas .org for tours and volunteer opportunities during other seasons.

Mussels found on the beach of North Brother Island, part of the Harbor Herons Preserve.

Four Sparrow Marsh Preserve in Brooklyn, 67 acres of saltmarsh

Named by naturalists Ron and Jean Bourque (who also help manage Floyd Bennett Field), Four Sparrow Marsh Preserve is home to four native species that require undisturbed marshland for breeding: sharp-tailed sparrows, seaside sparrows, swamp sparrows, and song sparrows. Located on the north shore of Jamaica Bay, and separated from residential areas in Brooklyn, Four Sparrow Marsh Preserve remains in a fairly natural state, ideal for nesting species, including several species of ducks, gulls, wading and woodland birds, as well as mollusks and crustaceans that the birds feed on. Rare birds such as the bobolink, common snipe, and little blue herons can be observed as well as 326 species of birds, which make Four Sparrow Marsh a stopover during fall and spring migration.

In 2004, the Parks' Natural Resources Group completed a three-acre saltmarsh restoration project at Four Sparrow Marsh, which included restoring tidal flow to previously filled areas and planting saltmarsh cordgrass. A small, adjacent woodland, which serves as an important buffer to the marsh, was also restored.

Forest Park, Queens, 274 acres of forest, and a newly restored kettle pond wetland

The Forest Park Preserve, in the eastern section of Forest Park, is home to some of the last undisturbed forest in the city. This mature oak forest is the largest wooded area in Queens, with many trees more than 150 years old. Beneath the soaring oaks and the hickories (mockernut, pignut, bitternut, and shagbark), lives a thriving understory of flowering dogwood trees and mapleleaf viburnum shrubs. On the forest floor grows a rich array of wildflowers, which completes the forest ecosystem and makes this forest an ideal spot for birding during fall and spring migration, when the rare cerulean, yellow-throated, and mourning warblers can be seen.

Forest Park Preserve is also the location of a freshwater wetland restoration by Parks' Natural Resources Group. In 2006, Strack Pond was restored and the site was re-dedicated in honor of Lawrence George E. Strack (1948–1967), the first Woodhaven, Queens, resident to die in Vietnam. The Strack Pond project restored a glacial kettle pond. Small kettle ponds teeming with emergent plants once dotted the floor of Forest Park, providing habitat for unique wildlife including frogs, birds, and other animals. This habitat restoration has brought back this precious wildlife.

The restoration also includes a walking trail and viewing areas, for bird, butterfly, and dragonfly watchers. Visitors to the site regularly see red-tailed Hawks, great blue herons, and great egrets, which are now sustained by the newly restored and diverse ecosystem.

The most common salamander found in New York City is the red-backed salamander.

Blue Heron Park, Staten Island, 169 acres of forest, grassland, shrubland, and freshwater wetland

Blue Heron Park is named for the great blue heron, the four-foot-tall wading bird that is commonly found throughout the New York

City area. From 1974 to 2001, the city acquired this parkland in several segments, because of an alliance between concerned residents of Staten Island who had worked hard to preserve and protect the land for thirty-three years and the New York City Department of Parks and Recreation. Blue Heron Park is now an exceptional wildlife sanctuary and educational resource. The park has been transformed from a wasteland filled with abandoned cars to a peaceful refuge of walking trails, meadows, ponds, streams, and woodlands. Park visitors can now walk three main trails through the park and discover wildflowers, including wild columbine, black-eyed Susan, and jack-in-the-pulpit.

Blue Heron Park contains six ponds, among them the 1.75-acre Spring Pond and the 1.4-acre Blue Heron Pond, crossed by a lovely footbridge.

These kettle ponds were formed fifteen thousand years ago by the retreating Wisconsin glacier. Today, they are teeming with life such as the glossy ibis, the black-crowned night heron, the wood duck, owls, osprey, various pond turtles, white water lilies, and the spring peepers and tree frogs that lay their eggs in the ponds.

Blue Heron Pond has a new nature center and handicapped-accessible trail. Each year more than ten thousand schoolchildren participate in the Park's nature education programs.

For detailed information on all forty-eight Forever Wild sites, go to the Forever Wild New York City Parks Department's website: http://www.nycgovparks.org/sub_about/parks_divisions/nrg/forever_wild/foreverwild_home.html.

The beautiful Blue Heron Park, a Forever Wild site, was transformed from a wasteland to a refuge with trails, meadows, ponds, streams, and woodlands.

FOREVER WILD SITES

	ACRES	WOODLAND	FRESHWATER WETLANDS	SALT MARSH	RARITAN BAY	ARTHUR KILL ESTUARY	JAMAICA BAY	HUDSON RIVER	LONG ISLAND SOUND	EAST RIVER	BRONX RIVER	MARINE INVERTEBRATES	HORSESHOE CRABS	MARINE FISH	FRESHWATER FISH	FROGS	TOADS	SALAMANDERS	SNAKES	TURTLES	WATERFOWL	SHOREBIRDS
BRONX																						
Bronx Park Preserve	35	•	•								•				•	•		•			•	
North Brother Island	20									•											•	•
Hunter I. Marine Sanctuary	138	•							•			•									•	•
Thomas Pell Wildlife Refuge	371	•	•						•			•		•	•							
Pelham Bay Park Preserve	883	•	•	•					•			•		•	•	•	•	•	•	•	•	•
Riverdale Park	110	•	•					•														
Seton Falls Park Preserve	36	•	•													•		•			•	
Van Cortlandt Park Preserve	573	•	•												•	•	•	•	•	•	•	
BROOKLYN																						
Four Sparrow Marsh	67	•	•	•			•					•		•								•
Fresh Creek Park Preserve	92			•			•					•		•								•
Paedergat Basin Park Preserve	161			•			•					•									•	•
Prospect Park Preserve	208	•	•																		•	•
MANHATTAN																						
Hallett Nature Sanctuary: CP	3.4	•																				
The Ravine: CP	119	•	•																			
Inwood Hill Park-Shorakapok	136	•		•				•													•	•
QUEENS																						
Alley Pond Park Preserve	549	•		•					•			•		•	•	•	•	•				
Cunningham Park Preserve	240	•												•								
Dubos Point Wildlife Sanctuary	33		•				•								•	•						
Flushing Meadows-Willow Lake	106		•												•					•	•	
Forest Park Preserve	274	•													•	•		•				•
Idlewild Park Preserve	242	•	•				•					•		•								
Rockaway Arverne Shorebird Preserve	84		•				•															•
Udalls Cove Park Preserve	31	•	•	•					•												•	•
Spring Creek Park Preserve	75		•				•														•	•
STATEN ISLAND																						
Arden Heights Woods Preserve	185	•	•																			
Blue Heron Park Preserve	169	•	•												•	•				•	•	•
Clove Lake Park Preserve	131	•	•	•											•						•	
Conference House Park Preserve	105	•	•		•								•	•							•	•
Deer Park Preserve	40	•	•																			
Eibs Pond Park Preserve	39		•												•	•				•	•	•
Evergreen Park Preserve	22	•	•												•					•	•	•
High Rock Park Preserve	90	•	•												•					•	•	
Isle of Meadows Preserve	100			•		•																•
Islington Pond Park Preserve	22	•	•												•	•				•		
Lemon Creek Preserve	16	•	•	•	•							•	•	•								•
Long Pond Park Preserve	115	•	•												•	•	•			•	•	
Pralls Island Preserve	74		•		•							•		•							•	•
Reeds Basket Willow Swamp	49	•	•													•		•				•
Saw Mill Creek Marsh Preserve	117	•		•	•																	•
Shooters Island Preserve	26			•	•																•	•
W.T. Davis Wildlife Refuge	428	•	•	•	•							•		•							•	•
Staten Island Greenbelt Preserve	1352	•	•	•											•	•	•	•	•	•	•	•
Sweet Bay Magnolia Preserve	241	•	•																	•		
Wolfe's Pond Park Preserve	207	•	•	•	•							•	•	•	•	•	•	•		•	•	•

Birds of Prey	Game Birds	Songbirds	Warblers	Bats	Chipmunks	Muskrat	Raccoons	Seals	Red Fox	Opossum	Freshwater Plants	Saltwater Plants	Native Wildflowers	Native Shrubs	Grassland	Manhattan Schist	Inwood Marble	Fordham Gneiss	Serpentenite	Hartland Formation	Acres	FOREVER WILD SITES
																						BRONX
		•	•																		35	Bronx Park Preserve
																					20	North Brother Island
•		•					•					•	•								138	Hunter I. Marine Sanctuary
•																					371	Thomas Pell Wildlife Refuge
•	•	•										•	•	•						•	883	Pelham Bay Park Preserve
		•											•	•		•		•			110	Riverdale Park
						•					•		•	•							36	Seton Falls Park Preserve
•	•	•	•				•		•	•	•		•	•		•	•	•			573	Van Cortlandt Park Preserve
																						BROOKLYN
•		•			•							•	•								67	Four Sparrow Marsh
•												•	•								92	Fresh Creek Park Preserve
													•		•						161	Paedergat Basin Park Preserve
		•	•																		208	Prospect Park Preserve
																						MANHATTAN
																•					3.4	Hallett Nature Sanctuary: CP
		•											•		•						119	The Ravine: CP
•		•										•	•	•		•	•				136	Inwood Hill Park-Shorakapok
																						QUEENS
																					549	Alley Pond Park Preserve
																					240	Cunningham Park Preserve
																					33	Dubos Point Wildlife Sanctuary
	•	•	•								•		•	•							106	Flushing Meadows-Willow Lake
•		•			•						•										274	Forest Park Preserve
															•						242	Idlewild Park Preserve
												•									84	Rockaway Arverne Shorebird Preserve
•							•				•	•									31	Udalls Cove Park Preserve
						•	•				•										75	Spring Creek Park Preserve
																						STATEN ISLAND
•				•							•										185	Arden Heights Woods Preserve
•		•									•		•	•	•						169	Blue Heron Park Preserve
		•	•																•		131	Clove Lake Park Preserve
•		•	•					•						•							105	Conference House Park Preserve
•		•	•		•								•	•							40	Deer Park Preserve
							•				•		•	•						•	39	Eibs Pond Park Preserve
		•	•								•		•	•							22	Evergreen Park Preserve
•		•	•										•	•							90	High Rock Park Preserve
												•									100	Isle of Meadows Preserve
		•	•																		22	Islington Pond Park Preserve
												•									16	Lemon Creek Preserve
		•	•										•	•	•						115	Long Pond Park Preserve
												•									74	Pralls Island Preserve
		•									•		•	•							49	Reeds Basket Willow Swamp
•		•				•	•				•										117	Saw Mill Creek Marsh Preserve
												•									26	Shooters Island Preserve
•		•				•	•		•	•	•		•								428	W.T. Davis Wildlife Refuge
•		•	•			•	•				•	•	•	•	•						1352	Staten Island Greenbelt Preserve
		•									•		•	•							241	Sweet Bay Magnolia Preserve
•		•	•				•		•	•			•								207	Wolfe's Pond Park Preserve

CHAPTER 4

animals

Earthworm: *Lumbricus terrestris*

ETYMOLOGY

Lumbricus: worm; *terrestris:* land

Description   An earthworm moves forward with its pointy end in the front. This is its mouth and *prostomium* (area in front of the mouth). There is a concentration of sensory cells around the prostomium. Though it has no eyes, the earthworm possesses light sensitive cells and can "sense" light. It cannot hear, but it feels vibrations of animals moving nearby. The worm's body is divided into segments. It moves forward by contracting and expanding its segments. *Setae*, pairs of bristles attached to each segment, push against the ground with each contraction and help the animal move. When a robin or other bird tries to pull an earthworm out of the ground, the worm uses these bristles to hold on to the wall of its home.

Common Locations   Earthworms live in the city's soil, forming deep, permanent burrows and coming to the surface to feed.

Notes of Interest   The earthworm has no lungs and takes in oxygen through its moist skin. If it dries out it will suffocate. Its skin is covered by mucus-secreting cells. The mucus lubricates the worm's body and eases its movement through its burrow. Earthworms are hermaphrodites, with both male and female reproductive organs. Once they have mated, the *clitellum*, the girdle-like ring around the front of the worm, slides along its body, picking up fertilized eggs. When the clitellum falls off into the soil, it forms an egg case within which the embryo worms develop.

Ecological Role   Earthworms are a sought-after prey by birds, burrowing mammals, turtles, and frogs. Earthworms are decomposers, turning decaying animal and plant material into rich, new soil.

KEY POINTS

- Earthworms were brought to North America by the early European settlers.
- In Central Park, abundant earthworms consuming the leaf litter may be disrupting the natural ecology of the forest floor.
- Earthworms are beneficial because they aerate the soil, which allows oxygen and rainwater in.

Plate 1   EARTHWORM

Horseshoe Crab: *Limulus polyphemus*

ETYMOLOGY

Limulus: sidelong motion; *polyphemus:* cyclops (One large eye is visible from the side of the horseshoe crab.)

Description Up to 20 inches long and 10 inches wide, the Atlantic horseshoe crab is named for the horseshoe-shaped front shield, or *carapace*, covering the *cephalothorax* (fused head and thorax).The crab has one large eye on either side of this shield and smaller eyes elsewhere. The rear shield is smaller, covering the abdomen, and beyond that is a long, pointed tail. The horseshoe crab has six pairs of joined legs. The first pair bears armlike claws used for feeding, four pairs are used for walking, and the long sixth pair is used for pushing. The crab's mouth is a narrow groove running between its legs. Behind the legs are gills housed in over-lapping plates, which are used for breathing. Females are larger than males.

Common Locations In May and June horseshoe crabs emerge from the sea onto New York City beaches, where each female lays thousands of eggs.

Notes of Interest Females leave the water with males grasping the backs of their shells. Females dig holes and lay up to twenty thousand tiny olive-green eggs, which the males fertilize. Humans depend upon horseshoe crabs for their value to the biomedical field. All vaccines and injections are tested for bacterial toxins using the blood of horseshoe crabs, because the animal's blood clots if bacteria are present. The 1967 Nobel Prize in Medicine was presented to scientists who used their studies of horseshoe crab vision to discover important principles regarding human eyesight.

Ecological Role Horseshoe crab eggs provide a banquet for migrating birds, which can double or even triple their weight during this spring feast. Horseshoe crabs are omnivores, feeding on marine worms, mussels, clams, dead fish, and algae. The middle segment of each leg is covered with spines that macerate the food, which is passed into the mouth located between the legs. Movement and feeding are related, and the horseshoe crab eats when it walks.

KEY POINTS

- Horseshoe crabs are not crabs.
- Their closest relatives are the arachnids, which include spiders and scorpions.

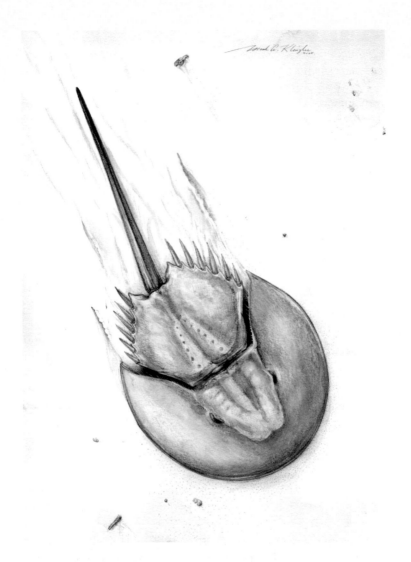

Plate 2 HORSESHOE CRAB

Daddy Longlegs: *Phalangium opilio*

ETYMOLOGY
Phalangium: spider; *opilio:* long legs

Description   The ⅛ to ¼-inch-long body of this arachnid is reddish brown with white spots. Unlike a spider's, a daddy longlegs' head, thorax, and abdomen form a compact, oblong body. The abdomen of the "harvestman" (seen in large numbers during fall or harvest season) is divided into segments and has no "waist." The daddy longlegs' long, curved, slender legs allow its body to be close to the ground. The legs, up to twenty times longer than the body, are seven-jointed and very fragile. The long second pair and their sensitive tips, are used to explore the arachnid's path, search for food, and warn of danger. Two shiny black eyes perch on top of the body. Protruding from its body are two tiny pincers, or *chelicera*, used to grasp, tear and push food into its mouth, to fight other harvestmen, and to clean its legs.

Common Locations   During summer and fall, daddy longlegs can be found throughout the five boroughs of New York City, in its parks, gardens, woods, and backyards.

Notes of Interest   The harvestman's long legs allow it to easily walk over the leaf litter. All of its legs have sense organs, but the longer second pair can be held high in the air, acting like antennae. They do not bite humans, but have glands at the base of the first pair of legs that emit an odor offensive to small animals as a defense against predators. Nocturnal foragers, daddy longlegs can roost in great numbers during the day on wood or tree trunks warmed by the sun, with their legs touching or intertwined.

Ecological Role   Daddy longlegs are omnivores, consuming insect pests such as aphids, decaying plants, and animals, thus helping to restore nutrients and minerals into the soil.

KEY POINTS

- Though they resemble spiders, daddy longlegs are not spiders. Like spiders, however, they are arachnids, possessing eight legs.
- Children often overcome their fear of spiders by holding the gentle, and common, daddy longlegs.

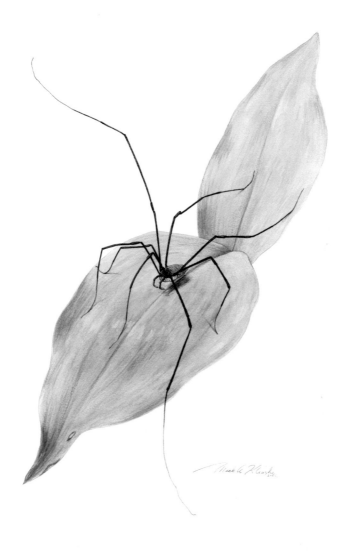

Plate 3   DADDY LONGLEGS

Garden Millipede: *Oxidus gracilis*

Description   The garden millipede is 1–1½ inches long. Its shiny, blackish brown body is rounded on top and flat on the bottom. It has twenty segments, with four small legs on each segment. Tiny *spiracles* (breathing pores) lie along each segment. Under magnification, the tan *keels*, extensions of the dorsal (back) segments, are visible. The garden millipede has a pair of antennae

Ecological Role   Millipedes are decomposers, feeding on decaying plant material. During the day they are found under moist leaf litter, rotting logs, bricks, and rocks. Millipedes will dry out and die if they are not in a moist environment.

Garden Centipede: *Lithobius forficatus*

Description   These common centipedes are long, thin, and reddish brown, with segmented bodies and one pair of legs on each segment. They are 2 inches long and typically have fifteen pairs of legs. (Centipedes of this species with fewer legs are immature and not fully grown.) Garden centipedes have two long antennae and a modified pair of legs at their head that function as jaws. These jaws are venomous and are used to attack small prey. The hind pair of legs projects backward and is as long as the centipede's antennae, making it difficult to tell which is the front end. Look for the small jaws in order to identify the head. The back two legs of centipedes are used to lasso prey and hold on until the centipede can bite.

Ecological Role   Garden centipedes are carnivores, feeding on insects, spiders, and other invertebrates.

Hoffman's Dwarf Centipede: *Nannarrup hoffmani*

Description   This tiny centipede was discovered living in Central Park in 2002 by scientists at the American Museum of Natural History during a study of the biodiversity of Central Park's leaf litter. Declared a new species, Hoffman's dwarf centipede is the smallest centipede known, at less than ½ inch long. Despite its diminutive size, it has forty-one pairs of legs. It is yellow, with short antennae.

Ecological Role   This tiny centipede is a voracious predator, killing and eating any animal it can get its tiny jaws around. It is common for scientists to find new species of invertebrates in wild

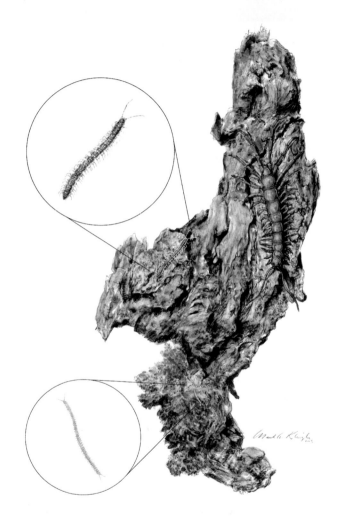

Plate 5   Clockwise from top left: GARDEN MILLIPEDE,
GARDEN CENTIPEDE, HOFFMAN'S DWARF CENTIPEDE

areas throughout the world. These discoveries are often used as a rationale for preserving wilderness. Discovering Hoffman's dwarf centipede in New York City is a reminder that conservation of urban parkland is important as well.

Pyralis Firefly: *Photinus pyralis*

Description   This beetle is about ¾ inch long. Its head is covered by a colorful *pronotum* (head and thorax cover) which is rosy pink, edged in yellow with a black spot in the middle. The *elytra* (wing covers) are black with yellow borders. At night, the very end (the last abdominal segment) of the firefly glows a bright yellow-green color. This light is called *bioluminescence.* The signal of the Pyralis firefly is easily identified, because it flies up as it flashes light. Males flash about every five seconds. Females do not fly, but flash from the ground about every two seconds. The flashes are mating signals. The female lays her eggs a few days after mating, on top of or in the soil. The eggs hatch in four weeks. The larvae, once hatched, feed until autumn. They burrow underground for the winter, and emerge in the spring to feed. Both eggs and larvae glow in the soil. Although other insects can produce light, fireflies are the only insects that can flash their light on and off in distinct signals.

Ecological Role   Firefly larvae are carnivorous, feeding on other insects and small invertebrates in the soil.

Two-Spotted Ladybug Beetle: *Adalia bipunctata*

Description   This species of ladybug is ¼ inch long and very round. It has a black head and thorax with white spots. The *elytra* (wing coverings) are reddish orange with two black spots: one on each elytron. After mating, the female lays pale yellow eggs on leaves near aphids. When the larvae hatch, they feed on the aphids. Larvae are up to ½ inch long, spiny, and black with yellow bands. After reaching full size, the larva attaches itself to a plant leaf or stem. The larval skin then splits down the back, exposing the pupa. The pupa is about the size of the adult but is all wrapped up, protecting the ladybug while it undergoes metamorphosis into its adult stage. This last metamorphic stage takes a few days.

Ecological Role   Both larvae and adults are carnivores, feeding on destructive plant invertebrates such as aphids, mealybugs, and mites: all garden pests. Ladybug larvae can eat about twenty-five aphids a day; adults can eat over fifty.

Plate 6

PYRALIS FIREFLY & TWO-SPOTTED LADYBUG BEETLE

Honeybee: *Apis mellifera*

Description   Introduced from Europe, honeybees are about ³/₄ of an inch long. Worker bees are female. Male bees are called *drones*, and their job is to mate with the queen to produce eggs. Female workers are slightly smaller than drones. All are reddish brown and black, with orangish yellow rings on their abdomen. The head, antennae, and legs are black. Honeybees have thick, pale hair on the *thorax* (middle body part). Like other social bees, a colony contains one breeding female, or "queen," a few thousand drones, and a large population of sterile female workers. The population of a hive can average between forty thousand and eighty thousand bees. The workers cooperate to find food and use a pattern of "dancing" to communicate the location of flowers. Their high level of social cooperation makes them one of the most advanced forms of insect life.

Ecological Role   Honeybees are important pollinators, enabling flowers to produce fruit and flowering plants to reproduce. Honeybees make the valued food, honey. Their numbers have been decimated by parasitic mites and colony collapse disorder.

Eastern Carpenter Bee: *Xylocopa virginica*

Description   The eastern carpenter bee, native to North America, is a 1-inch-long bee. Its most distinguishing feature is its long, shiny, bare, black abdomen. Having no stingers, males are harmless. The female does sting, but only if held. Carpenter bees chew 1- to 3-foot-long tunnels into wooden telephone poles, frames and other structures. The entrance hole and tunnels are round with a small finger-sized diameter. The tunnels terminate in several cells and cause little damage to the structure. The female carpenter bee collects pollen and nectar from nearby flowers and stores pollen in the cells for her larvae.

Ecological Role   Eastern carpenter bees are important pollinators, particularly today when North American honeybee populations have been severely depleted by mite infestations and disease.

Yellow Jacket: *Vespula maculifrons*

Description   Introduced from Europe, the ¹/₂-inch-long yellow jacket wasps have black and yellow stripes on their abdomen.

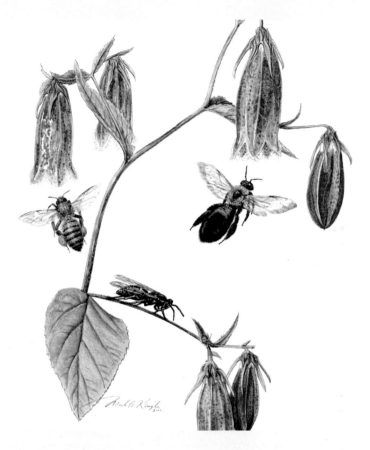

Plate 7 *Clockwise from left:* HONEYBEE,
EASTERN CARPENTER BEE, YELLOW JACKET

They are not as hairy as bees. Yellow jackets are social insects that
build enclosed paper nests below or above ground. A colony can
have up to five thousand wasps, with one queen. Female workers
hunt and kill prey for their larvae.

Ecological Role   Yellow jackets are pollinators and carnivores,
feeding on nectar and large quantities of insects. The females can
sting repeatedly. The painful bite causes swelling, redness, and an
itchy rash.

Common Green Darner Dragonfly: *Anax junius*

Description   Nicknamed "darning needle," the common green darner has a three-inch long thin body and up to a $4\frac{1}{2}$-inch wingspan. The wide wingspan makes the green darner one of the fastest-flying dragonflies. It is a colorful dragonfly, with a yellowish green head, a green thorax, and a violet-blue abdomen. Its clear wings have yellow tips. Females lay their eggs in stems of submerged plants. Nymphs hatch from their eggs and spend their larval stage underwater, using gills to breathe. Fully grown, the nymphs climb up the stem and out of the water. The winged dragonfly emerges from the exoskeleton of the nymph, dries its wings and flies off.

Ecological Role   Flying over ponds, streams, and meadows, the common green darner is a carnivore, hunting for mosquitoes, midges, flies, and other invertebrates. The aquatic nymph, also a carnivore, feeds on tadpoles, small fish, mosquito larvae, and other small aquatic invertebrates.

Eastern Forktail Damselfly: *Ischnura verticalis*

Description   One of the most common damselflies in New York City, the male has a lime green and black thorax and a blue-tipped abdomen. They are described as looking like "a little green dot being followed by a smaller blue dot." Females vary in color from the colors of males to blue to orange. Eastern forktails have clear wings, which they hold horizontally over their bodies when they are at rest. Eastern forktails are diminutive, reaching approximately 1 inch long

Ecological Role   The adults feed on small invertebrates, and nymphs feed on small aquatic invertebrates.

Eastern Amberwing Dragonfly: *Perithemis tenera*

Description   The eastern amberwing dragonfly is $\frac{3}{4}$ to 1 inch long, with a wingspan to $1\frac{3}{4}$ inches. It is yellowish brown, with a yellow face, a brown thorax and a brownish yellow abdomen. Its legs are yellowish with black spines, and its wings are amber. This low-flying skimmer usually flies in sunshine and close to water. It perches with its forewings held slightly higher than its hindwings. When laying eggs, the female flies over water, touching the surface with the tip of her abdomen and laying ten to twenty eggs with each dip.

Plate 8   Clockwise from top: COMMON GREEN DARNER
DRAGONFLY, EASTERN FORKTAIL DAMSELFLY,
EASTERN AMBERWING DRAGONFLY

Ecological Role   The eastern amberwing is a carnivore
through every stage of metamorphosis. Nymphs and adults feed
upon insects.

Polyphemus Moth: *Antheraea polyphemus*

Description The female polyphemus moth lays three to five eggs on the underside of a leaf. The host plants include trees and shrubs such as oaks, maples, birches, American hornbeam, haw-thorns, American beech, ash, witch hazel, tulip tree, black cherry, elderberry, sassafras, willows, hickories, elms, and sycamores. Cat-erpillars eat their eggs as they hatch, and then start feeding on leaves. As they grow they become large—up to $3^{1}/_{2}$ inches, and colorful: bright green with yellow stripes and red and silver spots. The cater-pillars wrap themselves in leaves and spin a silken, white cocoon, which hardens and turns brown. If the cocoon forms in late summer or fall, the pupa will overwinter and emerge in spring. If it forms in early summer, the adult will emerge, mate and lay eggs.

Tannish yellow with black and white wavy lines on its wings, the polyphemus moth is one of our largest and most colorful moths. Adults can have a 6-inch wingspan. The eyespots are yellow on the forewings and blue, black, and yellow on the hindwings. From below, the wings look like brown leaves, which helps them camou-flage. Males have large, feathery antennae, which detect the female's pheromones (scent). Adults do not feed, and have no mouthparts. They mate, lay eggs, and die.

Ecological Role Caterpillars are an important prey animal for birds, bats, mice, squirrels, and carnivorous invertebrates.

Eastern Tent Moth: *Malacosoma americana*

Description Female moths lay egg masses of up to three hun-dred eggs around a twig in midsummer. The egg mass is dark and shiny and overwinters, hatching in spring. Eastern tent larvae, or caterpillars, grow up to 2 inches long and are black with a white stripe down their back. Blue spots and red or yellow stripes run along their sides. Upon hatching, they immediately climb up the tree to a crotch of branches and build a silk tent, which they use for protection. They leave the tent during the day to feed and return to it at night. In large numbers, this caterpillar is capable of defoliating a forest. As the caterpillars feed and grow, the tent grows larger. Caterpillars spin a yellowish silk cocoon, emerging as adults in three weeks. The reddish brown adult moths have white bands on their forewings. They have feathery antennae and a hairy thorax.

Plate 9
From top: POLYPHEMUS MOTH & EASTERN TENT MOTH

Cabbage White Butterfly: *Pieris rapae*

Description   About 2 inches wide, the cabbage white is the most commonly seen butterfly in New York City. It is white with black spots on the forewings and charcoal wingtips. Males have one black spot on each forewing, and females have two. They can be seen flying from early spring through late fall. Caterpillars are green with a light yellow stripe and short white hairs. They grow to $^3/_4$ inch long. Cabbage white pupae form *chrysalids* (moth pupae form cocoons, while butterfly pupae form chrysalids) that are green or brown with points. The pupa hibernates over the winter and emerges as an adult butterfly in the spring. An interesting behavior of cabbage white butterflies is the dancing, spiral flight in which a male and female engage. When a male approaches a female that has already mated, she communicates her disinterest by ascending. The butterflies circle each other until the male loses interest, dropping down. The female descends slowly. European cabbage whites were introduced to North America around 1860 and have replaced our native cabbage white.

Ecological Role   After mating, females lay a single egg on the underside of a leaf of a host plant belonging to the mustard family, such as wild mustard, shepherd's purse, pepperweed, sweet alyssum, moneyplant, kale, cabbage, or broccoli plants. The adult butterflies are pollinators, feeding on the flower nectar of dandelions, red clover, asters, and other flowers.

Mourning Cloak Butterfly: *Nymphalis antiopa*

Description   The mourning cloak is a large butterfly, with a wingspan up to 4 inches. It is purplish brown above, with a wide yellow border and a row of blue spots within black just inside the border. The wings are irregular, with a short projection extending from each wing. Below, it is grayish black, bordered in yellowish gray with a row of bluish chevrons just inside the border. The mourning cloak is long-lived for a butterfly. It overwinters as an adult, and some may be eleven months old when observed the following summer. On sunny days in early spring, the mourning cloak's dark coloration and basking behavior helps raise its temperature above the air temperature. The wings become solar collectors, warming the *hemolymph* (blood) in the wing veins and pumping the warmed fluid to the body until the butterfly is warm enough to fly. The black

Plate 10   *From top:* CABBAGE WHITE BUTTERFLY
& MOURNING CLOAK BUTTERFLY

caterpillars have branched spines, white speckles, and rows of red spots along their backs.

Ecological Role   Mourning cloak caterpillars feed on the leaves of trees such as tulip, cottonwood, willow, elm, and birch. Butterflies feed on tree sap, fruit, and occasionally on flower nectar.

Eastern Tiger Swallowtail Butterfly:
Papilio glaucus

Description   This large ($4\frac{1}{2}$ inch) butterfly is yellow with wide vertical black stripes down the forewings and thin black stripes down the hindwings. The bottom edges of the hindwings have some orange and many blue spots. Borders of the wings have yellow spots outlined in black. Some adult females are a dusky brown with blue hindwings, mimicking the pipevine swallowtail, which feeds on Dutchman's pipevine, a plant that contains a foul-tasting chemical. Predators learn to avoid the imitators the same way they avoid the real pipevine swallowtails. The caterpillar is green with a large head with black and orange eyespots and blue dots on its body.

Ecological Role   Eastern tiger swallowtails lay their eggs on the leaves of tulip trees, and black cherry, American hornbeam, red maple, spicebush, American elm, and sassafras trees. The adults are pollinators, feeding on flower nectar.

Eastern Black Swallowtail Butterfly:
Papilio polyxenes

Description   Both male and female eastern black swallowtails are bluish black with yellow spots on their wings. Along the midline of the hindwings there are two orange eyespots with black dots. On the hindwings, the male has a yellow band with small blue spots below, and the female has yellow dots with a large band of blue dots. You can identify this butterfly as male if it has more yellow on its hindwings and female if it has more blue. On each of its segments, the green caterpillar is boldly patterned with bands of alternating yellow and black spots.

Ecological Role   Eastern black swallowtails lay their eggs on the leaves of plants that are members of the carrot family, such as Queen Anne's lace (wild carrot), fennel, dill, and parsley. The adults are pollinators, feeding on flower nectar.

Common Locations   These swallowtail butterflies are commonly seen during summer in city gardens throughout the five boroughs.

Plate 11   From top: EASTERN TIGER SWALLOWTAIL
& EASTERN BLACK SWALLOWTAIL

Monarch Butterfly: *Danaus plexippus*

Description   Monarchs go through four stages of metamorphosis. Female butterflies lay their eggs on milkweed leaves. The eggs hatch in three to five days and the tiny, 1/8-inch-long caterpillar eats its way out of the egg and proceeds to eat the milkweed leaf its egg was laid on. The caterpillar is colorful with black, white, and yellow bands. It has two long filaments near its head and two more on its next-to-last abdominal segment. It has eight pairs of legs. The first three pair of legs becomes the butterfly's legs. With sharp nippers in its jaws it cuts holes in leaves. It eats almost nonstop until it is too big for its skin, growing to about 2 inches long.

When it is two to three weeks old, the caterpillar spins a sticky knob, hooks its back feet into the knob, and hangs with its head down in a "J" formation. It splits its larval skin from the head to the tail. Its new skin is soft and damp but becomes dry when it hardens. The monarch chrysalis is one of the most beautiful objects in the natural world. It is jade and emerald green with glittering gold and black dots. Inside the chrysalis miraculous changes take place. The animal inside is transforming from a crawling insect to a butterfly capable of flying over two thousand miles. By seven days the colors of the chrysalis change, and the dark orange and black of the wings begins to show. Within ten to twelve days the shiny, translucent skin of the chrysalis splits, revealing the butterfly.

The butterfly is damp and crumpled when it emerges. It pumps liquid into the black veins of its wings to stiffen them. White spots border the two pairs of orange and black wings and dot the black head and thorax. Fine, dusty scales cover the monarch's wings. The scales overlap like shingles on a roof so that they can shed rain. The monarch's *proboscis* (tongue) is a coiled tube. As a caterpillar, it was a chewing insect; as a butterfly, it is a sipping insect.

Common Locations   Throughout New York City's parks, the monarch visits gardens and roadside flowers, particularly milkweed.

Ecological Role   Important pollinators, monarchs are the only butterflies that migrate. They fly thousands of miles to Mexico in late summer, where they overwinter until spring when they begin their return journey to gardens, roadsides, and fields throughout the United States, including the five boroughs of New York City.

Plate 12 MONARCH BUTTERFLY

Pillbug: *Armadillidium vulgare*

ETYMOLOGY
Armadillidium: armadillo-like; *vulgare*: common

Sowbug: *Porcellio scaber*

ETYMOLOGY
Porcellio: little pig; *scaber*: scaly
COUNTRY OF ORIGIN
European

Description   Pillbugs (not shown in illustration) and sowbugs are terrestrial (land) isopods. All isopods are crustaceans, but most are marine—very few live on land. Slate gray, pillbugs and sowbugs have at least ten plated segments and seven pairs of short legs emerge from beneath seven of these segments. They have a pair of long, jointed, sensory antennae. As the animals walk, the antennae touch the ground. Pillbugs and sowbugs breathe through special gilled appendages called *pleopods* on the underside of the abdomen. When disturbed, pillbugs curl up into a tight ball, and sowbugs run.

Common Locations   Pillbugs and sowbugs live in the soil, beneath leaf litter, stones, and bricks. They need high humidity or they will dry out. They also need moisture to breathe through their pleopods.

Notes of Interest   Females have a *marsupium*, a brood pouch, in which the eggs are incubated until they hatch. They live in family groups until the young are grown. Each family has a chemical "badge" which distinguishes it from the rest of the population. Pillbugs mate for life. The father is head of the family and guards the family's burrow. The mother and father gather food for the family. The entire family cleans the burrow, depositing waste pellets outside the entrance. Although the young leave the burrow in midwinter to make new families, they continue to stay within 30 yards of the family's main burrow.

Ecological Role   Pillbugs and sowbugs are omnivores, feeding mainly on leaf litter, dead and decaying material like rotting wood, and fungi. Their burrowing helps aerate and circulate the soil.

KEY POINTS
  · Pillbugs and sowbugs can only survive in moist places.

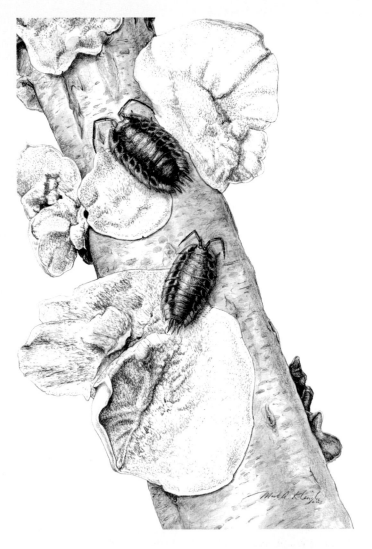

Plate 13 SOWBUGS

- They are active at night, avoiding the sun.
- Look for pillbugs and sowbugs under rotting logs.

Blue Crab: *Callinectes sapidus*

Description   The blue crab is a crustacean. It has a brownish blue, 9-inch-wide carapace covering its fused head and thorax, and five pair of legs. The first pair, the large and powerful pincers, is used for grabbing and crushing prey. The blue crab belongs to a family of swimming crabs but also uses its legs for walking. The fifth pair of walking legs, flat and paddle-shaped, is used for swimming and for fanning pheromones (scent) during courtship. Males have bright blue claws and females have red tipped claws. Males have a rocket-shaped abdomen, and females have a triangular-shaped abdomen, which rounds out when they are carrying eggs.

Ecological Role   Blue crabs live in brackish water (fresh water mixed with salt water) in the Hudson River and the brackish bays, sounds, and shores of New York City. Omnivores, adult crabs feed on fish, algae, and detritus (dead organic material). Along the Atlantic Coast they are the much-valued soft-shelled crabs that people love to eat. When the female molts and becomes soft-shelled she is able to mate, and she does so once in her life. The male carries her around until she sheds her shell. They mate, and he continues to carry and protect her until her shell hardens again and they separate. The following spring or summer she lays her eggs.

Northern Rock Barnacle: *Balanus balanoides*

Description   The rock barnacle is a small marine crustacean that lives in colonies permanently attached to rocks, boat hulls, docks, and underwater pilings. They also live on the surfaces of sea turtles, whales, and horseshoe crabs. The soft-bodied animal lives within a hard shell made up of many plates. The top plates open to allow the feeding appendages to capture food.

Ecological Role   When submerged, barnacles are filter feeders, "combing" the water with their feathery *cirri: thoracic* leglike feeding appendages that reach out to capture *zooplankton* (microscopic animals and protozoans) and food particles. When the tide is out and the barnacles are exposed to air, the top plates of their shells close to protect the animal within from drying out and from predation. Barnacles can spend many hours each day high and dry, protected within their shells. When the tide comes in, the cirri protrude from the plates and they are able to feed once again.

Plate 19   BLUE CRAB & NORTHERN ROCK BARNACLE

Spiny Cheek Crayfish: *Orconectes limosus*

ETYMOLOGY
Orco: Latin for God of the underworld; *nectes*: swimmer;
limulus: muddy

Description   *Orconectes limosus* is one of several species of
crayfish living in freshwater ponds, streams, and lakes of New York
City. Crayfish have a hard carapace over their cephalothorax (head
and thorax). The head has two pairs of sensory antennae and a pair
of eyes on movable stalks. The thoracic appendages include four
pairs of walking legs that are also used to probe streambeds for food.
The pond crayfish is 4 to 5 inches long. Crayfish have one pair of
clawed *chelipeds*, adapted from walking legs for grabbing prey and
for defense, which they extend in front of them while walking on the
streambed. These strong pincers can cut, capture food, attack, and
defend against predators. The crayfish also has several pairs of
appendages which cycle water over its gills, and five pairs of *swim-
merets*, which are under the abdomen and help the crayfish swim.
Crayfish have a hard external skeleton. This jointed exoskeleton provides protection and allows movement, but it is shed or molted as
the crayfish grows. Molting occurs six to ten times during the first
year of rapid growth, but less often during the second year. For several days following the molt, crayfish have soft exoskeletons, are
more vulnerable to predators, and will hide.

Common Locations   Crayfish are found throughout the five
boroughs in freshwater streams, ponds, and lakes. In Central Park
they live in the Model Boat Pond and the Ravine.

Notes of Interest   Crayfish commonly hide under rocks or logs
in their ponds or streambeds. Young crayfish feed during the day,
while adults (one year old and older) are more active on cloudy days
and during the night. Their movement is a slow walk. When startled,
they rapidly flip their tail, swimming backward to escape danger.

Ecological Role   Crayfish are omnivores and feed on snails,
algae, aquatic plants, insect larvae, worms, tadpoles, and dead fish.
They are important prey animals for fish, frogs, salamanders, turtles,
water snakes, wading birds, and aquatic mammals.

KEY POINTS:
- Crayfish look like tiny lobsters and, in fact, are members of
  the same family.

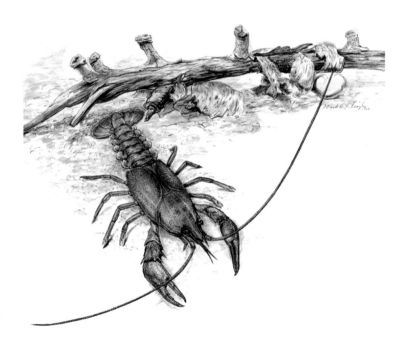

Plate 15   SPINY CHEEK CRAYFISH

American Eel: *Anguilla rostrata*

ETYMOLOGY

Anguilla: eel; *rostrata:* long nose

Description   The American eel grows up to 3 feet long. Smooth, tiny scales cover its long and slender body, making it slippery and almost impossible to grab. A long, low dorsal fin extends over at least two-thirds of its back, connecting with the *caudal* (tail) fin and the anal fin on the underside. It has no pelvic fins, but a pair of strong, well-developed pectoral fins. The American eel has diminutive eyes, a long, tapered head, and a small mouth with a lower jaw that sticks out farther than the upper jaw. Eels are yellowish brown to dark-olive above and paler below. Females grow larger than males.

Common Locations   American eels live in the Hudson River and other freshwater and brackish rivers of New York City.

Notes of Interest   American eels are *catadromous*. That is, they spawn in the ocean and males spend their lives in brackish to fresh water, while females move to freshwater rivers. It was not until the early twentieth century that scientists discovered that both the American eel and European eels spawned in the Sargasso Sea near Bermuda. Young eels begin their journeys back to the rivers their parents lived in. What has not been discovered is how young eels of each species know which continent to go to. After remaining in rivers for up to thirty years, adult females migrate in the fall back to the Sargasso Sea to lay their eggs. Mature female eels may contain two million or more eggs.

Ecological Role   American eels are omnivores. They consume a wide variety of aquatic insects, shrimp, crayfish, and other crustaceans, fish, fish eggs, frogs, and worms. They feed mainly at night.

KEY POINTS

- Although they look snakelike, American eels are fish.
- During winter, the American eels of New York City hibernate in the deep sediment of the Hudson and other rivers.
- American eels can "walk" on land by "slithering" on wet grass using their strong body muscles to move from one body of water to another or to get above waterfalls.

Plate 16   AMERICAN EEL

Striped bass: *Morone saxatilis*

ETYMOLOGY
Morone: unknown; *saxatilis:* rock-dwellers

Description   The mature striped bass can attain 70 pounds and reach 5 feet in length by the age of seventeen. Females grow larger than males. The striped bass has a long head, pointed snout, and a projecting lower jaw. The two dorsal fins are of equal length and are triangular. The striped bass is dark olive green to steel blue or almost black above, silvery on the sides, and white on the belly. The sides have seven or eight longitudinal dark stripes. Three to four stripes are above the lateral line, one is on it, and three are below. The upper stripes are the longest and may reach to the caudal fin (the tail).

Common Locations   Striped bass spawn in the fresh waters of the Hudson, 60 miles north of New York City. The Hudson River has become well known as a spawning area for the striped bass. Rebuilding of the West Side Highway was stopped in the mid-1970s because of the potential harm to the juvenile striped bass living along the shoreline piers of Manhattan's West Side. An alarming decline of striped bass in the late 1970s, due to pollution, over-fishing, and habitat loss, caused Congress to enact the Emergency Striped Bass Act. The cleanup of PCBs (polychlorinated biphenyls) and other pollutants in the Hudson River after the Clean Water Act of 1972, has helped bring the population of striped bass back.

Notes of Interest   Striped bass are *anadromous,* which means they migrate from the sea into an *estuary* ("arm of the sea") like the Hudson to spawn. Three-year-old juvenile females migrate to the ocean where they mature. After four or five years, females return to spawn. A mature female can produce three million eggs. The semi-buoyant eggs require strong freshwater currents to stay suspended for two or three days until they hatch.

Ecological Role   The striped bass is an omnivore. It eats small crustaceans and fish, including herring, menhaden, flounder, eel, shad, anchovies, fish eggs, crabs, shrimp, soft clams, and mussels. The striped bass has been one of the most sought-after commercial and recreational fish since colonial times.

KEY POINTS
- A large, silvery-sided fish with seven or eight dark stripes on its side.

Plate 17   STRIPED BASS

Pumpkinseed Sunfish: *Lepomis gibbosus*

Description   Pumpkinseeds (not shown in illustration) average 6–10 inches in length. They are colorful freshwater fish with wavy, interconnecting blue-green lines over their golden brown sides. Above they are brownish olive. They have red spots on the rear portion of their gill flaps and wavy emerald or blue streaks on the sides of their heads. Pumpkinseeds have long, pointed pectoral fins and no spots on the soft portion of their dorsal fins.

Ecological Role   Pumpkinseeds are omnivores. They consume insects, crustaceans, and small fishes.

Bluegill: *Lepomis macrochirus*

Description   Bluegills are greenish brown above, bluish green on the sides, and golden-orange below. The sides of their heads are bluish green. The large, square-shaped, blue-black gill flap and conspicuous dark blotch on the back of the soft-rayed portion of their dorsal fins distinguishes bluegills from other sunfishes. Bluegills average 6–10 inches in length.

Ecological Role   Bluegills are omnivores. Introduced from western New York State, bluegills eat mostly insects and crustaceans. The bluegill will also consume some plant material.

Largemouth Bass: *Micropterus salmoides*

Description   The largemouth bass is the largest member of the sunfish family, reaching 20 inches. The largemouth bass is greenish with a prominent black stripe running along the side. Its lower jaw juts out.

Ecological Role   Introduced to New York City from the central and southeastern United States, largemouth bass are omnivores. They lie in wait and ambush prey such as crayfish, frogs, salamanders, mice, and other small mammals.

Common Locations   Sunfish can be found throughout New York City's ponds and lakes.

Notes of Interest   Male sunfish use their fins to dig bowl-shaped nests by fanning the pond or lakebed and removing material. The males' nests are often close together. Females may deposit their

Plate 18 From top: BLUEGILL & LARGEMOUTH BASS

eggs in several nests. Males remain in one nest and guard the eggs and young until the young swim off.

American Bullfrog: *Rana catesbeiana*

ETYMOLOGY

Rana: frog; *catesbeiana:* for German naturalist Mark Catesby

Description   The American bullfrog, the largest frog in North America, grows to more than 10 inches. With its hind legs outstretched it can be 18 inches long. It is mottled green above and pale below. The males have yellow throats, and the females have white throats. Their eyes are gold and their head and body are broad. The *tympanic membrane* (eardrum) helps identify the frog's gender: The female's membrane is equal to the size of her eye. In males the membrane is larger.

Common Locations   Throughout the five boroughs in fresh-water ponds, lakes, and slow-moving streams

Notes of Interest   The American bullfrog is native to the eastern United States. The male attracts the female using deep vocalizations that sound like *jug-o-rum.* From June through August females lay between ten thousand and twenty-five thousand eggs in a mass of jelly. These hatch into tadpoles within a week if air and water temperatures are warm. Metamorphosis from tadpole to frog can take two years, during which time the tadpole can grow to 6 inches long. American bullfrogs become mature in four to five years, at which time the male finds a territory from which he attracts females and defends it against other males.

Ecological Role   American bullfrogs are carnivores and will eat anything they can swallow, including invertebrates and small vertebrates such as mammals, birds, reptiles, fish, turtles, and frogs. Bullfrogs are consumed by herons, egrets, raccoons, and snakes. Tadpoles are eaten by predacious diving beetles, dragonfly larvae, and frogs, including adult bullfrogs.

KEY POINTS

- The American bullfrog is a large, mottled green frog.
- Its long, strong hind legs make it a powerful swimmer and jumper.
- The bullfrog hibernates below the muddy pond or lakebed.
- Frogs take oxygen in through their skin and can stay submerged throughout their winter hibernation.

Plate 19 AMERICAN BULLFROG

Fowler's Toad: *Bufo fowleri*

ETYMOLOGY

Bufo: toad; *fowleri:* named for naturalist Samuel P. Fowler, who discovered this toad in Massachusetts in 1843

Description   Fowler's toads are brownish gray or olive green with dark spots and a light stripe down the center of their backs. They are 3–4 inches long. In each of the dark spots there are three or more warts. The belly is white with one dark spot. Males have a dark throat and are darker overall than females. The toads have golden eyes flecked with black. The parotid glands of Fowler's toads are two bumps on the back of the head that lie directly behind the eye ridges. These glands store a toxin, which is released when a predator picks them up in their mouths. Birds and reptiles are not as affected as mammals by this toxin, which irritates the predator's mouth, forcing them to drop the toad.

Common Locations   Woodlands and fields of city parks in the Bronx, Brooklyn, Queens, and Staten Island.

Notes of Interest   Male Fowler's toads call females to ponds and lakes with a high-pitched trilling *waaah* produced by their round vocal sacs. Males will clasp females in an embrace called *amplexus.* The female lays long double strings of seven thousand to ten thousand eggs, which the male fertilizes externally. The female then returns to her life on the land. The eggs hatch in two to seven days. The tiny, dark tadpoles change into miniature toads in thirty to forty days. Maturity may be reached as young as one year but typically takes two years.

Ecological Role   Fowler's toads are carnivores, feeding on insects, worms, and other invertebrates they find in the soil where they live. They hibernate in cold weather by burrowing into the soil. Fowler's toads are consumed by garter snakes, water snakes, large frogs, birds, and raccoons, who eat the toad's underside to avoid the toxins in the parotid glands.

KEY POINTS

- Like all toads, Fowler's toads have dry, bumpy skin.
- They store water in their bladder, and their thick skin keeps water from leaving their bodies, which is why, unlike frogs, they can spend their lives on land.
- Fowler's toads return to the water to mate and lay eggs.

Plate 20 FOWLER'S TOAD

Red-Backed Salamander: *Plethodon cinereus*

Plethodont: full of teeth, referring to the rough pads in the roof of the mouth of some amphibians; *cinereus*: ash-colored, referring to the dark phase of this salamander

Description Growing up to 5 inches long, this native salamander occurs in two color phases. The "redback" phase has a reddish stripe down its back and tail. The "leadback" phase lacks the stripe and has a dark back, sometimes speckled with faint light spots. In both, the abdomen is mottled with a white and gray salt-and-pepper-like pattern. Red-backed salamanders are members of the lungless group of salamanders. They breathe through their skin and membranes in their mouth, which must be moist in order to absorb oxygen. Glands in their skin help maintain moisture. Salamanders have no external ears but sense vibrations from the ground. They have good vision and an excellent sense of smell and taste. The mouths of red-backed salamanders contain small teeth implanted on the margins of the upper and lower jaws and, in some cases, on the roof of the mouth.

Common Locations This slender salamander is found under rocks, leaf litter, and rotting logs in moist wooded areas of city parks in all five boroughs. It is our most common salamander.

Notes of Interest The breeding period is October to April. A group of five to twelve eggs is laid in a rotting log, a tree stump, or under rocks from May through July. Not requiring water to reproduce, the young go through their larval stage inside the egg. The female remains with the eggs through hatching, protecting them from predators. The young salamanders hatch in August and September. Females begin laying eggs at the age of four years. Males mature a year earlier.

Ecological Role Red-backed salamanders are carnivores, consuming tiny arachnids, insects, and other small invertebrates of the leaf litter. The presence of red-backed salamanders indicates a healthy forest. As indicator species, their presence verifies the health of New York City's woodlands.

KEY POINTS

- Look for this salamander in habitats where it spends its entire life, from egg to adult: under moist logs, rocks, and leaf litter.

VERTEBRATES: AMPHIBIANS

Plate 21   RED-BACKED SALAMANDER

Eastern Spotted Newt:
Notophthalmus viridescens

ETYMOLOGY

Notophthalmus: eyelike round markings; *viridescens:* green

Description The eastern newt goes through several different life stages during metamorphosis. The adult newt can grow up to 5 inches long. It is yellowish brown or olive above with small black spots. It is yellow below, with small black and red spots. The larval or tadpole stage is different from frog or toad tadpoles in that newts hatch with all four legs. They have feathery gills on the outside of their heads. Once the eastern spotted newt tadpoles develop lungs and move onto the land, they go through their *eft* stage, at which time they are a bright orangish red. The efts live on land for up to four years. They do not have gills, but like all newts and salamanders must keep their skin moist because they absorb oxygen through their skin. They are most often seen crawling around after a heavy rain. As they grow older, the efts grow darker, looking more like adult eastern spotted newts. Eventually, they return to the water as adults. Not all eastern spotted newt larvae become efts; especially in coastal areas, some larvae transform directly to the aquatic adult. In winter, efts hibernate under logs or stones. When they mature, they return to the pond where they mate and lay or fertilize eggs.

Common Locations Eastern spotted newts can be found in ponds in Brooklyn, Manhattan, and Queens.

Notes of Interest Newts in the red eft stage have toxins in their skin as a defense against predators. The aquatic adults remain active year-round and can even be seen swimming under ice.

Ecological Role Eastern spotted newts are carnivores during all three stages of metamorphosis. Efts eat small insects and snails. Adult newts consume worms, insects, small crayfish and other crustaceans, snails, mussels, tadpoles, amphibian eggs, and fish eggs. Adult newts and larvae are eaten by fish, turtles, birds, and other predators.

KEY POINTS

- In New York City, the eastern spotted newt is most often seen in its adult stage in ponds.

Plate 22 EASTERN SPOTTED NEWT

Common Snapping Turtle:
Chelydra serpentina serpentina

ETYMOLOGY

Chelydra: turtle; *serpentina:* serpent

Description   Native to North America, the common snapping turtle is one of the world's largest freshwater turtles, reaching a shell length of 19 inches and weight of 50 pounds. Its large head has strong jaws and a pointed nose, which sticks out of the water in order to breathe. The snapper's *carapace* (top shell) is brownish black when immature and olive or tan as it matures, with nine spiked edges toward the rear. Its *plastron,* or bottom shell, is small, yellow, or cream-colored with dark markings. Its flesh can be brown, black, gray, or tan. With large, strong, heavily scaled legs and webbed feet for swimming, the snapper's toes possess long thick claws. Its long tail has three rows of spikes. The snapper's eyes are small, but have a strikingly patterned black and gold "sunburst" design.

Common Locations   The common snapping turtle can be found in freshwater ponds in all five boroughs of the city. They prefer muddy bottoms where they can hibernate in winter and camouflage themselves as they lie in wait to ambush prey.

Notes of Interest   The snapping turtles have an incredibly wide throat, and can gulp down huge pieces of food. The windpipe opening is in the middle of the mouth, so when their mouth is full of food they can still breathe. The female leaves the water in late spring or early summer to dig a nest and lay her twenty to forty ping-pong-ball-shaped eggs, which she covers with dirt. The eggs are left to hatch on their own, which happens after about two or three months.

Ecological Role   The common snapping turtle is an omnivore. Adult snappers consume frogs, fish, newts, tadpoles, toads, crayfish, snakes, small turtles, small mammals, and birds.

KEY POINTS

- In June 2003 a 35-pound snapper was hit by a car in Central Park. Named "Myrtle," the turtle went to Connecticut for rehabilitation.
- Although mostly nocturnal, common snapping turtles feed underwater during the day, ambushing their prey from below.
- On land, snappers can be aggressive toward humans.

Plate 23   COMMON SNAPPING TURTLE

Diamondback Terrapin: *Malaclemys terrapin*

ETYMOLOGY

Malaclemys: soft turtle; *terrapin:* turtle

Description   The adult female has a shell up to 10 inches long, while the male's shell is only 5 inches. Its grayish white head, neck, and legs are dotted with black spots and streaks. The *carapace* (upper shell) is sculpted, with concentric rings of diamond-shaped *scutes* (scales). The color of diamondback carapaces can vary widely, from black, brown, or gray, to orange, olive, or tan. The *plastron* (lower shell) is usually yellowish or greenish gray. They have large black eyes and cream-colored jaws. Their webbed feet, designed for swimming, bear strong claws for climbing up banks.

Common Locations   This beautiful turtle can be found year-round in the bays and estuaries of Gateway National Recreation Area, a federal park that includes Jamaica Bay Wildlife Refuge (Queens), Floyd Bennett Field (Brooklyn), and several parks in Staten Island, as well as Alley Pond Park, Queens.

Notes of Interest   These terrapins can live in salt water, but mainly inhabit brackish marshes, where aquatic marsh plants such as saltmarsh cordgrass provide important feeding habitat. In summer, females come on shore to dig their nests in sand or gravel and lay three to eighteen eggs. After nesting, females join the males in the deeper bays and estuaries, where they feed until hibernation. Eggs take more than two months to hatch. Hatchlings emerge in late summer and early fall. Some hatchlings overwinter in their nests and emerge the following spring. Many hatchlings are preyed upon by raccoons.

Ecological Role   Terrapins are primarily carnivores, feeding on worms, snails, crabs, and fish. Occasionally they feed on aquatic plants. Predators such as raccoons pose a serious threat to terrapins. Highly prized for their meat from the 1880s through the 1930s, terrapins were harvested in huge numbers to make turtle soup, which almost led to their extinction. In 1990 regulations in New York State became effective, protecting the diamondback, whose populations are still small.

KEY POINTS

- The diamondback terrapin, one of the few saltwater turtles, has characteristic diamond-shaped scutes.

Plate 29 DIAMONDBACK TERRAPIN

- Since human disturbance can prevent females from
  nesting, the best way to view terrapins is with binoculars
  from 150 feet.

Eastern Painted Turtle: *Chrysemys picta picta*

Chrysemys: yellow turtle; *picta:* painted, embroidered

Description   The native eastern painted turtle is beautifully patterned. Up to 9 inches long, their greenish black *carapace* (upper shell) is flat and smooth with yellow lines between the *scutes* (scales). The carapace is bordered with red markings, and the *plastron* (lower shell) is yellow. The greenish black face is covered with broad, yellow stripes with yellow spots behind the eyes. The neck, legs, and tail have yellow and red stripes.

Common Locations   The eastern painted turtle can be found in freshwater ponds and lakes throughout the five boroughs of the city.

Notes of Interest   Eastern painted turtles prefer water bodies with aquatic plants for food and shelter, and logs and rocks that they can climb out on to bask. Sitting in the sun helps them digest food, warm their muscles, and rid themselves of parasites such as leeches, which dry up in the sun. Sometimes painted turtles bask with other turtles, such as the red-eared slider, and several turtles may sit on top of one another on logs or rocks. If the turtles sense danger they quickly escape into the water. In spring and summer, females dig nests on the shore and lay their eggs. Some hatchlings may overwinter in the nest and emerge the following spring. As with some other turtles and snakes, the gender of the hatchling is determined by temperature. Warm temperatures produce females and cooler temperatures produce males.

Ecological Role   The eastern painted turtle is an omnivore, consuming aquatic plants such as duckweed, algae, and water lilies, along with earthworms, insects, leeches, snails, crayfish, fish, tadpoles, frogs, and carrion (dead animals). Predators of the eastern painted turtle, especially juveniles, include fish, bullfrogs, turtles, snakes, herons, hawks, crows, raccoons, and foxes.

KEY POINTS

- Eastern painted turtles are colorful, with bright yellow stripes on their heads and red markings along the border of their carapace.
- Look for them basking on rocks and logs in city ponds and lakes.

Plate 25 EASTERN PAINTED TURTLE

Eastern Garter Snake: *Thamnophis sirtalis*

ETYMOLOGY
Thamnophis: bush snake; *sirtalis:* garter-like, referring to striped pattern of old-fashioned sock garters

Description The eastern garter snake grows up to $4^{1/2}$ feet long. Its pattern can vary but generally it consists of three pale stripes on a dark body. One narrow stripe runs down the center of the snake's back, and one broad stripe runs along each side. The stripes are usually yellow. Between the center and side stripes are two rows of alternating black "checker" spots. The scales of the eastern garter snake are *keeled* (ridged), and the snake's belly is yellow or pale green. Garter snakes, like all snakes, smell by using their tongues. When a snake flicks its forked tongue, each fork picks up chemicals from the air. The snake puts one fork in each of two holes in the roof of its mouth called the Jacobson's organ, which then sends a smell signal to its brain. Garter snakes, like all snakes, do not have ears. Their skulls and jawbones pick up vibrations from the ground.

Common Locations Eastern garter snakes can be found in city parks in all five boroughs, particularly near ponds and in moist woodlands and fields.

Notes of Interest Eastern garter snakes mate in spring. The young are born live in late summer or autumn. Garter snakes begin to hibernate in October. The snakes will go into any burrow that goes below the frost line: chipmunk and woodchuck burrows and basements are often used as hibernation dens.

Ecological Role Eastern garter snakes, like all snakes, are carnivores. Eastern garter snakes feed on a wide variety of animals: earthworms, fish, frogs, toads, salamanders, mice, and birds. They are not venomous, nor are they constrictors. They grasp their prey with strong jaws and sharp teeth that slant back to hook and hold the prey. Then the snake swallows the animal whole.

KEY POINTS

- The eastern garter snake is a medium-sized checkered and yellow-striped snake.
- It is commonly found in a wide variety of habitats, including wetlands, woods, and parks.

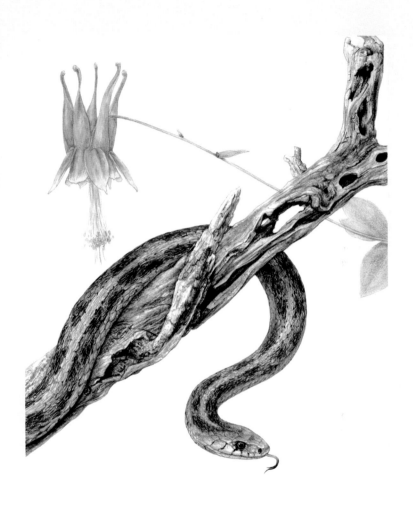

Plate 26   EASTERN GARTER SNAKE

Double-Crested Cormorant:
Phalacrocorax auritus

ETYMOLOGY
Phalacrocorax: bald raven; *auritus:* crested
Double-crested: ear tufts; *cormorant:* sea crow

Description This cormorant has a large black body with a long black tail, a bare, orange throat patch, emerald green eyes, and black legs and feet. The two crest feathers appear during breeding season. Males and females are alike. Immature double-crested cormorants have a light brown, sometimes white, throat, and chest.

Size Double-crested cormorants are 29–36 inches long. Their wingspan is 54 inches.

Common Locations During the summer, these water birds can be found and observed throughout the city's rivers, lakes, ponds, sound, bays, and ocean. Whenever you see a large black bird swim partially submerged in the water, dive, and then resurface, you are seeing a double-crested cormorant. Most cormorants migrate south in the fall.

Notes of Interest Double-crested cormorants do not have oil in their feathers. It is thought that they do not have to waterproof their feathers, as do most other birds, because they need wet feathers to more easily dive and stay submerged to find fish. Cormorants nest on small islands around the city. U Thant Island, which lies in the East River across from the United Nations and was named for the former Secretary General, has at least ten nests of double-crested cormorants. Some can be seen from the water.

Ecological Role A carnivore, the double-crested cormorant can dive down to 25 feet and stay submerged for several minutes as it hunts for fish. In fresh water the cormorant hunts for fish, amphibians, crayfish, and other aquatic invertebrates.

KEY POINTS
- As they perch, cormorants hold their wings out to dry.
- When the cormorant swallows, you can see the fish— often an American eel—moving down inside its throat.
- Usually silent, the cormorant can make deep grunting sounds when threatened or during courtship.

Plate 27   DOUBLE-CRESTED CORMORANT

Mute Swan: *Cygnus olor*

ETYMOLOGY
Cygnus: swan; *olor:* swan

Description The mute swan is a large white swan with an orange bill, a black triangle between the eyes and the bill, and a black knob above the bill. *Cygnets* (immatures) have gray-brown feathers and a gray-brown bill with a small black knob.

Size Mute swans are 56–62 inches long. Their wingspan is 7–8 feet. Males and females look alike, but males are larger.

Common Locations Manhattan: For six years during the harsh winters of the mid-1990s, a pair of mute swans wintered at the 79th Street Boat Basin. Each fall they would bring their cygnets to this city marina. Mute swans can be found during the warm seasons on many of the city's ponds and lakes, such as those in Inwood Hill Park in Manhattan and Van Cortlandt Park in the Bronx. During late fall, winter, and early spring they can be seen on the West Pond of Jamaica Bay Wildlife Refuge.

Notes of Interest Mute swans mate for life. If their mate dies, they have been known to grieve and die soon after. Mute swans are not mute. They have a call that is a soft purr, which they use with each other, with their cygnets, and with humans who feed them and whom they trust. Mute swans were introduced to the United States from Europe in the 1800s.

Ecological Role Mute swans are herbivores, feeding mainly on aquatic plants. Humans mistakenly feed them white bread, which is a very poor diet for these birds. If you feed them bread, make sure it is whole grain.

KEY POINTS
- The wings of mute swans make a humming sound in flight.
- When chicks first hatch, their feathers are not waterproof, and they ride on their parents' backs in the water.
- Mute swans often swim with their bills pointed down, their necks held in a graceful curve, and their wings arched over their backs.
- They have enormous black paddle-shaped webbed feet. Sometimes they will hold one foot straight out above the water as they paddle with the other foot.

Plate 28   MUTE SWAN

Canada Goose: *Branta canadensis*

ETYMOLOGY

Branta: burned (charcoal coloration); *canadensia:* from Canada

Description The Canada goose has a long black neck, white cheek patches, white throat (chin strap), and a black head. Their bodies are large and are brown-gray above with a whitish chest and belly. They have large, black, webbed feet. Males and females look alike. Goslings (babies) are a greenish yellow, round, and covered in down feathers.

Size Canada geese are 26–45 inches long. Their wingspan is 54–84 inches long. The male is larger than the female.

Common Locations The Canada goose can be found throughout the city on rivers, bays, sounds, ponds, and lakes. Here are a few locations: In Manhattan, Central Park's lakes, Riverside Park, and up and down the Hudson River; in Queens, Alley Pond Park and Jamaica Bay Wildlife Refuge; in Staten Island, Clove Lakes Park and Goethals Pond; in the Bronx, Van Cortlandt Park Lake and Pelham Bay Park; and in Brooklyn, Prospect Park Lake.

Notes of Interest Canada geese mate for life and are devoted to their goslings. The family stays together for one year before the yearlings separate from their parents and form groups with other yearlings. When mature, generally by age 3, they find their own mates and start families. Many Canada geese stay in New York City year-round. Others migrate.

Ecological Role Canada geese are omnivores. They feed on mollusks, crustaceans, and aquatic plants and graze on land grasses and other plants.

KEY POINTS

- The voice of the Canada goose is a two-note honk— *haronk*. Males have a deeper voice than females, whose honk is higher pitched. Canada geese are vocal, honking when they fly, or when they are on the water or on the land.
- When a goose family paddles together, they form a line: one parent swims in front, the goslings swim in the middle, and one parent takes up the rear.
- As the female and goslings feed, the male often stands guard, protecting the family.

Plate 29 CANADA GOOSE

Brant Goose: *Branta bernicula*

ETYMOLOGY

Branta: burned (charcoal coloration); *bernicula:* barnacle, from the Irish legend that these geese hatched from barnacles

Description   Adult brant geese have black necks, heads, and breasts. Their bellies can range from pale gray to nearly black, and their small bills and webbed feet are black. Their primary feathers (large flight feathers) and tail are also black, but the tail *coverts* (small feathers, coverings) are bright white, giving them a white-rumped appearance when in flight. The brant has a white "necklace" set against a black neck. This white ring is paler on juveniles.

Size   The brant geese are 22–26 inches long. Their wingspan is 42 inches.

Common Locations   Brant geese winter along the shores of Staten Island, Brooklyn, Queens, and on the Hudson River in Manhattan. They can be seen flying in huge flocks over the salt marshes of Jamaica Bay in Brooklyn and Queens, and in Wolfe's Pond Park in Staten Island.

Notes of Interest   Brant geese mate for life. Their eggs are incubated by the female, but the goslings are cared for by both parents and remain with their parents until the following breeding season.

Ecological Role   Brants are mainly herbivores, feeding on grasses, mosses, lichens, and aquatic plants during the warmer months and on marine algae and seaweed during winter. Their feeding and resting patterns depend on the tides; they feed at any time of the day or night that they have access to submerged algae and other vegetation.

KEY POINTS

- Brant geese are smaller than Canada geese.
- Their voice is a throaty *cur-onk.*
- Brant geese are rarely found in fresh water and winter in New York City along ocean and bay shorelines and the Hudson River.
- Arctic brants undertake one of the longest migrations of any waterfowl: some fly nonstop for three thousand miles across the Pacific Ocean to wintering grounds on the coast of Mexico.

Plate 30 BRANT GOOSE

American Black Duck: *Anas rubripes*

ETYMOLOGY
Anas: duck; *rubripes*: red foot

Description Both males and females have dark brown bodies, pale brown heads, and white under their wings. Males are darker than females and have a yellower bill. Both males and females have reddish feet and legs and a purple *speculum* (wing patch).

Size American black ducks are 20–24 inches long; their wingspan is 32–36 inches.

Common Locations Black ducks can sometimes be seen with mallards throughout the city's saltwater and freshwater wetlands. Some well-known places for viewing black ducks are the Lagoon in Pelham Bay Park in the Bronx; Marine Park and Floyd Bennett Field's Return-A-Gift-Pond in Brooklyn; the Hudson River and Central Park's Row Boat Lake, the Meer, Turtle Pond, and the Pool in Manhattan; and Prall's Creek and Goethals Pond in Staten Island.

Notes of Interest Black ducks can interbreed with mallards. They and other dabbling ducks can "jump" vertically from the water and take flight. The black duck is the only northeastern American duck where the males and females look alike.

Ecological Role Black ducks are omnivores and feed on aquatic plants as well as aquatic insects, tadpoles, small frogs, and salamanders. They are dabbling ducks, often feeding by "tipping up"—a method of feeding on the bottom with their rumps straight up and their webbed feet paddling the surface of the water.

KEY POINTS

- The black duck's voice is similar to the mallard's. Females make a throaty *quack*, and males have a more reedy *quack*.
- The black duck is shy and will swim away if approached.

Plate 31   AMERICAN BLACK DUCK

Mallard Duck: *Anas platyrhynchos*

ETYMOLOGY

Anas: duck; *platys:* broad or flat; *rynchos:* beak. *Mallard:* male.

Description The male has a metallic emerald green head, white neck ring, reddish brown chest, and grayish body. Besides the distinctive green head, all male mallards have two curly tail feathers. Males have bright orange legs and webbed feet. The female mallard has brown feathers edged in buff. Females have a dark line from the beak across the eye toward the back of the head. Females have white tail feathers, and both male and female have a blue *speculum* (wing patch) edged in black and white.

Size Mallard ducks are 21–28 inches long. Their wingspan is 30–40 inches.

Common Locations The most commonly seen ducks in New York City, mallards can be found throughout the five boroughs of the city on rivers, bays, sounds, ponds, and lakes.

Notes of Interest Mallards can be found year-round on the city's wetlands. During the spring and summer, females line their nests with their own down feathers. When the ducklings hatch, their mother leads them to water. Ducklings are brown with yellow spots.

Ecological Role Mallards are omnivores, feeding on aquatic and land plants and seeds, aquatic mollusks, insects, tadpoles, and fish. Like black ducks, they are dabbling ducks, often feeding by "tipping up" with their rumps straight up and their webbed feet paddling the surface of the water.

KEY POINTS

- The call of the female mallard is a loud *quack quack.* When she calls to her ducklings, her voice is deeper and more hoarse.
- Males have a more "reedy" voice.
- Ducklings have a loud, piercing *peep* that can be heard for quite a distance. This helps the mother find them if they are separated.

Plate 32   MALLARD DUCK

Wood Duck: *Aix sponsa*

ETYMOLOGY
Aix: a water bird; *sponsa:* betrothed, referring to the brilliant colors of the bird's plumage, as though it were dressed for a wedding. *Wood:* these ducks nest in trees.

Description   A native of North America and considered by many to be the most beautiful bird in North America, the wood duck is a freshwater dabbling duck. The male wood duck is colorful and intricately patterned, with a brilliant green iridescent head and crest that falls down to its back. The male's chest is wine colored, covered with white starlike points. The male's bill is red-orange, outlined with yellow and white, and has a black tip. His eyes are a brilliant orange-red. His back is dark purplish blue and iridescent. His throat and belly are white and his flanks are tan, crisscrossed with brown and outlined in black and white. The female's head and crest are grayish with a conspicuous white ring around her eyes. Her bill is dark and her throat is white.

Size   The wood duck is 17–20 inches long. Its wingspan is 28–30 inches.

Common Locations   Wood ducks can be found at Van Cortlandt Park in the spring and New York Botanical Garden in the winter. Brooklyn: The ducks live in the ponds in Brooklyn Botanical Garden and Floyd Bennett Field. Manhattan: The ducks can be found in the Lake in Central Park in winter. Queens: Alley Pond Park. Staten Island: Bunker Ponds Park during spring, Long Pond Park, and Clove Lakes Park.

Notes of Interest   These ducks make their nests in the cavities of trees up to 50 feet above ground, sometimes near the water, but sometimes more than a mile from water. After the eggs hatch, the mother wood duck leaps from the nest and calls to her ducklings who jump from the nest and follow her to water.

Ecological Role   As an omnivore, the wood duck feeds on aquatic plants, especially duckweed, and aquatic insects and tadpoles. On land they feed on all kinds of berries, seeds, nuts and acorns.

KEY POINTS:
- In some places, the wood duck is also called the acorn duck or the bridal duck.
- The male's call is a high-pitched *jeeeee*.

Plate 33 WOOD DUCK

Canvasback Duck: *Aythya valisineria*

ETYMOLOGY
Aythya: a seabird; *valisineria:* wild celery which is what the canvas-back loves to eat; Canvasback: feathers on back and flanks resemble canvas.

Description The male is white, with a red head and neck and black breast. His eyes are ruby red. The female has a brown head. Both male and female have sloping foreheads and sloping bills.

Size The canvasback duck is 19–24 inches long, with a wing-span of 28–35 inches. The female is larger than the male.

Common Locations In winter, Bronx: mouth of the Bronx River at Soundview Park; Manhattan: the Hudson River at Inwood Hill Park and the 79th Street Boat Basin in Riverside Park. Queens: Alley Pond Park and Jamaica Bay Wildlife Refuge. Staten Island: southern tip on Raritan Bay and Mariners Marsh Preserve.

Notes of Interest The canvasback is a great flier, traveling up to 72 miles per hour. During winter, huge numbers of canvasbacks raft up together, diving for food and bobbing up to the surface.

Ecological Role Canvasbacks are carnivores and can dive down to 30 feet hunting for fish and mollusks.

KEY POINTS

- Canvasbacks migrate to the Midwestern prairie and plains pothole region where they raise their families each spring and summer.
- Canvasbacks used to be seen by the thousands during winter in New York City wetlands. Their numbers are greatly reduced.

Plate 39   CANVASBACK DUCK

Bufflehead Duck: *Bucephala albeola*

ETYMOLOGY
Bucephala: buffalo-headed, large-headed; *albeola:* white; *bufflehead:* buffalo-head

Description   A tiny duck, the smallest of the North American diving ducks, male buffleheads are black and white with a blue bill. Males are black above and white below, with a puffy black head capped with a white crest. In sunlight, the black head has a greenish red iridescence. The females are dark above and pale below with a white cheek patch and white wing patches.

Size   The bufflehead duck is 13–16 inches long, with a wingspan of 20–24 inches.

Common Locations   In winter, bufflehead ducks can be seen on most wetlands in the city. The Bronx: Pelham Bay Park on the Long Island Sound and the Lagoon. Brooklyn: Prospect Park and Dead Horse Bay. Manhattan: the Hudson River at the 79th Street Boat Basin in Riverside Park and the Lake and Turtle Pond in Central Park. Queens: Alley Pond Park and Jamaica Bay Wildlife Refuge. Staten Island: the Atlantic Ocean off the southern tip near Conference House Park, and Prall's Creek.

Notes of Interest   Buffleheads are tiny but active ducks, scurrying across the water's surface or diving for food. Buffleheads can take off from the water like a dabbling duck, without having to run on its surface, as do most diving ducks. They are fast swimmers and can dive down to 15 feet.

Ecological Role   Buffleheads are omnivores. In their summer breeding grounds, they can be found in fresh water feeding on aquatic insects, snails, fish, and aquatic plants. They spend winter in salt water diving for shrimp, snails, and other crustaceans and mollusks.

KEY POINTS
- Male buffleheads are small black-and-white ducks with puffy black and white heads.
- Female buffleheads nest in woodpecker holes in trees in their northern summer breeding grounds near ponds, lakes, and freshwater rivers.
- Fast fliers, buffleheads can fly close to 50 miles per hour.

Plate 35   BUFFLEHEAD DUCK

Red-Breasted Merganser: *Mergus serrator*

ETYMOLOGY
Mergus: diver: *serrator:* one who saws

Description   The red-breasted mergansers are the largest of all the diving ducks. The male has a white collar above a speckled red breast and an iridescent, greenish black head with a ragged, wispy crest. He is black above and gray below with square, white wing patches. The female has a pale reddish brown neck and head with a shorter, shaggy crest and gray body. Both male and female have narrow, serrated red bills. Their eyes, legs, and feet are red.

Size   The red-breasted merganser is 16–18 inches long; its wingspan is 31–35 inches.

Common Locations   In winter: the Bronx: Pelham Bay Park. Brooklyn: Dead Horse Bay. Manhattan: The Lake and Turtle Pond in Central Park and the Hudson River south of the 79th Street Boat Basin in Riverside Park. Queens: Alley Pond Park, Breezy Point, and Jamaica Bay Wildlife Refuge.

Notes of Interest   The red-breasted merganser, along with the other diving ducks, is a winter resident of the city. In saltwater marshes, rivers, and bays and freshwater lakes, they are strong swimmers above and under water. They fly in single file low over the water.

Ecological Role   The red-breasted mergansers are carnivores who use their serrated bills to catch fish and aquatic crustaceans. Flocks may form a single file line to drive fish toward the shallows for easier capture.

KEY POINTS

- Red-breasted mergansers have a raked appearance.
- Males have a white, wide neck ring, or collar, above a reddish brown breast.
- The bill has sharp, backward-pointing serrations.
- Winter residents of city's rivers, bays, marshes, and lakes.

Plate 36   RED‑BREASTED MERGANSER

Hooded Merganser: *Lophodytes cucullatus*

ETYMOLOGY

Lophodytes: crested diver; *cucullatus:* hooded; *hooded:* high crest resembles a hood

Description The male hooded merganser has a fan-shaped white crest, bordered in black and a black head, neck, back, and tail. His breast is white and so is his belly. He has two black stripes extending diagonally from his back, down across his white breast. His flanks are reddish brown and his eyes are bright yellow. The female has a reddish brown crest, dark back, and a gray belly and flanks.

Size The male hooded merganser is 16–19 inches long, with a wingspan of 24–26½ inches.

Common Locations In winter: the Bronx: Pelham Bay Park and Van Cortlandt Park. Brooklyn: Floyd Bennett Field's Return-A-Gift Pond. Manhattan: The Lake in Central Park. Queens: Jamaica Bay Wildlife Refuge. Staten Island: Goethals Pond and Arlington Marsh.

Notes of Interest The hooded merganser is a striking and beautiful bird. Their crests are surprisingly large and flexible and can be raised and lowered.

Ecological Role Omnivores, the hooded mergansers dive for fish, crustaceans, aquatic insects, frogs, tadpoles, mollusks, and aquatic plants.

KEY POINTS

- Winter residents, the hooded mergansers can be found in the city's saltwater marshes and bays and in freshwater lakes.
- Because of their large crests, both males and females have a striking appearance.

Plate 37 HOODED MERGANSER

Great Blue Heron: *Ardea herodias*

Ardea: heron; *herodias:* heron; *great blue:* large and grayish blue

Description   Our largest long-legged wading bird, and most commonly seen heron, the great blue heron stands 4 feet tall. It is mostly gray-blue with a black cap, white around its head, neck, and chest with some cinnamon striping on its neck. It has long legs and an elongated, sharp, spear-shaped bill. In flight, the great blue heron holds its head folded back in an s-shape on its shoulders and trails its outstretched legs behind. Great blue herons migrate south in the fall and are found in the city during spring and summer.

Size   Great blue herons are 42–52 inches long and have a wingspan of about 7 feet.

Common Locations   Found along the shores of the city's freshwater and saltwater wetlands. The Bronx: Pelham Bay Park and Van Cortlandt Park. Brooklyn: Floyd Bennett Field, Four Sparrow Marsh, Marine Park; Manhattan: The Lake in Central Park. Queens: Alley Pond Park. Staten Island: Mount Loretto Unique Area, Saw Mill Creek Park.

Notes of Interest   When it is fishing, the great blue heron usually stands still as it waits for its prey to swim close enough for it to strike with its spearing bill. This heron moves in what seems like slow motion to stalk prey. The great blue heron is usually a solitary hunter.

Ecological Role   Great blue herons are carnivores and feed on fish, frogs, salamanders, crabs, crayfish, grasshoppers, dragonflies, and mice.

KEY POINTS
- The large, grayish blue heron has long legs and a long sharply pointed bill.
- In flight, it folds its head back in an s-shape, with its long legs trailing behind and its huge wings beating slowly.
- Great blue herons fish along the shore or in shallow water.

Plate 38   GREAT BLUE HERON

Black-Crowned Night Heron:
Nycticorax nycticorax

Nycticorax: night raven

Description   The black-crowned night heron is a medium-sized, stocky heron. It has a short, thick neck that gives it a hunched appearance. It has a black cap with several long, trailing white plumes at the back of its head. It is dark gray above and white below. The eyes of the black-crowned night heron are ruby red, and its legs and feet are pink. Immatures are brown with white streaks.

Size   Black-crowned night herons are 23–28 inches long; their wings span 45 inches.

Common Locations   In the summer, black-crowned night herons can be found throughout the city's rivers, bays, salt marshes, lakes, and ponds. The Bronx: Pelham Bay Park and Van Cortland Park. Brooklyn: Marine Park, Four Sparrow Marsh, Prospect Park, and Floyd Bennett Field. Manhattan: Central Park's The Lake, the Meer, and Turtle Pond, Inwood Hill Park, and the Hudson River at the 79th Street Boat Basin in Riverside Park. Queens: Alley Pond Park and Jamaica Bay Wildlife Refuge. Staten Island: Saw Mill Creek Park and Wolfe's Pond Park.

Notes of Interest   The black-crowned night heron is known as the "quark" bird, because of the call it makes as it hunts, mainly at night. The black-crowned night heron appears short and stocky when it is standing still or stalking prey. However, in flight, it is an impressive bird, with broad wings.

Ecological Role   The black-crowned night heron remains perfectly still as it waits for prey to swim toward it. It then thrusts its heavy bill into the water seizing fish, its main food. As omnivores, they also feed on algae and aquatic plants, frogs, toads, crayfish, blue crabs, shrimp, mollusks, and aquatic insects.

KEY POINTS
- Black-crowned night herons can often be seen standing still on the shores of wetlands or stalking prey.
- Black-crowned night herons appear hunched over, with long white breeding plumes hanging from the back of their heads.

Plate 39   BLACK-CROWNED NIGHT HERON

· Black-crowned night herons are identified by their black
crown and back and white neck and belly.

Red-Tailed Hawk: *Buteo jamaicensis*

ETYMOLOGY
Buteo: a kind of hawk; *jamaicensis:* the Island of Jamaica where specimens were given their scientific name

Description   This is the city's largest hawk. Although the red-tailed hawk is dark brown above, a key feature is its white chest with brown streaks. The chestnut red on the upper side of its tail gives this hawk its name. Immature red-tailed hawks are similar to adults, but the tail is banded with brown with no chestnut red coloration.

Size   The red-tailed hawk is 19–25 inches long, with a wingspan of 46–58 inches.

Common Locations   The Bronx: Pelham Bay Park. Brooklyn: Prospect Park; Floyd Bennett Field Grasslands during winter. Manhattan: the Ramble in Central Park and the 927 Fifth Avenue ledge nest during spring when the nest is active. The nest can be viewed from the model boat pond inside Central Park around East 72nd Street. Riverside Park: Riverside Church; near the 79th Street Boat Basin during winter; Inwood Hill Park. Queens: Fort Tilden during winter. Staten Island: Saw Mill Creek Park.

Notes of Interest   The red-tailed hawk has a varied diet. Common food items within the city include rodents, particularly rats and squirrels, pigeons, doves, and other songbirds. When you hear crows or see a flock of pigeons in flight, this large hawk is probably nearby. Crows try to "mob" it by attacking as a group. Red-tails nest in the tallest trees in the area. They mate for life. The celebrated red-tail hawk Pale Male and his mate built a ledge nest on an apartment house at 927 Fifth Avenue near 74th Street in Manhattan. Pale Male and his nest gained fame in 2004 when the nest was removed by the co-op association. Pressure from the birding community resulted in the association allowing the hawks to rebuild the nest on a reconstructed platform.

Ecological Role   Red-tailed hawks are successful carnivores, hunting pigeons and rats in the city.

KEY POINTS
- Red-tailed hawks are large and commonly seen.
- The red-tailed hawk has a mottled white chest and a reddish brown upper tail.

Plate 10   RED-TAILED HAWK

Osprey: *Pandion haliaetus*

ETYMOLOGY
Pandion was king of Athens; *haliaetus:* sea eagle

Description   The osprey is a large raptor, almost eagle size, dark brown above, and white below. Its head is capped by a white crest with a black cheek patch from its beak across its eye to the back of its head. Viewed from below, ospreys have arched, narrow white wings with dark wrist patches.

Size   Ospreys are 21–24½ inches long; with a wingspan of 54–72 inches. Females are larger than males.

Common Locations   Brooklyn: Floyd Bennett Field during spring migration. Bronx: the Lagoon in Pelham Bay Park. Queens: nesting on human-made platforms in Jamaica Bay Wildlife Refuge and Alley Pond Park where Alley Creek flows into Little Neck Bay. Staten Island: the ponds at Mount Loretto Nature Preserve. Manhattan: Belvedere Castle's Hawkwatch during fall migration in Central Park.

Notes of Interest   Osprey perch on dead tree branches near water and fly out over water to hunt for fish. When fish are sighted they will hover and dive, often completely submerging themselves. They rise with fish in their talons and in midair arrange the fish in their talons so that they fly with it head first, reducing air resistance as they fly to a perch or nest to feed the female and chicks. Ospreys mate for life. During the middle of the twentieth century, osprey, like other birds of prey—the bald eagle and the peregrine falcon— were almost driven to extinction by the pesticide DDT, which collected in the tissue of the fish they ate. Since DDT was banned and the 1973 Endangered Species Act created, ospreys have made a comeback, with more than eight thousand nesting pairs in the United States alone.

Ecological Role   Ospreys are carnivores and feed predominately on fish, such as herring, bluefish, eel, flounder, menhaden, perch, shad, and bass.

KEY POINTS
- Ospreys are large, hawklike birds, brown above, white below, with black patches at the bend of their wrists.
- Ospreys make a high-pitched *cheep-cheep-cheep* noise.
- Ospreys build huge nests atop trees or on human-made platforms near water.

Plate 41 OSPREY

- Ospreys are fast fliers during migration, reaching speeds up to 80 miles per hour.

Peregrine Falcon: *Falco peregrinus*

ETYMOLOGY
Falco: falcate or hooked shape of talons; *peregrinus:* "wandering" as peregrines can be found worldwide

Description   The peregrine falcon is a large, powerful raptor, with sharply pointed wings, a narrow tail, white chest, and an abdomen heavily spotted with dark gray bars. Its head has a black crown, with black cheek patches, or "sideburns."

Size   The peregrine falcon is 15–20 inches. Its wingspan is 40 inches.

Common Locations   Peregrine falcons can be found on the ledges of skyscrapers and on bridges. Several peregrine falcon nesting sites can be found in the city, including the towers of the Marine Parkway Bridge, which can be viewed from the beach at Rockaway Inlet in Brooklyn, Riverside Church at 120th Street and Riverside Drive in Manhattan, the MetLife Building at 1 Madison Avenue in Manhattan, and the Goethals Bridge in Staten Island.

Notes of Interest   By the early 1970s, peregrine falcons were nearly driven to extinction. Not one could be found east of the Mississippi River because of the insecticide DDT, which worked its way up the food chain to the peregrine falcons and caused their eggshells to be so thin that the incubating females would break them. The banning of DDT and the Endangered Species Act helped bring the peregrines back from near extinction.

Ecological Role   Peregrine falcons are powerful carnivores feeding on pigeons, mourning doves, and a variety of songbirds.

KEY POINTS:

- More peregrine falcons live in New York City than any other place in the world.
- Peregrines can fly at speeds exceeding 200 miles per hour when diving for prey. They are the fastest animals on earth.
- Peregrine falcons mate for life. If one dies, the other will seek out a new mate.

Plate 12 PEREGRINE FALCON

Barn Owl: *Tyto alba*

ETYMOLOGY
Tyto: owl; *alba:* white; *barn owl:* nesting in barns

Description   The barn owl has a distinctive heart-shaped white face with no ear tufts. Its upper body is tawny. Below, its white breast and belly are dotted with black, and its long, white wings are edged with black stripes. The barn owl's long legs are pale.

Size   The barn owl grows to 14–20 inches long. Its wingspan can range from 43–47 inches.

Common Locations   The Bronx: Hunter Island and the Landfill in Pelham Bay Park; Brooklyn: Floyd Bennett Field Grasslands; Queens: Forest Park and Jamaica Bay Wildlife Refuge; Staten Island: Mariners Marsh Preserve and Saw Mill Creek Park.

Notes of Interest   In the summer of 2003, as part of a wildlife restoration program by the New York City Department of Parks and Recreation's Urban Park Rangers, barn owls were released in Van Cortlandt Park in the Bronx, Alley Pond Park and Forest Park in Queens, and Marine Park in Brooklyn.

Ecological Role   Barn owls are carnivores and feed predominantly on rodents. When a nest box in Jamaica Bay Wildlife Refuge was cleaned out after one season, close to forty pounds of remains were found. The bones belonged to more than five hundred house mice, more than two hundred Norway rats, and close to two thousand meadow voles.

KEY POINTS

- The barn owl's voice is a long, loud shriek.
- The barn owl has a heart-shaped face and long wings and legs.
- When perched, the barn owl lowers its head and swings it from side to side.

Plate 43   BARN OWL

Monk Parakeet: *Myiopsitta monachus*

ETYMOLOGY
Myia: a fly; *psitta:* parrot; *monk:* monk's hood look of gray forehead and neck

Description The monk parakeet is bright green above with a long, pointed, green and blue tail. Their upper belly is lemon to olive yellow; their lower belly is bright green. Their wings are blue. The very top of their heads, necks, and breasts are gray. Their bills are large and flesh colored.

Size Monk parakeets are 8–12 inches long, with a wingspan of up to 21 inches.

Common Locations Brooklyn: Greenwood Cemetery, Brooklyn College, Marine Park. Manhattan: Central Park. New Jersey: River Road in Edgewater.

Notes of Interest Monk parakeets are native to South America. It is believed that the population of monk parakeets living in the New York area descended from a group that escaped from a shipping crate at Kennedy Airport in the early 1970s when they were being brought in for the pet trade. Able to survive subfreezing temperatures because of the enormously large colonial nests that they construct and roost in, monk parakeets are successfully living and breeding in the Northeastern United States. Parakeets worldwide usually construct nest cavities in trees. Monk parakeets are the only parrots in which colonies cooperate to build stick nests. Thorny sticks are preferred as they help deter predators. Their enormous, moundlike nests are often more than 6 feet long and 3 or 4 feet wide. The nests keep them warm in the winter and cool in the summer. Pairs mate for life and construct separate nesting chambers within these huge nests with separate entrances.

Ecological Role Monk parakeets are omnivores that feed on seeds, fruit, berries, nuts, flowers, and invertebrates.

KEY POINTS

- Monk parakeets spend much of their time repairing and adding to their nest. In fact, cooperative nest building is the main activity for these very social birds.
- As they work on their nests, the noise level is high: Their screeching and squawking can be heard from half a mile away.

Plate 11 MONK PARAKEET

Ruby-Throated Hummingbird:
Archilochus colubris

ETYMOLOGY
Archilochus: first in importance and an ambush; *colubris:* South American Indian name for this bird

Description　Both male and female ruby-throated humming-birds are metallic green above and gray below. The male has a gorget (pronounced: gor jet; iridescent throat feathers) that are brilliant red in the sun and black in the shade. Females have a white throat. The male's tail is slightly forked, but the female's tail is not.

Size　The ruby-throated hummingbird is 3–3¾ inches long, with a wingspan of 4–4¾ inches.

Common Locations　These tiny birds can be found through-out the summer months in city parks and community gardens, feed-ing on the nectar of flowers. The Bronx: Van Cortlandt Park, Bronx Botanical Garden, and Wave Hill. Brooklyn: Prospect Park and the Brooklyn Botanic Garden. Manhattan: Central Park, Riverside Park, and Fort Tryon Park.

Notes of Interest　Despite their tiny size, they travel hundreds, sometimes thousands, of miles during their fall and spring migra-tions. When they return to the city in the early spring, they follow the yellow-bellied sapsucker—a woodpecker—as it drills sap holes in tree trunks. The hummingbirds then visit the sap holes to drink the sap until the flowers they depend on bloom. Ruby-throated hummingbirds have powerful wing muscles allowing them to beat their wings more than seventy times per second and more than two hundred times per second during courtship displays. They get their common name from the humming sound of their wings.

Ecological Role　Ruby-throated hummingbirds are pollina-tors; they feed on the nectar of flowers and carry pollen from flower to flower. They also consume insects and spiders, which they feed to their babies.

KEY POINTS
- Ruby-throated hummingbirds are the only hummingbirds that live east of the Mississippi River.
- The white eggs are the size of jellybeans.
- Usually two eggs are laid in the nest made of spider silk, thistledown, and camouflaged with lichen.

Plate 95   RUBY-THROATED HUMMINGBIRD

· Spider silk is used to bind the nest together and helps the
nest expand as the baby birds grow.

Red-Bellied Woodpecker: *Melanerpes carolinus*

ETYMOLOGY

Melanerpes: black-headed creeper; *carolinus*: where this bird was first illustrated in 1758 and named by Linnaeus; *red-bellied*: this woodpecker has a red spot on its lower belly

Description The red-bellied woodpecker is large with a brilliant red crown and nape (back of head down to the shoulders). The female has a red nape. Both male and female have the black and white pattern of most woodpeckers known as a "zebra-back." Their tails have a similar black and white pattern with a white rump patch.

Size The red-bellied woodpecker is 9–10½ inches long, with a wingspan of 15–18 inches.

Common Locations The red-bellied woodpecker lives throughout the five boroughs in the large and smaller parks. The Bronx: Pelham Bay Park and Van Cortlandt Park. Brooklyn: Prospect Park. Manhattan: Central Park, Inwood Hill Park, and Riverside Park. Queens: Alley Pond Park, Cunningham Park, and Forest Park. Staten Island: Mount Loretto Unique Area.

Notes of Interest Both males and females use their chisel-like bills to excavate nesting cavities in dead trees. They nest in softwood city trees such as basswood, maple, and sycamores and in the decayed tops or branches of dead trees.

Ecological Role The red-bellied woodpecker is an omnivore, feeding on invertebrates, berries, fruit, nuts, and seeds. It uses its powerful bill to hammer on tree trunks and branches for wood-boring insects. During winter, these woodpeckers will visit feeding stations for seeds and suet.

KEY POINTS

- Both males and females hammer on trees and lampposts to assert dominance in their territories.
- The male red-bellied woodpecker has a brilliant red "mohawk" cap.
- The red-bellied woodpecker has a small red mark on its lower belly that can be seen when the bird is above you.

Plate 16   RED–BELLIED WOODPECKER

Blue Jay: *Cyanocitta cristata*

ETYMOLOGY
Cyanocitta: chattering blue bird; *cristata:* crested

Description The blue jay is a beautiful bird. Its crest, nape, back, and tail are a brilliant blue, often with shades of purple. The tail and wings have black bars and white spots. Their face, chest, and belly are white. They have a black "necklace" that extends up the sides of their face to their crest.

Size The blue bird can grow to 11–12½ inches long, with a wingspan of 15¾–17½ inches.

Common Locations The blue jay can be seen in the wooded areas of the city's parks in all five boroughs.

Notes of Interest Blue jays, like their relative the crow, are intelligent and curious birds. They are devoted mates. The blue jay's blue feathers are actually brown. Light refracted off their feathers scatters blue wavelengths of sunlight so that the bird appears blue.

Ecological Role The blue jay is an omnivore feeding on insects, seeds, nuts, and berries. Although considered by some to be aggressive pests, research has shown that only 1 percent of jays feed on bird eggs or other birds. Blue jays help the oak forests grow because of the "forgotten" acorns they bury. The blue jay is also valued for the harmful insects it consumes such as Japanese beetles and tent and gypsy moth caterpillars.

KEY POINTS

- The blue jay is one of the few "blue" birds that lives in our area.
- The blue jay has a loud, raucous call: *jay, jay.*
- Another one of its calls is a soft, musical *tull lull.*

Plate 47   BLUE JAY

Black-Capped Chickadee: *Parus atricapillus*

ETYMOLOGY
Parus: titmouse; *atricapillus:* black crown

Description   The black-capped chickadee is a tiny gray bird with a black cap, black bib, and white cheeks. It has a long gray tail and white chest and belly.

Size   The black-capped chickadee is $4^{3}/_{4}-5^{3}/_{4}$ inches long, with a wingspan of $7^{1}/_{2}-8^{3}/_{4}$ inches.

Common Locations   The black-capped chickadee can be seen in the wooded areas of the city's parks in all five boroughs throughout the year.

Notes of Interest   Black-capped chickadees are monogamous, and their pair bond lasts until one of the pair dies. Pairs establish and defend a territory, remaining on or near their territory for life. Black-capped chickadees often nest in cavities they excavate themselves. They also nest in natural cavities, abandoned woodpecker holes, and nest boxes.

Ecological Role   Black-capped chickadees are omnivores. They feed on invertebrates such as spiders, insects, millipedes, and mollusks; seeds; berries; and nuts.

KEY POINTS

- Chickadees are frequent visitors to bird feeders. They fly in and take one seed at a time. Holding the seed between their feet, they hammer it with their beaks until they crack it open.
- The white cheeks separating the black cap and chin make chickadees easy to identify at a distance.

Plate 98   BLACK–CAPPED CHICKADEE

Tufted Titmouse: *Parus bicolor*

ETYMOLOGY
Parus: titmouse; *bicolor:* two colors; *tufted:* crested; *titmouse:* small, insectivorous bird

Description   The tufted titmouse is a small, crested bird. Both males and females have a characteristic black forehead and gray crest. The upperparts are gray, with darker gray flight feathers. The face and underparts are white with russet flanks. The dark eye and eye ring are conspicuous on the white face.

Size   The tufted titmouse is 6–6½ inches long, with a wingspan of 9¼–10¾ inches.

Common Locations   The tufted titmouse can be seen through the four seasons in the wooded areas of the city's parks in all five boroughs.

Notes of Interest   Tufted titmice breed during the spring and summer. Pairs mate for life. Titmice build their nests in tree cavities. These cavities are made by woodpeckers, fungus, and other organisms. The female usually lays five or six white eggs with brown spots. Eggs take about two weeks to hatch, and both parents feed their young.

Ecological Role   Tufted titmice are omnivores that feed on spiders and their egg cases, caterpillars, wasps, bees, scale insects, ants, beetles, treehoppers, other insects, snails, acorns, beechnuts, blackberries, elderberries, blueberries, grapes, serviceberries, ragweed, sunflower seeds, pine seeds, Virginia creeper berries, hackberries, and mulberries. They eat more animal protein during the warm seasons and nuts, berries, and seeds in winter. Tufted titmice cache (store) seeds in cracks in trees.

KEY POINTS
- Tufted titmice are one of the few crested birds in our area.
- Titmice can be "whistled" down from trees by people who mimic their calls.
- They are tame and intelligent birds.
- Hawks and falcons prey on tufted titmice.

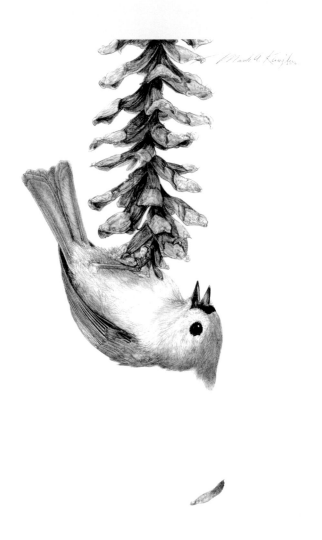

Plate 49 TUFTED TITMOUSE

White-Breasted Nuthatch: *Sitta carolinensis*

ETYMOLOGY
Sitta: nuthatch; *carolinensis:* from Carolina where bird was identified and named; *nuthatch:* using the bill to open nuts

Description   Both the male and female white-breasted nuthatch have a blue-gray back, a white breast and belly, and tawny flanks. They have a black cap and nape with a white face and throat. Their dark eyes stand out against an unmarked white face. Their tail feathers are black patterned with white bands. The central tail feathers are pale bluish gray. Undertail coverts (small feathers) are white marked with reddish orange.

Size   The white-breasted nuthatch is 5–6 inches long, with a wingspan of $9^{1}/_{4}$–11 inches.

Common Locations   White-breasted nuthatches can be seen through the four seasons in the wooded areas of the city's parks in all five boroughs.

Notes of Interest   The white-breasted nuthatch collects insects from the bark of trees, usually creeping head first down the trunk. It often calls *yank, yank* while feeding. In winter, it may feed in flocks with chickadees and titmice. At feeders, the nuthatch often picks up one seed at a time and flies away with it to a tree where it hacks it open with its beak. The white-breasted nuthatch is a cavity nester, using old woodpecker holes.

Ecological Role   White-breasted nuthatches are omnivores, feeding on insects and spiders during the summer and nuts, berries, and seeds in the winter.

KEY POINTS
- Nuthatches are often seen moving head first down the trunk of a tree.
- White-breasted nuthatches work their way down a tree trunk searching for grubs and insects in the bark crevices that other up-climbing tree foragers, such as the woodpecker, would miss.
- The nuthatch can hang upside down, swinging from tiny branches.
- You will often hear the nuthatch's nasal call—*yank, yank*—before you see it.

Plate 50   WHITE‑BREASTED NUTHATCH

Gray Catbird: *Dumetella carolinensis*

ETYMOLOGY
Dumetella: thicket dweller; *carolinensis:* of Carolina; *catbird:* named for their catlike *meow* call

Description The gray catbird is a medium-sized gray bird with a black cap and tail and russet undertail coverts. Its eyes and legs are dark.

Size The catbird is 8–9¼ inches long, with a wingspan of 11–12 inches.

Common Locations Gray catbirds can be found in thickets and shrubs throughout meadows and fields of the city's parks in all five boroughs.

Notes of Interest The gray catbird belongs to the mockingbird family and is a great mimic, often imitating the calls of jays, hawks, whippoorwills, a variety of songbirds, the kingfisher, and occasionally tree frogs. They are named for their meowlike calls.

Ecological Role The gray catbird is an omnivore. During spring, the majority of their food consists of a variety of invertebrates, including ants, caterpillars, grasshoppers, beetles, spiders, and millipedes. When feeding on the ground, catbirds will toss leaves aside with their bills to expose prey. As fruit becomes available it makes up more of the catbird's diet. By summer, fruit makes up more than half of the adult's diet. Fruits consumed include honeysuckle, grapes, dogwood, and poison ivy berries. Nestlings are fed insect food almost exclusively until just before fledging, when fruit is introduced. Catbirds migrate south before the winter, and in their winter feeding grounds fruit makes up 80 percent of their diet.

KEY POINTS

- If you hear a meowing coming from a shrub in a city park, it is probably the call of the gray catbird.
- The other songs of the catbird are rich and complicated, as they rarely repeat phrases.
- The gray catbird is our only gray bird with a black cap and rusty undertail coverts.

Plate 51 GRAY CATBIRD

Northern Mockingbird: *Mimus polyglottos*

ETYMOLOGY
Mimus: mimic; *polyglottos:* many-tongued

Description The northern mockingbird is a medium-sized bird, gray above and pale below. It has a long, gray tail and a slender black bill. Its white outer tail feathers and white wing patches are conspicuous during flight.

Size Northern mockingbirds are about 9–11 inches long, with a wingspan of 13–15 inches.

Common Locations Northern mockingbirds can be seen year-round in the wooded areas of the city's parks, gardens, and residential areas in all five boroughs.

Notes of Interest Mockingbirds are known for the complicated variations of their song. On summer nights when the moon is full, the male will sit in a tree and sing all night. They can sing up to two hundred songs. Mockingbirds mate in the spring and build nests in shrubs and understory trees. A pair of mockingbirds often has more than one nest at a time. The male watches over fledglings (older young with feathers) while the female incubates a new clutch of eggs. Females lay three to five blue-green eggs with brown spots. Eggs hatch in less than two weeks.

Ecological Role Mockingbirds are omnivores. During fall and winter, the mockingbird feeds mainly on wild berries, including holly, blackberry, pokeberry, sumac, poison ivy, and Virginia creeper. Throughout the spring and summer and especially during the breeding season, their diet consists of insects found on lawns and meadows.

KEY POINTS

- Mockingbirds sing throughout most of the year, except during the "dog days" of late July through August.
- Mockingbirds mate for life, sometimes separating during the winter season and then reuniting in the spring.
- Scientists have found that female mockingbirds are attracted to males whose songs have the greatest variety.

Plate 52 NORTHERN MOCKINGBIRD

American Robin: *Turdus migratorius*

ETYMOLOGY

Turdus: a thrush; *migratorius:* wandering; *robin:* early American settlers named this bird after the English robin red breast

Description   The American robin is a medium-sized bird. It is the largest member of the thrush family. The male is grayish brown above. Its head and tail are almost black, and it has a partial white eye ring. Its breast is a brick red. Females are paler. Robins' throats are white with dark streaks and their lower belly, where it meets the tail, is white. Robins have white outer tail feathers that are visible when birds are in flight. Their bill is yellow. Immature robins have the speckled breast of other thrushes. As they mature their breasts gain the brick red plumage.

Size   American robins are 9–11 inches long; their wingspan is $14^{3}/_{4}$–$16^{1}/_{2}$ inches.

Common Locations   American robins can be seen year-round in the wooded areas of the city's parks, gardens, and residential areas in all five boroughs.

Notes of Interest   Robins have sturdy legs with muscles designed for running or hopping, allowing them to escape predators and quickly cover open ground while hunting. Their syrinx ("song box") has complex muscles allowing them to sing complicated songs that carry a long distance.

Ecological Role   The American robin is an omnivore. Worms are a large part of its diet, but it also consumes other insects, including beetles, grasshoppers, ants, cicadas, termites, caterpillars, butterflies, and fruit and berries, including holly berries, pokeberries, and grapes.

KEY POINTS

- When the robin is hunting and it cocks its head to the side toward the ground, it is watching the ground for tiny movements that indicate a worm is traveling close to the surface.
- American robins' eggs are pale blue-green, known as "robin's-egg blue."

VERTEBRATES: BIRDS

Plate 53 AMERICAN ROBIN

Black-and-White Warbler: *Mniotilta varia*

Mniotilta: moss-plucker; *varia* variegated

Description   Black-and-white warblers are small birds with lengthwise black-and-white stripes above and below. They have conspicuous white stripes above and below each eye. Their legs are short and their feet have extended hind claws for clinging to bark. Their bills, slightly curved and unusually long for a warbler, are adapted for probing bark crevices for insects. The female resembles the male but has a dull white belly.

Size   Black-and-white warblers are $4\frac{1}{2}-5\frac{1}{2}$ inches long, and their wingspan is $8\frac{1}{4}-9$ inches.

Common Locations   Black-and-white warblers can be found in city parks and wooded areas of all five boroughs. They are among the early spring migrants, using their long, curved bills to probe for dormant insects in and under tree bark.

Notes of Interest   The black-and-white warbler's short legs and long hind claws help them creep up, down, and around tree trunks and branches, searching for insects. In this regard, they are very similar to nuthatches and brown creepers. They are able to arrive earlier in the spring than other warblers who consume active insects dependent on flowering plants. The black-and-white warbler feeds on insects still dormant from overwintering in tree bark.

Ecological Role   The black-and-white warbler is an insectivore whose diet consists primarily of beetles, ants, and caterpillars, including the destructive gypsy moth caterpillars. It also feeds on spiders and daddy longlegs.

KEY POINTS

- The black-and-white warbler acts more like a nuthatch or creeper than a warbler, as it creeps around tree trunks and branches searching for invertebrates.
- The song of the black-and-white warbler is *weesee, weesee, weesee, weesee, weesee* and sounds like a squeaky wheel.

Common Yellowthroat: *Geothlypis trichas*

ETYMOLOGY
Geothlypis: ground bird; *trichas:* thrush (an inappropriate name)

Description   Common yellowthroats are tiny birds. The male has a distinctive black mask across his face, with a white band above and a yellow throat and breast. He is olive green above, with yellow undertail coverts and a white belly. The female lacks the black mask and has an olive green face and crown.

Size   Yellowthroats are 4–5 inches long, with a wingspan of 6–7 inches.

Common Locations   The common yellowthroat is seen from April through September in city parks in all five boroughs. It often constructs its nest close to the ground in shrubs and thickets near saltwater marshes and freshwater ponds, lakes, and streams. It also nests in thickets along woods and paths.

Notes of Interest   Yellowthroats are careful when they approach their nests. They do not fly directly to them; instead, they fly to the ground and walk into the underbrush to their nests. They leave the same way to keep predators from locating their nests.

Ecological Role   The common yellowthroat is an insectivore that consumes various insects, including grasshoppers, dragonflies, damselflies, mayflies, beetles, caterpillars, moths, butterflies, flies, ants, aphids, and leafhoppers. It also feeds on spiders.

KEY POINTS

- The yellowthroat is often heard before it is seen.
- The call of the yellowthroat is a commonly heard *witchity, witchity, witchity, witchity.*
- Another common call of the yellowthroat is a scolding *chack!* which it says as it appears from, and disappears into, dense underbrush.

Yellow Warbler: *Dendroica petechia*

ETYMOLOGY
Dendroica: tree-dweller; *petechia:* red spots on the skin

Description   The yellow warbler appears all yellow from afar. However, on closer inspection, the wings and back are greenish yellow. The male's breast and flanks have reddish brown streaks. The tail has yellow spots, visible on the underside.

Size   Yellow warblers are $4\frac{1}{2}-5\frac{1}{2}$ inches long, with a wingspan of 8 inches.

Common Locations   Yellow warblers can be found during spring and fall migrations in thickets, along streams, in gardens, and in wooded areas of city parks, in all five boroughs.

Notes of Interest   May is the best month to see the yellow and other warblers. In spring, these tiny, colorful, insect-eating birds migrate to New York City from Central and South America, where they have spent the winter. The yellow warbler is often seen in shrubby areas near water. It is a common and widespread warbler in North America, building its nest just 3 to 12 feet off the ground in a shrub or small tree.

Ecological Role   The yellow warbler is an insectivore; however, on occasion, it will supplement its diet with berries. It forages for insects and spiders on tree limbs and bushes but prefers small insect larvae and caterpillars.

KEY POINTS:

- The yellow warbler is a small yellow bird.
- It feeds destructive tent and gypsy moth caterpillars and other insects to its nestlings.

Plate 59 Clockwise from top left: YELLOW WARBLER,
BLACK-AND-WHITE WARBLER, COMMON YELLOW THROAT

Red-Winged Blackbird: *Agelaius phoeniceus*

ETYMOLOGY
Agelaius: belonging to a flock; *phoeniceus:* deep red

Description   The red-winged blackbird is a medium-sized bird. The male is glossy black all over, except for his "epaulets," or shoulder patches, which are red, bordered with yellow. Sometimes the red is concealed and only the yellow is visible, until they fly, when the full, brilliant scarlet can be seen. The female is a streaked brown above and below with a distinctive light streak over the eyes. Immature males resemble females until they are two years old, when they start to attain their adult plumage. Then they are black with red shoulder patches bordered with orange.

Size   Red-winged blackbirds are 7–9½ inches long, with a wingspan of 12–14½ inches.

Common Locations   Red-winged blackbirds are commonly seen in understory trees and shrubs near marshes, ponds, lakes, and streams in city parks throughout the five boroughs.

Notes of Interest   Migrating males return in the spring to set up and defend their territories in order to attract a female. Their courtship displays and territorial defenses include spreading their tail and wings, raising their scarlet epaulet feathers, and singing their *o-ka-lee* song. The red epaulets remain covered when they want to avoid conflict with other males. Red-winged blackbirds are fierce defenders of their nests and will mob hawks, crows, and other predators, chasing them from their territory. In the fall, they migrate south in enormous flocks of a thousand or more birds.

Ecological Role   Red-winged blackbirds are omnivores. In the summer, they feed on invertebrates, consuming flies, beetles, moths, butterflies, gypsy moth and tent caterpillars, grubs, grasshoppers, snails, millipedes, and spiders. Their diet also includes blackberries, blueberries, and seed they find at bird feeders.

KEY POINTS

- Red-winged blackbirds are often perched on cattails during the breeding season.
- Red-winged blackbirds are sometimes heard singing their buzzy *o-ka-lee* before they are seen.

Plate 55   RED-WINGED BLACKBIRD

European Starling: *Sturnus vulgaris*

ETYMOLOGY

Sturnus: starling; *vulgaris:* common; *starling:* "little star" referring to the white spots on the starling's plumage

Description   In fall and winter, the European starling is dark brown, speckled with white spots. Its bill is gray. However, in spring and summer, the starling's plumage is a glossy, iridescent black, showing purple and green in the sunlight, and its bill is yellow. Immatures are a dull brown.

Size   European starlings are 7½–8½ inches long, with a wing-span of 15½ inches.

Common Locations   European starlings live year-round throughout the five boroughs, inside and outside city parks. They are everywhere.

Notes of Interest   In the early 1890s, one hundred European starlings were released in Central Park by a society that introduced into America all of the birds mentioned in the works of Shakespeare. Now there are over 200 million European starlings living through-out the United States. One of their first nesting sites was under the eaves of the American Museum of Natural History, across the street from Central Park. The starling is considered a pest as it successfully competes with native cavity nesters, often commandeering the nests of less aggressive woodpeckers.

Ecological Role   The European starling is an omnivore that feeds on various insects, including pests such as weevils and Japa-nese beetles, ants, flies, bees, wasps, grasshoppers, millipedes, snails, spiders, and earthworms. Fruit, berries, and seeds are also consumed.

KEY POINTS

- Starlings are cavity nesters and can be found nesting in hollow pipes of lampposts on street corners and woodpecker holes in trees.
- In flight they have a triangular appearance.
- Starlings are natural mimics and have been known to imitate the songs of flickers, phoebes, crows, barking dogs, and meowing cats.
- Starlings are extremely intelligent birds.

Plate 56   EUROPEAN STARLING

Baltimore Oriole: *Icterus galbula*

ETYMOLOGY

Icterus: jaundice (ancient Greeks believed that yellow birds cured jaundice); *galbula:* small, yellow, bird; *Baltimore:* during the colonial era, the baron of Baltimore's colors were orange and black

Description The male Baltimore oriole is a brilliant orange with a black head and wings. The wings have a white wing bar. Females and immatures have a yellow face, chest, and belly with an olive head and dark wings. Their wings have two white wing bars.

Size Baltimore orioles are 7–8 inches long, with a wingspan of $11\frac{1}{4}$–$12\frac{1}{4}$ inches.

Common Locations Baltimore orioles can be found during spring, summer, and fall in city parks throughout the five boroughs.

Notes of Interest The woven-basket nest is suspended from the tip of a branch. Female orioles weave the nest from plant fibers, hair, and string, which they collect from their habitat. They line the inside of their nests with fine grasses, synthetic fibers, and hair.

Ecological Role The Baltimore oriole is an omnivore that feeds on insects, fruit, berries, and seeds. It forages on trees and shrubs for tent and gypsy moth caterpillars, beetles, ants, aphids, grasshoppers, and wood borers. Its diet also includes wild cherries, juneberries, blackberries, and grapes. It collects nectar from flowers.

KEY POINTS
- The Baltimore oriole is a beautiful orange bird with a black head, neck, and nape.
- Its song is clear, flutelike, and varied.
- The Baltimore oriole's woven-basket nest is one of the more unusual bird nests.

Plate 57   BALTIMORE ORIOLE

Scarlet Tanager: *Piranga olivacea*

ETYMOLOGY

Piranga: South American name for a bird; *olivacea:* olive; *tanager:*
tangaras: Amazon Indian word for brilliantly colored birds

Description   The male scarlet tanager has a scarlet red body
with black wings and a black tail. Females, immatures, and non-
breeding males are dull olive-green above and pale yellow below
with dark wings and a dark tail.

Size   The scarlet tanager can reach $6^{1}/_{2}-7^{1}/_{2}$ inches long, with a
wingspan of 11–12 inches.

Common Locations   During spring, summer, and fall, scarlet
tanagers can be seen in the wooded areas of city parks throughout
the five boroughs.

Notes of Interest   Although it is brightly colored, the scarlet
tanager is often hidden because it spends most of its time foraging
for insects in the tops of tall trees. The scarlet tanager migrates to
South America each winter and returns to our area in the spring.
When females arrive, the males court them by singing and hopping
around on perches low to the ground, spreading their black wings
and displaying their brilliant scarlet backs.

Ecological Role   The scarlet tanager is an omnivore, feeding
on invertebrates and fruit. During summer, it consumes insects and
spiders, earthworms, mulberries, and other wild fruit. It gleans
insects from trees and forages for invertebrates in shrubs and on the
ground.

KEY POINTS

- The scarlet tanager is one of our most colorful
  spring migrants.
- It is the only North American bird with a red body
  and black wings and tail.
- The song of the scarlet tanager, which is sung from
  the treetops, sounds like the song of the American robin.

Plate 58   SCARLET TANAGER

House Sparrow: *Passer domesticus*

ETYMOLOGY
Passer: sparrow; *domesticus:* belonging to a house

Description   The male house sparrow has a gray crown, with chestnut patches bordering the crown and extending down to the pale gray cheek and neck. The black stripe in front of the eye extends to the beak and meets the black bib. The thick bill is grayish black, and the legs are pale brown. The rump and tail are gray, the shoulders are chestnut brown, and the wings are brownish with a white wing bar. The female has gray checks, neck, and breast without the black bib. She has a buffy stripe between a brown eye stripe and brown crown.

Size   House sparrows are 5½–6¼ inches long, with a wingspan of 9½–10 inches.

Common Locations   The house sparrow is the most commonly seen bird throughout the five boroughs of New York City, inside and outside city parks. They nest inside street corner lamppost pipes, over air conditioners, and inside any cavity they can find on building exteriors. They are everywhere!

Notes of Interest   One hundred house sparrows were introduced from Europe into Brooklyn in the fall of 1851 and the spring of 1852. From this initial introduction, the species expanded throughout America and Canada. The North American house sparrow population is estimated at 150 million birds. They thrive in New York City on a diet of food garbage, as well as seeds, berries, and insects.

Ecological Role   House sparrows are omnivores, feeding on invertebrates such as beetles, grasshoppers, crickets, aphids, spiders, flies, and moths in the summer. They consume fruit in the summer, and dried berries and grass seeds in the winter.

KEY POINTS

- House sparrows are the most commonly seen birds in the city.
- Males have a black bib, chestnut nape, and gray cheeks and neck.
- Females are pale gray overall with a light tan stripe above the eye.
- The house sparrow's voice is a series of almost identical chirps.
- House sparrows "bathe" in sandy soil, throwing dust over their feathers as though it was water.

Plate 59   HOUSE SPARROW

Dark-Eyed Junco: *Junco hyemalis*

ETYMOLOGY
Junco: a rush or marsh bird; *hyemalis:* winter

Description   Male dark-eyed juncos have a dark gray head, back, and upper breast. The lower breast and belly are white in stark contrast to the dark upper breast. Their bills are pink. Females and immatures are paler and browner than the males. Dark-eyed juncos have white outer tail feathers that are conspicuous in flight.

Size   Dark-eyed juncos are $5^{1}/_{2}$–$6^{1}/_{4}$ inches long; with a wing-span of $9^{1}/_{2}$–10 inches.

Common Locations   During winter, the dark-eyed juncos can be found in large flocks foraging among the leaf litter in the wooded areas of city parks throughout the five boroughs.

Notes of Interest   The voice of the dark-eyed junco is a prolonged trill on the same pitch. Members of a foraging flock keep in contact through a *chip* call back and forth to each other.

Ecological Role   Dark-eyed juncos are omnivores. During winter, they forage on the ground in leaf litter and snow for grass seeds, and the seeds of ragweed, smartweed, pigweed, lamb's quarters, chickweed, sorrels, thistles, and sweet gum trees. During summer, they consume insects such as beetles, grasshoppers, ants, and spiders. Berries are also part of their diet.

KEY POINTS
- The dark-eyed junco is a small, dark gray bird with a white belly.
- They feed mainly on the ground, scratching at the leaf litter with both feet, foraging for seeds.
- Dark-eyed juncos forage in flocks.
- In flight their white outer tail feathers flash conspicuously.

Plate 60   DARK-EYED JUNCO

Northern Cardinal: *Cardinalis cardinalis*

Cardinalis: red of a Roman Catholic cardinal's robe

Description The male Northern cardinal, except for the black around his bill, is a completely red bird. Its thick, conical bill, crest, head, back, underparts, and tail are a brilliant cardinal red. The female cardinal is olive-tan above and below with a red bill, reddish crest, and reddish wings. Immature cardinals resemble females, but are browner and have darker bills. The cardinal can raise and lower its crest at will.

Size The Northern cardinal is 7¹/₂–8¹/₂ inches long; its wing-span is 10¹/₄–12 inches.

Common Locations The Northern cardinal can be seen year-round throughout the woodlands, meadows, and gardens of city parks in all five boroughs.

Notes of Interest Cardinals mate for life. When you see a cardinal, it is likely that its mate is nearby. During courtship the male often will feed the female. The female lays three to five eggs at one time and incubates them while the male brings her food. Cardinals build their nests in shrubs or understory trees. The cardinal nest is an open bowl of weed stems, twigs, leaves and bark, and is lined with grass. Their nests often contain paper or plastic in the outer layer.

Ecological Role The Northern cardinal is an omnivore. It consumes a variety of invertebrates, including beetles, cicadas, dragonflies, leafhoppers, aphids, ants, termites, grasshoppers, crickets, spiders, snails, and slugs. It also consumes about thirty kinds of wild fruit and nearly forty types of weed seeds, blossoms, tree seeds, and maple sap from holes made by sapsuckers. The Northern cardinal is a frequent visitor to bird feeders and particularly enjoys sunflower seeds.

KEY POINTS
- The Northern cardinal is a brilliant red bird with a red crest.
- The song of the cardinal is a rich *hoit, hoit, hoit, hoit; what cheer, what cheer; wheat, wheat, wheat; pret-ty, pret-ty, pret-ty.* Their alarm call is a sharp *tsip.*
- Both males and females sing, often back and forth to each other.

Plate 61 NORTHERN CARDINAL

House Finch: *Carpodacus mexicanus*

ETYMOLOGY

Carpodacus: fruit-eater; *mexicanus:* Mexican; *house:* lives near and on buildings

Description   The male house finch has a bright red head, nape, breast, and rump. He is streaked reddish brown above, with brown and white streaking on his flanks. His wings are brown, with two white wing bars. The female and immature house finch is streaked brown, paler below, with darker wings and two white wing bars. The bill of the house finch is thickly conical and downcurved. The tail of the house finch is brown, with a shallow notch, in contrast with the tail of the purple finch, which is more deeply notched.

Size   House finches are 5–5³⁄₄ inches long, with a wingspan of 9 inches.

Common Locations   The house finch can be seen year-round throughout city parks and streets in all five boroughs.

Notes of Interest   In 1940, a small number of finches brought in from southern California for the pet trade were turned loose in Long Island. Since then they have spread across the eastern United States and southern Canada. The red color of the male comes from carotenoid pigments in its food. The more pigment in the food, the redder the male. Females prefer to mate with the reddest male they can find. House finches frequently fall victim to the avian eye disease conjunctivitis, which is contagious for other types of finches but not for humans.

Ecological Role   House finches are herbivores that feed on the seeds of weeds such as thistle, dandelion, ragweed, goldenrod, and wild fruit. House finches are frequent visitors to bird feeders.

KEY POINTS
- The house finch is a small brown bird with a red head, breast, and rump.
- House finches often nest in roof gardens of New York City apartment buildings, in ivy-covered walls, in hanging and potted plants, under eaves, and behind air conditioners.

Plate 62 HOUSE FINCH

American Goldfinch: *Carduelis tristis*

ETYMOLOGY

Carduelis: thistle (they eat thistle seeds); *tristis:* sad (in reference to its call)

Description   During the breeding seasons of spring and summer, the male American goldfinch is a small, bright yellow bird with a black cap and forehead, white rump, black wings, and a black tail with white edges. During winter, females and males are a dull, pale yellowish tan with black wings, black tail, and white wing bars.

Size   American goldfinches are $4\frac{1}{2}-\frac{1}{2}$ inches long, with a wingspan of $8\frac{3}{4}-9$ inches.

Common Locations   The American goldfinch can be found year-round at backyard feeders and throughout city parks in all five boroughs.

Notes of Interest   American goldfinches travel in small flocks. Their soprano song *per-chick-o-ree* is often repeated at each dip of their undulating flight. Pairs nest close to thistle plants and sometimes in thistles. Their nests, made of woven plant fibers and lined with the down of milkweed plants, are so thick walled that they will temporarily hold water. They use spider silk and caterpillar webs to bind the rim of their nests with bark or strong plant fibers such as grape or hawthorn.

Ecological Role   Mainly an herbivore, the American goldfinch feeds on the seeds of wildflowers, weeds, and trees. Thistle seeds are their favorite, but they can often be seen feeding on the seeds of dandelion, sunflower, chicory, ragweed, goldenrod, and a variety of grasses. In spring and early summer, they feed on some insects and fruit.

KEY POINTS

- Bull and Canada thistles bloom in midsummer and fertilized seeds form downy "parachutes" (similar to dandelion "fluff") that help them travel on the wind. Goldfinches gather this downy material and use it to line their nests.
- To attract American goldfinches, plant thistles or put out thistle seed in your bird feeders.

Plate 63   AMERICAN GOLDFINCH

White-Throated Sparrow: *Zonotrichia albicollis*

ETYMOLOGY
Zonotrichia: striped head; *albicollis:* white neck

Description   The white-throated sparrow is a small, plump sparrow. Both males and females have black and white or black, brown, and tan stripes on their heads; white throats; and conspicuous yellow spots (lores) between their eyes and bills. They are streaked rusty brown above and gray below. Their wings are streaked rusty brown with two white wing bars.

Size   White-throated sparrows are 6–7 inches long, with a wingspan of 8³/₄–10 inches.

Common Locations   White-throated sparrows can be found year-round throughout the woodlands and city parks of the five boroughs. They spend most daylight hours foraging among leaf litter.

Notes of Interest   The white-throated sparrow comes in two color morphs: white striped and tan striped. The color forms are genetically determined. Research has shown that they typically mate with a bird of a different morph. Males generally prefer females with white stripes, and females prefer tan-striped males.

Ecological Role   White-throated sparrows are omnivores. They can be heard scratching noisily among dry leaves foraging for weed seeds. They consume the fruit of dogwood, elder, cedar, and spicebush understory trees. They are frequent visitors to the soil beneath bird feeders, consuming sunflower and mixed seed that has fallen to the ground. Their diet also includes insects such as ants, beetles, and flies.

KEY POINTS
- White-throated sparrows forage together in small flocks.
- Their striped crowns; bright, white throats; yellow lores; and plump bodies are conspicuous.
- The voice of the white-throated sparrow is a pleasing *Old Sam Peabody, Peabody, Peabody.*

Plate 69 WHITE-THROATED SPARROW

Eastern Red Bat: *Lasiurus borealis*

Description   Males are bright red or orange-red; females are dull red, brick, or chestnut. Males and females have frosted white on their backs and breasts and a whitish patch on their shoulders. Their heads are round and furry. Red bats migrate, but some remain during winter and hibernate in hollow trees or leaf litter. The red bat is hardy. On warm winter afternoons it may be seen flying.

Common Locations   Bats live in all five boroughs of New York City.

Notes of Interest   The bat is the only mammal that flies. The flight membranes are extensions of its skin, connecting the body with its wings, legs, and tail. Bats, unlike birds, use both their legs and wings during flight. They have elongated fingers that support the wing membrane. Bats feed at night; they find food and navigate by echolocation—they utter a continuous series of inaudible cries that echo when they hit solid objects. In the daytime, they shelter under the eaves of buildings, in tree cavities, rock crevices, and under tree bark and foliage. When hibernating, bats can lower their body temperature just above freezing and lower their metabolism to conserve energy. "Bat" comes from Old Norse "ledhrblaka," or "leather flapper." This became "bakka" and then "bat."

Ecological Role   Bats are insectivores, consuming more than 50 percent of their body weight each night. Bats nurse their young, and in the evening, the baby bat clings to its mother as she flies from the roost to feed on insects. One bat can eat five hundred mosquitoes in an hour.

Little Brown Bat: *Myotis lucifugus*

Description   The most common bat, the little brown bat, grows to 4 inches with a 3-inch wingspan. Little brown bats have long ears; long, glossy brown fur above; and light buff-colored fur below; they hibernate in large groups during winter and establish large maternity colonies in summer. The little brown bat lives twenty to thirty years.

Big Brown Bat: *Eptesicus fuscus*

Description   Big brown bats grow to 5 inches long, with a 13-inch wingspan. Females are larger than males. Big brown bats have

Plate 65 *Clockwise from top:* EASTERN RED BAT,
LITTLE BROWN BAT, BIG BROWN BAT

brown fur above and paler fur below. The hairless parts of its face,
ears, wings, and tail are black.

Common Raccoon: *Procyon lotor*

ETYMOLOGY

Procyon: (evolved) before dogs; *lotor:* washing, referring to the raccoon's habit of washing its food; *raccoon:* Algonquin word "arakun"—he scratches with his hands

Description　The common raccoon is about 3 feet long, with a black mask across its eyes and a bushy tail, with black rings. It has shiny black eyes; white stripes above and below the black mask; and a round, black nose. The raccoon's fur is a grizzled grayish brown. Its front paws resemble human hands and are extremely dexterous.

Common Locations　Raccoons live in the parks of all five boroughs. About fifty raccoons live in Central Park.

Notes of Interest　Raccoons live on the edges of wetlands. As nocturnal animals, they are active at night and spend the days sleeping in tree cavities. Their dens also include rock crevices, caves, or woodchuck burrows. Raccoons are intelligent, curious, and agile and can climb trees forward or backward. They can descend a tree headfirst. They are fast runners (15 mph), excellent swimmers, and are known to have superb night vision and an acute sense of hearing. A solitary animal, the only real social groups raccoons form are mothers and their kits. Female raccoons are protective of their young: they care for their kits for about a year, even though they are weaned and begin hunting at two or three months. During extremely cold or snowy periods, raccoons may sleep for long periods. However, they do not hibernate.

Ecological Role　Raccoons are omnivores. They consume crickets, grasshoppers, grubs, worms, dragonfly larvae, clams, wasps, salamanders, frogs, crayfish, snakes, turtles and their eggs, bird eggs and nestlings, fish, voles, and squirrels. They often eat garbage and, occasionally, carrion (dead animals). Raccoons have been seen washing their food in water during captivity.

KEY POINTS
- Raccoons are black-masked, ring-tailed mammals.
- On a mild winter day, you might see one sleeping near the hole of its den in a hollow tree.
- Other animals seldom attack an adult raccoon because they are such courageous fighters.

Plate 66   COMMON RACCOON

Eastern Chipmunk: *Tamias striatus*

ETYMOLOGY
Tamias; a hoarder; *striatus:* striped

Description   The eastern chipmunk, a native rodent, grows to 10 inches long, including the tail. Small, reddish brown, chipmunks have little pointy faces, with two white stripes, one above and one below the eye. Five black stripes bordered by white run down the back and along the sides. The belly and sides are pale, and the tail is dark above and reddish brown below. You will often hear the sharp *chip* call before seeing the little chipmunk.

Common Locations   Chipmunks can be found in most city parks. In 1998, they were reintroduced into Central Park, though they are rarely seen there.

Notes of Interest   The eastern chipmunk excavates a series of tunnels with two or three burrow entrances hidden under rocks, vegetation, or logs. Its primary chamber, the nest chamber, is 10 inches in diameter and is lined with dried leaves. It may be as deep as 3 feet below the ground and 6–12 feet away from the burrow entrance. Chipmunks dig food storage chambers and chambers for discarded soil from tunnel building.

Ecological Role   The eastern chipmunk is an omnivore and consumes acorns, nuts, and seeds from oaks, maples, American beech, sweet gum, black cherry, flowering dogwood, and hickory trees; wild strawberries, buttercup and other plants, berries, grasshoppers, beetles, katydids, cicadas, slugs, snails, insects, baby birds, bird eggs, salamanders, small snakes, young mice, mushrooms, and carrion (dead animals). Chipmunks pack food into their cheek pouches and return to their burrows to store their cache, much of which will be eaten during winter. Some of these seeds sprout and become new trees. Chipmunks are prey for hawks, owls, and crows.

KEY POINTS

- The eastern chipmunk dashes around with its tail straight up in the air.
- During hibernation they awaken every few weeks to feed on stored food.
- Nesting chambers are kept clean: shells, husks, and waste are taken to refuse tunnels.

Plate 67   EASTERN CHIPMUNK

Eastern Gray Squirrel: *Sciurus carolinensis*

ETYMOLOGY

Sciurus: in the shadow of the tail; *carolinensis:* first identified in the Carolinas

Description Members of the rodent order, eastern gray squirrels can grow to 20 inches. They are grayish brown above and white below. Their tails are bushy, with silver-tipped hairs. They hold their tails over their bodies as protection from sun and rain. Tails are used for balance when running and leaping from tree to tree. They possess excellent vision and a keen sense of smell and hearing. Gray squirrels are highly adapted for climbing trees; they have curved claws, and the ability to reverse their hind feet 180 degrees, which permits them to hang upside down from branches and bird feeders, collecting nuts, berries, and seeds.

Common Locations The eastern gray squirrel is the most frequently seen mammal and is a fixture in every city park. Colonies of black squirrels can be found in Washington Square Park and Inwood Hill Park in Manhattan.

Notes of Interest Squirrels live in two types of homes. One is a den in a tree cavity. The other is a large leafy nest built in the tops of tall trees, consisting of piles of leaves layered over a frame of twigs, with a nest hollowed out in the center. Females nest alone when pregnant, usually in the tree den. They have two litters per year: one in winter and one in spring or early summer. The young are cared for by their mother until they are ten to twelve weeks old. Many New Yorkers love feeding the squirrels.

Ecological Role Eastern gray squirrels are omnivores, consuming nuts, flowers, and buds of twenty-four oak tree species. Acorns are their main source of food. Other food items include the fruits, seeds, and flowers of maples, mulberry, hackberry, elms, horsechestnut, wild cherry, dogwood, hawthorns, and ginkgo trees. They will also feed on bones, bird eggs, and nestlings.

KEY POINTS

- Eastern gray squirrels communicate using a variety of vocalizations and postures, such as tail flicking.
- By burying acorns, they help plant future oak trees.

Plate 68   EASTERN GRAY SQUIRREL

Red Fox: *Vulpes vulpes*

ETYMOLOGY

Vulpes: fox

Description   The red fox has rusty, reddish fur with a white chin, throat, belly, and tip of its tail. With long, pointy ears, a narrow snout, and a bushy tail, they can stand 16 inches tall and grow to $3^1/_2$ feet long. They can weigh up to 15 pounds. Red foxes, like wolves and coyotes, look like dogs, which they are related to.

Common Locations   Red foxes are not commonly seen because they are shy and generally nocturnal. However, fox sightings have occurred in Van Cortlandt Park in the Bronx and Alley Pond Park in Queens.

Notes of Interest   The red fox lives alone until it pairs up with its mate during breeding season. After mating, they find and enlarge an abandoned woodchuck burrow or dig a new maternity den. The main entrance is about 3 feet wide, and has one or two escape holes. It is lined with grass and dry leaves. The litter is from one to ten pups. When pups are weaned at eight to ten weeks old and old enough to eat meat, the mother regurgitates meat she has eaten for them. Later, she carries live prey to the den so pups learn how to kill. Next, they hunt with their parents. At seven months, the pups leave the den and are on their own. The parents separate until the next mating season and may use the same maternity den for years.

Ecological Role   Foxes are opportunistic omnivores, feeding on whatever is available such as mice, voles, shrews, moles, squirrels, rabbits, woodchucks, opossums, raccoons, skunks, muskrats, beaver, waterfowl, turkey, and other birds, turtles, lizards, snakes, crayfish, caterpillars, grasshoppers, beetles, and other insects. During summer and fall, foxes will eat grapes, acorns, cherries, berries, grasses, sedges, and nuts. They will also eat carrion. Foxes hunt some prey by stalking. They move as close to the animal as possible, and then try to catch it. Red foxes have keen hearing and can detect digging, gnawing, or rustling of small animals underground and will dig them up.

KEY POINTS

- Usually nocturnal, they hunt at sunset, night, and dawn.
- Red foxes do not hibernate, but hunt year-round.

Plate 70 RED FOX

CHAPTER 5

plants

AQUATIC PLANTS

Common Cattail: *Typha latifolia*

ETYMOLOGY

Typha: bulrush or cattail; *latifolia:* broadleaf

PLACE OF ORIGIN

Native to America

Description Common cattail is a perennial growing up to 7 feet tall. The flat leaves are up to ¾ of an inch wide. The brown cigar-shaped female flower sits on the end of a spike and is capped by the male flower spike. Plumed cattail seeds float on the water, and drift away to start new plants. Cattails also have rhizomes, which are underground stems that spread horizontally to start new plants.

Common Locations Cattails are found along the edge of wetlands in city parks in all five boroughs. Common cattail grows mostly in fresh water but also thrives in slightly brackish marshes.

Notes of Interest Cattail plants spread from floating seeds but also by rhizomes so that an acre of cattail may consist of only a few individual plants.

Ecological Role Cattail root systems help prevent erosion, and the plants are often home to red-winged blackbirds and geese.

KEY POINTS

- Cattail stands provide important food and cover for wildlife. The rhizomes are eaten by Canada geese, snow geese, and muskrats.
- Muskrats also use the foliage to construct their lodges, and muskrat dens can provide resting and nesting sites for waterfowl.
- Cattail seeds are eaten by green wing teal ducks, some sandpipers, Canada geese, and snow geese.
- Native Americans used cattail for food. Rhizomes were dried and ground into flour or eaten as cooked vegetables. Young stems were eaten raw or cooked, and immature fruiting spikes were roasted. The leaves were made into woven mats, and the soft down from ripe fruiting heads was used as padding and in baby diapers.

Plate 71 COMMON CATTAIL

Common Reed: *Phragmites australis*

ETYMOLOGY
Phragmites: to grow like a fence
PLACE OF ORIGIN
Europe

Description   Common reed is a perennial grass growing up to 12 feet tall. The leaves are blue-green, long, flat, and sharply pointed. The flowers are tiny and form silky purplish panicles or plumes as they mature. Common reed flowers August through September. Although the leaves fall off in autumn, the stems and plumes remain throughout the winter. Common reed spreads by means of underground stems called rhizomes.

Common Locations   Common reed can be found growing in freshwater ponds and lakes and in brackish marshes throughout city parks in all five boroughs.

Notes of Interest   Although common reed is considered an invasive plant it can be beneficial to wildlife by providing habitat for many native species of birds and other animals. Golden-crowned kinglets feed on insects that live on phragmites. An array of animals forage on the young stems and seeds. Phragmites serves a vital role by filtering pollutants from the water.

KEY POINTS

- Native people wove floor mats and baskets from the hollow stems of a native variety of common reed.
- Common reed controls erosion by stabilizing the soil.
- As an invasive plant, common reed engenders a loss of biodiversity of plant life.
- Common reed thrives in waste areas and spreads from underground rhizomes as well as from seeds.
- Common reed crowds out other wetland plant species such as cattails.

Plate 72 COMMON REED

Red and White Clover: *Trifolium sp.*

ETYMOLOGY
Trifolium: leaves are divided into three leaflets

PLACE OF ORIGIN
Europe

Description   Red clover is a perennial that grows from 6–18 inches. The fragrant flower heads are made up of many tiny, pealike magenta flowers clustered together at the top of the hairy stem. The three leaflets bear a chevron, or a pale V shape.

Description   White clover is a perennial with creeping stems between 4 and 10 inches long. The flower heads are made up of clusters of tiny, white pealike flowers. The leaves are composed of three leaflets.

Common Locations   Both clovers are widespread throughout the five boroughs of New York City.

Notes of Interest   Clover is a member of the legume family. All members of this family are beneficial to the soil. Bacteria, living in nodes on the roots of clover and other legumes, have the ability to transform atmospheric nitrogen into nitrogen in the soil, thus improving soil fertility that benefits other plants.

Ecological Role   Red and white clover are important food sources for many mammals, including the white-tailed deer, wild turkey, red fox, eastern cottontail, and woodchuck. Caterpillars of the common sulphur and eastern tailed blue butterflies feed on the leaves of clover. Some species of adult butterflies that visit clover flowers include monarch, eastern black swallowtail, pearl crescent, spicebush swallowtail, cabbage white, great spangled fritillary, painted lady, and red admiral. Bees, butterflies, and other insects help pollinate clover.

KEY POINTS

- Nitrogen-fixing bacteria living on the roots of clover help put nitrogen into the soil.
- Clover flowers are important sources of nectar for bees and butterflies.
- Red and white clovers are the sources of the four-leaf clover.

Plate 73   RED CLOVER & WHITE CLOVER

Common Milkweed: *Aesclepias syriaca*

ETYMOLOGY

Aesclepias from Aesculapius, Greek god of healing; *syriaca*: Syrian (this plant is native and was mistakenly thought to be Syrian by Linnaeus who named it)

PLACE OF ORIGIN

Native to North America

Description   Common milkweed is a perennial plant growing up to 5 feet tall. The opposite leaves are up to 10 inches long with a prominent midvein. The fragrant, pinkish white flowers hang in clusters (umbels). The fruits are large, green hairy pods, which turn brown in the fall. Pods can contain two hundred seeds or more. In the fall, they split open and silky floss carries each seed with the wind. Milkweed can spread underground by rhizomes, which are underground stems that sprout new plants. Through rhizome spreading, common milkweed forms a colony.

Common Locations   Common milkweed grows in open, sunny areas in city parks and gardens throughout the five boroughs.

Notes of Interest   Common milkweed is the host plant for monarch caterpillars. It produces a white, milky sap that contains toxins, which make the caterpillars poisonous to predators. The monarch butterfly retains these poisons, which repel predators. Once a bird tastes a monarch it learns to avoid these black and orange butterflies.

Ecological Role   Monarch butterfly caterpillars, milkweed bugs, and milkweed leaf beetles only feed on milkweed leaves and could not survive without them. Other species of insects, such as bees, wasps, sphinx moths, and the milkweed tiger moth, use milkweed as their primary or major food source.

KEY POINTS

- The beautiful, fragrant pink flowers attract a long list of pollinating animals, including butterflies, honeybees, lacewings, and the ruby-throated hummingbird.
- Female monarch butterflies will only lay their eggs on the leaves of the milkweed.

Plate 79 COMMON MILKWEED

Common Mullein: *Verbascum thapsus*

ETYMOLOGY

Verbascum: corruption of *barbascum:* beard (shaggy leaves); *thapsus:* ancient North African town where this plant was native; *mullein:* from Latin *mollis:* soft

PLACE OF ORIGIN

North Africa

Description   Common mullein grows 3 to 6 feet tall. The leaves are alternate and are stalkless, hairy, and very soft. The small yellow flowers are borne on a single stalk. A biennial, common mullein produces a large basal rosette the first year, with long, narrow leaves. The flowering stalk appears in the second year. Common mullein flowers are yellow with five petals. Flowers are about an inch wide. They bloom a few at a time from June to September.

Common Locations   Common mullein grows along sunny paths and streets throughout city parks in all five boroughs.

Notes of Interest   Common mullein was brought to America by the Puritans, who used the plant as a medicinal herb. Teas and ointments made from the leaves are used to this day to treat lung problems.

Ecological Role   Common mullein is a pioneer plant: it is one of the first plants to grow in a place that has burned or been disturbed. American goldfinches, indigo buntings, and other birds eat mullein seeds. Common mullein provides shelter for insects in the winter. Since rosettes survive through the cold weather, leaves provide warmth and protection for ladybugs and other insects.

KEY POINTS

- Mullein is known as the candlestick plant because the downy hairs on the leaves were used for lamp wicks.
- The flowery ends of the long flower stalks were dipped in oil, lighted, and used as torches.
- The soft leaves have been used to line the inside of shoes.

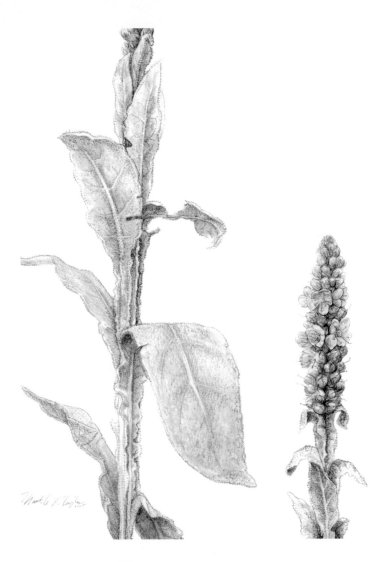

Plate 75 COMMON MULLEIN

Dandelion: *Taraxacum officinale*

ETYMOLOGY

Taraxacum: treating disorders; *officinale:* medicinal; *dandelion:* from the French *dent de lion:* tooth of the lion for the toothlike shape of the leaves

PLACE OF ORIGIN

Europe and Eurasia

Description   The dandelion is a perennial plant with a long taproot. The sharply toothed leaves form a basal rosette, and bright yellow flower heads sit on top of long, hollow stems, which exude a white, milky fluid. The flower head is made up of numerous florets (small, complete flowers), each producing a single seed. When dandelions go to seed, the flower heads close and then reopen showing the commonly seen "puffballs," each seed attached to a separate "parachute" that children love to blow.

Common Locations   Flowering in spring, summer, and fall, the leaves of the dandelion are among the first greens to emerge in late winter and early spring. Dandelions can be found through out the five boroughs of the city, growing in sunny, open places, including city sidewalks, along streets, in backyards, and through out city parks.

Notes of Interest   The flower heads open in the morning and close by late afternoon. They will also close during cloudy or rainy days and reopen the next day.

Ecological Role   The dandelion's flower is a source of nectar for insects from early spring through late fall. Small birds feed on the dandelion's seeds. Dandelion leaves, roots, and flowers have been part of humans' diets for centuries.

KEY POINTS

- Early settlers brought the dandelion to America for food and medicine.
- Dandelions reproduce by windblown seeds and also by regeneration from the taproot, even if the flower and leaves are cut off.
- Children love picking the pretty yellow flowers.

Plate 76 DANDELION

Black-Eyed Susan: *Rudbeckia hirta*

ETYMOLOGY

Rudbeckia: Olaus Rudbeck was a botanist and professor of Medicine at Uppsala University in Sweden in the early eighteenth century; *hirta*, Latin for hairy

PLACE OF ORIGIN

Native to North America

Description The black-eyed Susan grows 2–3 feet tall. Yellow ray flowers surround the characteristic brown, domed center.

When it first germinates, the seedling grows into a rosette with oblong leaves. Sometimes flowers will appear in the first summer but usually the blooms appear in the summer of the second year. The flower heads are 2–3 inches across with dark brown disk flowers forming the "cone" in the center, making it more of a "brown-eyed" Susan. The leaves are long, rough, and hairy.

Common Locations Black-eyed Susan flowers can be seen from June through October in city parks throughout the five boroughs.

Notes of Interest This plant is covered with hairs, making it feel slightly rough. Black-eyed Susans attract many birds, including finches, black-capped chickadees, northern cardinals, sparrows, and nuthatches.

Ecological Role Black-eyed Susan is often planted on hillsides and along roads to control erosion. This beautiful wildflower offers food and shelter to several song and game birds. Although it appears to die every winter, the black-eyed Susan is a perennial that returns in the spring.

KEY POINTS

- This yellow daisylike wildflower provides beauty, prevents erosion, and attracts birds.
- The raised center is made up of a multitude of tiny disk flowers.
- The black-eyed Susan is really "brown-eyed."

Plate 77   BLACK–EYED SUSAN

TREES

Conifers

Conifers (evergreens) are cone-bearing trees with needle leaves that are, with some exceptions, green year-round.

Eastern White Pine: *Pinus strobus*

Description The native eastern white pine grows to 100 feet. The 3–5-inch-long needles are in bundles of five and stay on the tree for two to three years. The mature bark is dark grayish brown and is broken into vertical ridges. The mature reddish brown cones are up to 7 inches long and are tipped by white resin.

Ecological Role The northern saw-whet owls roost in young eastern white pines in Pelham Bay Park during winter.

Austrian Pine: *Pinus nigra*

Description The European Austrian, or black pine grows to 60 feet. The long, shiny needles are in bundles of two and remain on the tree for several years. The yellow cone scales have small spines at their tips. With maturity, the outer bark becomes chalky white, and the inner bark darkens to almost black, creating a platelike black and white pattern.

Ecological Role The Austrian pine is the most commonly found pine tree in Central Park. In winter, long-eared owls roost in a grove of black pines located just south of Bow Bridge.

Bald Cypress: *Taxodium distichum*

Description The bald cypress, related to the giant sequoia tree, can reach 140 feet tall. Although considered conifers because they possess needlelike leaves and bear cones, they are deciduous in that they shed their leaves in autumn. The soft needles are less than an inch long and arranged in two rows, one on either side of the branch. Even the fibrous, reddish brown outer bark is soft on this tree. The 1-inch round woody cones contain up to thirty samaras (winged seeds). When standing in water, the bald cypress produces "knees," wooden knobs that protrude from shallow water or soil surrounding the tree. Some scientists believe they anchor the tree, while others think they help the tree "breathe" by taking in oxygen.

White Pine

Austrian Pine

Bald Cypress

Plate 78   *From top*: WHITE PINE,
AUSTRIAN PINE, BALD CYPRESS

Some believe they do both. The bald cypresses are long-lived trees; some live a thousand years.

   Ecological Role   Although typically a tree of the south, the bald cypress can tolerate the cold and grow well in wet, low-oxygen habitats and in poor, compacted soil in the city. The decay-resistant wood is widely used to build the wooden water tanks that sit atop city apartment buildings.

Ailanthus: *Ailanthus altissima*

ETYMOLOGY

Ailanthus: sky tree; *altissima:* the tallest

PLACE OF ORIGIN

China

Description   A tall tree with the common name "Tree of Heaven," the ailanthus grows to 80 feet. Ailanthus grows fast, climbing 3 feet per year for the first four years. The ailanthus has fast-growing roots, which burrow into cracks in the sidewalks and building foundations. It has a straight trunk and wide branches forming a broad crown. The mature gray bark bears pale, vertical fissures. The alternate compound leaves can reach up to 2 feet long with twenty five to thirty pointed leaflets. The female trees produce inconspicuous, tiny green flower clusters that bear more than three hundred thousand 1 ½-inch-long, reddish to yellow-green samaras (winged seeds), each with a centrally placed seed.

Common Locations   The ailanthus tree grows throughout the five boroughs and in all city parks.

Notes of Interest   Because of its tolerance of heat, drought, cold, pollution, and poor soil, the ailanthus is often the only tree that can survive in certain urban sites. It is the tree in the classic book, *A Tree Grows in Brooklyn.*

Ecological Role   The ailanthus is considered a weed tree because it grows anywhere and so quickly. The hundreds of thousands of seeds produced by each female ailanthus tree are dispersed by the wind. Its profuse flowers are a source of nectar for bees. Birds such as pine grosbeaks and crossbills consume the seeds. In Asia, it is considered an important medicinal tree.

KEY POINTS

- The Ailanthus tree grows in vacant lots, city backyards, and alongside buildings.
- Its long compound leaves give the tree a lacy, tropical look.
- In midsummer look for numerous clusters of thousands of colorful samaras (winged seeds) on the female trees.

Ailanthus

Plate 79   AILANTHUS

American Elm: *Ulmus americana*

ETYMOLOGY

Ulmus: Elm; *americana:* from America

Description The American elm is a tall, stately tree growing up to 100 feet. Its distinctively elegant form is easily recognized from a distance. The elm's trunk divides into large ascending branches that arch over city streets and support slender, graceful branches that flow down toward the earth. The crown can be plume-shaped or spreading. The gray bark forms deeply furrowed ridges and diamond-shaped fissures. The oval leaves are doubly toothed, 3–6 inches long, and lopsided at the base. The tiny green flowers are clustered along the twigs and produce flat, oval keys (samaras, or winged seeds) with hairy edges. The keys are deeply notched with inward-curved points.

Common Locations Although American elms can be found in all five boroughs, some prominent locations include the Bronx: Seton Falls Park and Wave Hill; Brooklyn: Prospect Park; Manhattan: Riverside Drive from 104th Street to Grant's Tomb; American elms line Literary Walk at the Central Park Mall and line 5th Avenue all along the park side; Queens: Forest Park.

Notes of Interest In the mid-twentieth century, Dutch elm disease wiped out the urban elm forests of many American cities. Disease-resistant elms are currently being planted.

Ecological Role The keys are consumed by small songbirds, including American goldfinches and purple finches. Keys and buds are eaten by the gray squirrel. Twigs and bark are fed on by the eastern cottontail rabbit in winter and the Baltimore oriole often builds its nest in the drooping branches in spring.

KEY POINTS

- Graceful and elegant, the American elm is highly prized as a shade and ornamental tree.
- The keys (winged seeds) fall in huge numbers in mid-spring.
- Dutch elm disease, spread by beetles, killed most American elms nationwide between 1930 and 1960.

American Elm

Plate 80 AMERICAN ELM

American Hornbeam: *Carpinus caroliniana*

ETYMOLOGY
Carpinus: hornbeam; *caroliniana:* from Carolina; *hornbeam:* strong tree

PLACE OF ORIGIN
Native to America

Description The American hornbeam tree, also known as ironwood for its extremely strong wood, is a short, understory tree, growing to 30 feet and occasionally reaching 60 feet tall. The smooth, dark gray trunk has a distinctly muscular appearance, with a deeply ridged and sinuous look, which gives it the common name of musclewood. The male flowers (staminate catkins) emerge in late March and hang down like long, slender, green chandeliers. The female flowers (pistillate catkins) emerge from the tips of the branches and, once pollinated, grow into small nutlets, each one enclosed in the base of three-lobed, leaflike bracts, which are borne in pairs in loose and drooping clusters. Alternate leaves, 2–4 inches long with pointed tips, are finely and sharply double toothed, thin, and translucent. Many leaves give the tree a dense appearance and provide abundant shade in summer. In late autumn, the leaves turn deep scarlet and orange.

Common Locations American hornbeam trees can be found throughout the five boroughs in most city parks.

Notes of Interest Hornbeam wood is so strong that early settlers used it to make mallet heads and plow blades when iron was not available.

Ecological Role The nuts are eaten by the eastern gray squirrel, ruffed grouse, bobwhite, ring-necked pheasant, and wild turkey. Cottontail rabbits and white-tailed deer feed on its twigs, shoots, and leaves.

KEY POINTS
- The hornbeam's ridged, sinewy bark looks muscular.
- The wood of hornbeams is among the hardest and strongest of most trees.
- Male and female flowers appear in early spring.

American Hornbeam

Plate 81   AMERICAN HORNBEAM

Ginkgo: *Ginkgo biloba*

ETYMOLOGY
Ginkgo: silver apricot; *biloba:* two-lobed (leaf shape)
PLACE OF ORIGIN
China

Description   The ginkgo biloba is a tall tree growing up to 80 feet. Although it is a deciduous tree, the ginkgo is related to conifers and bears leaves that have parallel veins, which some scientists believe evolved from the fused needles of evergreen trees. The fan-shaped leaves, attached to spurs on twigs, are notched in the middle and turn a beautiful yellow in autumn. The female trees produce inconspicuous flowers, which form 1-inch plumlike fruit. The male cones are on separate trees. The bark of the mature ginkgo is reddish brown and deeply fissured.

Common Locations   In Manhattan street after street and avenue to avenue contain at least some ginkgo trees. Ginkgo trees have been planted in city parks in all five boroughs. An enormous ginkgo tree can be found on the Western Ridge walk in Inwood Hill Park.

Notes of Interest   Charles Darwin considered the ginkgo tree to be a "living fossil" because it was the only tree of a large family of prehistoric trees to survive the last ice age. Trees from the ginkgo family lived two hundred million years ago when dinosaurs roamed the earth. Europeans first encountered ginkgo trees growing in monasteries in the mountains of eastern China in the early eighteenth century where they were tended by Buddhist monks. Ginkgo trees were brought to Europe in the early 1700s and to America in 1784. The ginkgo tree is a commonly planted street tree in New York City because it resists drought, air pollution, insects, and disease.

Ecological Role   The fruit of the ginkgo tree is valued as a delicacy, and is sold as the "white nut" in Asian markets. The nuts are collected in the parks when they fall to the ground. Crows and eastern gray squirrels also feed on ginkgo nuts.

The edible kernel lies within a pulp covering that has an unpleasant odor. When planting ginkgo trees on the street, male trees are preferred over the females, which produce the malodorous fruit that litters the ground, covering cars below. Available in health food stores and other shops, the ginkgo is considered medicinal and is used by some to improve memory.

Ginkgo

Plate 82 GINKGO

KEY POINTS
- Ginkgo trees bear fan-shaped leaves with parallel veins.
- The seed within the malodorous fruit is edible.

Horsechestnut Tree: *Aesculus hippocastanum*

ETYMOLOGY
Aesculus: edible (although the nut is *unfit* as human food); *hippocastanum:* horsechestnut.

PLACE OF ORIGIN
The horsechestnut is an Asian relative of the American buckeye tree and is not a chestnut tree at all.

Description The beautiful horsechestnut tree grows to a height of 85 feet. Its opposite leaves are palmately compound with five to seven leaflets. The mature scaly bark is grayish brown and broken into shallow fissures. Horsechestnut tree flower clusters are white, speckled with red or yellow and appear on an erect spike that looks like a candelabra. The flowers produce spiny seedpods encasing a hard, shiny, brown nut that looks like a chestnut but is not. This brown nut bears a dull, rough, pale brown scar where it has been attached to the inside of the nut case or pod. The pod, a large, green husk protected with short, sharp spines, splits into three parts when it falls to the ground, freeing the nut inside.

Common Locations The Bronx: Van Cortlandt Park; Brooklyn: Fort Green Park; Prospect Park; Manhattan: Central Park, Riverside Park; Queens: Kissena Park; Staten Island: Clove Lakes Park.

Notes of Interest The tree gets its name from the shape of the leaf scars covering the twigs and branches, which look like tiny horseshoes. Turks used the seeds in a cough remedy for horses with respiratory problems.

Ecological Role Squirrels feed on the nuts and plant the ones they don't eat. Butterflies, bumblebees, and other insects are attracted to the honeylike scent of the flowers.

KEY POINTS
- The nuts, called *conkers*, are poisonous to humans.
- After pollination the flowers' yellow speckles turn red.
- Horsechestnut flowers are known as "candles."

Horsechestnut

Plate 83 HORSECHESTNUT

Lindens: *Tilia* spp.

Description   Linden trees can reach 100 feet at maturity. Their tapered trunks form widespread drooping branches at the lower level and ascending branches above, which create a rounded crown. Some trees have several trunks. The alternate, coarsely toothed leaves are generally heart shaped, dark green above and pale, or silvery, below. The extremely fragrant yellow flowers bloom in late June and produce one or two nutlets suspended from a leafy bract, which spins in the wind when the seeds are mature, dispersing them from the tree. The grayish brown bark is fissured into long ridges.

American Linden: *Tilia americana*

Description   The leaves of this native linden grow up to 10 inches long and have an unequal base.

Bigleaf Linden: *Tilia platyphyllos*

Description   The leaves grow up to 5 inches and have a sharply pointed tip (not shown).

Littleleaf Linden: *Tilia cordata*

Description   Small, heart-shaped leaves growing to 3 inches with sharply pointed tips.

Silver Linden: *Tilia tomentosa*

Description   The round or oval-shaped leaves grow up to 5 inches, are dark green above, silver below, and have an uneven base.

NOTES OF INTEREST
Linden wood is soft and has been used by woodcarvers throughout the old and new world for thousands of years. The Iroquois carved masks from the linden. The fibrous inner bark was woven into cord, rope, and rope bags. The fiber, called *bast*, has given this tree the common name of basswood. During the flowering period, perfumers collect the heady scent for their products. Linnaeus's family took their name from a linden tree.

Linden

Plate 81   From top: AMERICAN LINDEN,
LITTLELEAF LINDEN, SILVER LINDEN

Ecological Role   The linden is also called the bee tree because its strong fragrance and nectar attract bees that produce a delicious honey. When lindens bloom, bees apparently forsake most other flowers. The white honey bees make from linden nectar is regarded as high quality.

KEY POINTS

- The linden tree is beautiful all year. The deeply furrowed and ridged bark stands out in winter; the green leaves flash silver in the wind in spring and summer; the flowers are among the sweetest smelling, pervading the air for blocks; and the leaves turn a lovely yellow in autumn.

Honey Locust: *Gleditsia triacanthos*

PLACE OF ORIGIN
America

Description   The honey locust grows up to 70 feet. The trunk and branches can have clumps of long, sharp thorns. The alternate, compound leaves are sometimes doubly compound and give the tree a delicate, lacy look. The bark has scaly plates. The inconspicuous, wind-pollinated flowers produce long, brown seedpods that contain a sweet pulp and seeds that resemble coffee beans.

Ecological Role   A commonly planted park and street tree, honey locust is resistant to drought, pollution, and salt. The sweet pulp inside the seedpod is eaten by white-tailed deer, gray squirrels, and eastern cottontail rabbits. Birds and mammals feed on the seeds and help disperse them. The enormous thorns are dangerous to humans and wildlife; therefore only thornless locusts are currently being planted in New York City.

Black Locust: *Robinia pseudoacacia*

PLACE OF ORIGIN
America

Description   The tall, gangly black locust tree grows up to 80 feet. Its alternate, compound leaves, sometimes more than a foot long, and bearing up to nineteen small, oval leaflets, open in April or May and are followed by gorgeous and fragrant clusters of pealike white flowers. The flat, brown seedpods produced by these flowers are up to 4 inches long. The thick bark is deeply furrowed and criss-crosses the trunk like woven braids.

Ecological Role   Black locust wood is hard and resistant to rot. During a late autumnal storm in the early 1990s, hundreds of black locust trees fell down in Van Cortlandt Park. The New York City Parks Department used the wood and beautiful bark to build fences and rustic benches and gazebos, some of which can be seen in the Central Park Ramble. The fragrant flowers attract pollinating animals in midspring. The black locust tree is a member of the legume family, and like all its relatives, bears nodes on its roots, which house nitrogen-fixing bacteria. These very important inhabitants take atmospheric nitrogen and fix it into the soil where plants can use it.

Honey Locust

Black Locust

Plate 85

From top: HONEY LOCUST & BLACK LOCUST

Sugar Maple: *Acer saccharum*

Description The sugar maple tree grows up to 100 feet tall. It has a wide trunk and rounded crown. Clusters of yellowish green flowers appear with new leaves in early spring and produce samaras (winged seeds) that fork almost straight down. The opposite leaves are up to 5½ inches wide with five lobes. The bark of the mature sugar maple is scaly, gray, and deeply furrowed.

Ecological Role In autumn, the sugar maple tree bears glorious red, orange, and yellow leaves. Like native people and colonists, contemporary farmers collect the sap to make maple syrup. Sugar maples make poor street trees because they are sensitive to road salt and pollution. The large branches of older trees often decay before the trunk, leaving nesting cavities for various birds and animals

Red Maple: *Acer rubrum*

Description The red maple tree grows up to 90 feet tall. Throughout the four seasons, the color red can be seen on this maple: red leaf buds in winter; red flowers produce red samaras (winged seeds) in spring; red leaf stems in summer; and red to orange leaves in autumn. The leaves are opposite, up to 4 inches long with three to five lobes. The bark of young trees is smooth and pale gray and becomes darker and roughly ridged with age.

Ecological Role The red maple is one of the first trees to flower in early spring and provides nutritious seeds for white-tailed deer, eastern cottontail rabbits, and gray squirrels.

Norway Maple: *Acer platanoides*

Description The Norway maple grows up to 60 feet tall. The small, yellowish green flowers appear in early spring before the leaves and produce samaras (winged seeds) that point away from one another. The opposite leaves are broad and up to 6 inches long, with five to seven lobes. The brown bark has narrow ridges

Ecological Role Botanist John Bartram introduced the quick-growing Norway maple to America in the 1750s. The shade of the Norway maple is so dense that nothing can grow underneath. Although the Norway maple is resistant to city pollutants, it is con-

Sugar Maple

Red Maple

Norway Maple

Plate 86 From top: SUGAR MAPLE,
RED MAPLE, NORWAY MAPLE

sidered an invasive tree and is being eradicated in some city parks to
make room for native trees.

Mulberry: *Morus spp.*

ETYMOLOGY
Morus: mulberry

White Mulberry Tree: *Morus alba*

PLACE OF ORIGIN
China

Red Mulberry Tree: *Morus rubra*

PLACE OF ORIGIN
Native to America

Description White and red mulberry trees, which grow to 40–50 feet tall, have short trunks. The leaves are alternate, 2–8 inches long, and can have no lobes, two lobes, or three lobes. The upper surfaces of white mulberry leaves are smooth. The upper surfaces of the leaves of red mulberry trees are rough. The flowers are small and green. The fruit of the mulberry trees are edible, juicy, and sweet and ripen by early summer. The bark is reddish brown.

Common Locations The Bronx: Van Cortlandt Park; Brooklyn: Prospect Park; Manhattan: Central Park, Riverside Park; Queens: Forest Park; Staten Island: Conference House Park where a 57-foot white mulberry stands tall over the Conference House.

Notes of Interest The white mulberry tree is resistant to pollution, compacted soil, heat, drought, and salt. White mulberry trees were raised in China close to five thousand years ago. The mulberry tree is the host plant for the silkworm caterpillars. In the early 1600s, the English King James I, shipped white mulberry trees and silkworms to the colony of Virginia to start silkworm production, which was unsuccessful. If you are raising silkworm caterpillars in New York City, it is relatively easy to find local mulberry leaves to feed the hungry caterpillars.

Ecological Role Birds love mulberries. American robins, wood thrushes, catbirds, and cedar waxwings, among other songbirds, consume the fruit of mulberries. Humans love the taste of the sweet, juicy berries. The white mulberry is often considered an invasive weed tree because birds disperse the seeds, and the trees

Mulberry

Plate 87   MULBERRY

pop up everywhere. It is one of the most common trees in New York City.

KEY POINTS

· In early summer, mulberry trees bear delicious juicy berries.

Eastern White Oak: *Quercus alba*

Description The eastern white oak grows over 100 feet tall. Its massive trunk and wide branches create a spreading crown. The bark is gray with vertical and horizontal fissures. Its leaves, up to 9 inches long, with five to nine rounded lobes, are bright green above, and whitish below. They turn red, then brown in the fall. The dead leaves will often stay on the branches through the winter.

Ecological Role This tree provides cover for many birds and small mammals throughout the seasons. Birds and mammals use white oak leaves and twigs as nesting material. Eastern cotton-tails, the white-footed mouse, gray squirrels, blue jays, northern bobwhite, wild turkeys, mallards, American crows, eastern chipmunks, and raccoons feed on its acorns, which are up to an inch and a half long and germinate in the fall. Eastern white oaks can live more than five hundred years and were an important food source for Native Americans.

Northern Red Oak: *Quercus rubra*

Description The northern red oak grows 70–90 feet tall. It has a straight trunk and rounded crown. The bark, with deep vertical fissures that resemble ski trails, is gray to reddish brown. The red oak leaves, up to 9 inches long with seven to eleven bristle-tipped lobes, turn red in autumn. The acorns are up to an inch long with shallow, saucerlike caps.

Ecological Role The northern red oak is the most common oak in the entire Northeast. Birds and mammals consume its acorns.

Pin Oak: *Quercus palustris*

Description The pin oak grows 60–70 feet tall. Its branches are studded with pinlike shoots. It has a straight mastlike trunk shooting up the center with grayish brown bark marked by narrow fissures. The pin oak's leaves, up to 5 inches long, bear five to seven bristle-tipped lobes that are separated by u-shaped sinuses. Their small ($^3/_4$ inch) acorns have shallow cups and take two years to mature. The lower branches droop down, the middle branches stick straight out, and the upper branches reach up.

Eastern White Oak

Northern Red Oak

Pin Oak

Plate 88   From top: EASTERN WHITE OAK,
NORTHERN RED OAK, PIN OAK

Ecological Role   The pin oak is tolerant of any kind of soil, drought, pollution, city air, storms, pests, and fungi. Waterfowl, wild turkeys, gray squirrels, and raccoons eat its small acorns. The pin oak is a commonly found tree in New York City.

Osage Orange: *Maclura pomifera*

ETYMOLOGY
Maclura: William Maclure, eighteenth-century American geologist; *pomifera:* applelike fruit

PLACE OF ORIGIN
Native to America, in the Oklahoma, Arkansas, and Louisiana area once inhabited by the Osage Indians.

Description   The Osage orange is a small tree that grows up to 50 feet. Its short trunk supports spreading branches, which form an uneven crown. The alternate leaves have no teeth, are between 2–5 inches long, and end in a tapered point. The bark is gray to orange brown, with deep, orange furrows. Leaves attach to the twigs with sharp, short spines. Tiny, inconspicuous wind-pollinated flowers produce large, green, coarse, and fissured fruit up to 6 inches in diameter that weighs up to 3 pounds. The fruit has an aromatic, citruslike scent. They ripen in the fall and litter the ground beneath the tree. Only the female trees produce fruit.

Common Locations   The Bronx: St. Mary's Park; Brooklyn: Brower Park; Manhattan: North of 72nd Street in Riverside Park, Marcus Garvey Park; Staten Island: some of the original Osage orange trees planted by Frederick Law Olmsted (co-designer and developer of Central Park) in the 1840s, are still standing on Sequine Avenue south of Hylan Boulevard.

Notes of Interest   The Osage Indians used the hard, yet flexible wood of this tree to make bows highly valued by the Plains Indians. The wood of Osage orange trees is reported to be stronger than oak (*Quercus*), as tough as hickory (*Carya*) and is considered by archers to be one of the finest native North American woods for bows. Osage orange trees are relatives of mulberry trees.

Ecological Role   The eastern gray squirrel feeds on the seeds. Yellow-orange dye is made from the root bark.

KEY POINTS
- Look for the large, green fissured fruit of the Osage orange tree in September and October.
- The spiny twigs, the bark's orange fissures, and the leaves without teeth are characteristic of this tree.

Osage Orange

Plate 89   OSAGE ORANGE

Eastern Redbud: *Cercis canadensis*

ETYMOLOGY
Cercis: ancient Greek name for Redbud; *canadensis:* of Canada

PLACE OF ORIGIN
Native to America

Description   The eastern redbud is a small tree that grows to 30 feet. Its small trunk, or trunks, and spreading branches form a low, broad crown. The gorgeous lavender-pink, pealike "red bud" flowers appear before the leaves in April, and produce 3-inch-long flat seedpods. The large, alternate, heart-shaped leaves are 2–5 inches long and wide, with smooth, untoothed margins. This small, understory tree is a legume and has nitrogen-fixing bacteria living in nodes in its roots.

Common Locations   In April, eastern redbud trees can be seen in bloom throughout the five boroughs in city parks. The Bronx: Pelham Bay Park; Brooklyn: Prospect Park; Manhattan: Riverside Park, Central Park; Queens: Flushing Meadows Corona Park; Staten Island: Clove Lakes Park.

Notes of Interest   Eastern redbud is planted as an ornamental tree. The redbud is also known as the Judas Tree. Its European cousin, *Cercis siliquastrum*, is said to be the tree from which Judas Iscariot hung himself. *Cercis siliquastrum* was once widely grown in the hills of Judea.

Ecological Role   Redbud seedpods are consumed by many birds, including northern cardinals, ring-necked pheasants, rose-breasted grosbeaks, and bobwhites. White-tailed deer and gray squirrels also feed on the seeds. Fragrant, early spring flowers are a source of nectar for bees. Birds such as the American robin build their nests in the redbud's low branches.

KEY POINT
- The eastern redbud's branches are covered in tiny, pealike lavender-pink flowers in April.
- The large, heart-shaped leaves are another distinctive characteristic of this small, ornamental tree.
- Wildlife feed on the seeds, pollinate the flowers, and build their nests in this beautiful little tree.

Eastern Redbud

Plate 90 EASTERN REDBUD

Sweetgum: *Liquidambar styraciflua*

ETYMOLOGY

Liquidambar: yellow sap; *styraciflua:* aromatic storax or resin; *sweetgum:* sweet sap can be chewed like gum

PLACE OF ORIGIN

America

    Description   The mature sweetgum tree grows to 100 feet tall with a pyramid-shaped crown. The alternate, finely toothed leaves have five to seven lobes. They are star shaped and aromatic. In the fall, they turn glorious shades of red, orange, yellow, and purple. The bark becomes scaly and deeply furrowed as the tree matures. The round male and female flowers produce single, green, spiny seed balls, which hang suspended from long stems months after the leaves fall.

    Common Locations   Sweetgum trees grow throughout the city's parks in all five boroughs.

    Notes of Interest   The wood is hard and durable and is used for furniture, barrels, wooden bowls, cabinets, and interior finishing. In addition to using the sap as chewing gum, Native Americans and settlers used the sap to treat a variety of ailments in both humans and domestic animals. Native Americans used the roots and bark to treat skin disorders, diarrhea, and fevers.

    Ecological Role   Each seed ball produces tiny seeds consumed by squirrels and winter birds such as northern juncos, tufted titmice, and white-throated sparrows.

KEY POINTS

- Brown, dried seed balls litter the ground beneath sweetgum trees in late winter.
- In autumn, the star-shaped leaves are some of the most beautiful foliage in the city.
- If you crush a sweetgum leaf you can smell its aromatic fragrance.

Sweetgum

Plate 91   SWEETGUM

London Plane: *Platanus × acerifolia*

PLACE OF ORIGIN
England

Description The London plane tree grows to 120 feet tall. It has a massive trunk and branches, covered in a pale green, brown, and tan bark that peels off as the tree grows. The alternate leaves are up to 10 inches long with three to five shallow lobes. The female flowers produce two or three seedpods on one stalk.

Common Locations Both Frederick Law Olmsted in the late nineteenth century, and Robert Moses in the twentieth century, planted London planes extensively throughout New York City's parks.

Notes of Interest The London plane is a hybrid of the American sycamore and the oriental plane. In the early seventeenth century, the gardener to Charles I, king of England, brought seeds of the American sycamore back from Virginia. It is believed that the trees from these seeds hybridized with the oriental plane trees in his garden and produced the London plane. The leaf of the London plane is the symbol of the New York City Department of Parks and Recreation.

Ecological Role The seedpods fall off in late winter and are consumed by birds. This tree is tolerant of pollution.

American Sycamore: *Platanus occidentalis*

PLACE OF ORIGIN
America

Description The American sycamore also grows to 120 feet, with a huge trunk and massive branches. The bark of the lower trunk is brown and scaly. The bark of the upper trunk and branches peels off exposing a pale, almost white, inner bark. The alternate leaves are up to 8 inches and are wider than they are long with three to five extremely shallow lobes. The inconspicuous female flowers produce a single seedpod dangling from the end of its stem.

Common Locations Brooklyn: Prospect Park; the Bronx: Van Cortlandt Park; Manhattan: Central Park, Inwood Hill Park, Riverside Park; Queens: Astoria Park; Staten Island: Conference House Park.

Notes of Interest A sycamore tree standing in St. Paul's Chapel graveyard protected the ancient tombstones and the chapel from falling debris when the World Trade Center towers fell on

American sycamore

Sycamore Roots sculpture

Plate 92   AMERICAN SYCAMORE

September 11, 2001. This tree is memorialized by a bronze sculpture of its roots by artist Steve Tobin, which now stands in the courtyard of Trinity Church.

Ecological Role   This huge tree can live up to five hundred years.

Tulip Tree: *Liriodendron tulipifera*

ETYMOLOGY
Liriodendron: lily tree (referring to the flowers); *tulipifera:* tuliplike flowers. The tulip tree is in the magnolia family and is not related to lilies or tulips.

Description   The tulip tree is the tallest deciduous hardwood tree in North America, growing to a height of 150 feet. The trunk is straight and sheds its lower branches as it grows. The grayish brown bark has deep furrows. Tulip tree leaves have a distinctive, almost squarish shape with four lobes and a notch between the top two lobes. They turn bright yellow in the fall. The showy flowers have green petals splashed with orange, a cluster of yellow stamens, and thick green pistils in the center, which produce stout, green cone-shaped fruit that mature into dried, brown samaras (winged seeds).

Common Locations   Throughout the woodlands of New York City's parks in all five boroughs. Queen's Alley Pond Park has a tulip tree over 133 feet tall.

Notes of Interest   The tulip tree is an example of a self-pruning species: Its lower limbs die and fall off as the tree grows. Native people, pioneers, and early colonists made dugout canoes from tulip tree trunks. Daniel Boone made a 60-foot tulip tree canoe to travel down the Ohio River with his family when he moved from Kentucky.

Ecological Role   Tulip tree flowers are a source of nectar for bees. In autumn, gray squirrels, purple finches, cardinals, and grosbeaks consume the seeds. White-tailed deer browse the twigs.

KEY POINTS
- Tulip trees are New York City's tallest trees.
- The notched, four-pointed leaves turn yellow in the fall.
- Beautiful green, orange, and yellow flowers can be seen in late May through mid-June.
- Seedpods litter the ground in autumn.

Tulip Tree

Plate 93 TULIP TREE

Weeping Willow: *Salix babylonica*

ETYMOLOGY

Salix: willow; *babylonica:* refers to the psalm in which the Hebrews mourn their captivity in Babylon by the willows

PLACE OF ORIGIN

Asia

Description   A medium-sized, broad tree with a rounded crown, the weeping willow grows to 50 feet tall, and has pendulous, gracefully drooping branches that can touch the earth. The alternate, toothed, lance-shaped leaves are up to 5 inches long and taper at both ends from slender, delicate branches that appear almost orange in winter. New spring leaves are a brilliant lime green. Inconspicuous flowers are wind pollinated. The bark is gray, rough, quite thick, and deeply furrowed.

Common Locations   Weeping willows can be seen near freshwater ponds and lakes throughout New York City's parks in all five boroughs. Brooklyn: Prospect Park on the shore of Prospect Lake; the Bronx: north end of Van Cortlandt Golf Course; Manhattan: Riverside Park South; Central Park: the Pool, Harlem Meer, and the Lake; Staten Island: Clove Lakes Park.

Notes of Interest   The weeping willow was planted as an ornamental tree along the shores of the city's ponds and lakes. Although it is a fast grower, it has a short life span.

Ecological Role   Weeping willows provide shade and help control runoff and erosion. Their roots hold soil and help stabilize pond and lake banks by trapping and using rainwater that otherwise would run off into ponds, causing erosion.

KEY POINTS

- Weeping willows are recognizable by their characteristic drooping, graceful branches.
- They are beautiful in all seasons with lime-green leaves and branches in spring; full, green crowns in summer; yellow leaves in autumn; and orange branches in winter.
- Aspirin was originally synthesized from salicylic acid, an ingredient in willow bark.

Weeping Willow

Plate 99   WEEPING WILLOW

Wild Cherry: *Prunus serotina*

ETYMOLOGY
Prunus: plum or prune; *serotina:* late flowering

PLACE OF ORIGIN
Native to America

Description   Urban wild or black cherry trees can grow to 80 feet tall and up to 100 feet in the forest. The alternate, fine-toothed, lance-shaped leaves are 2–5 inches long, with long, pointed tips. In April or May, after the leaves unfold, drooping white flower clusters emerge, covering the tree and producing pea-sized green fruit that turns black in late summer. The crown is oblong with an irregular shape. The dark bark on a mature tree is scaly and broken into plates, which resemble burned potato chips.

Common Locations   The Bronx: Pelham Bay Park and Van Cortlandt Park; Brooklyn: Prospect Park; Manhattan: Central Park, Inwood Hill Park, Riverside Park, Tompkins Square Park; Queens: Alley Pond Park; Staten Island: Wolfe's Pond Park.

Notes of Interest   The wild cherry is valued for its hardwood, which is used for fine furniture and scientific instruments. Cherry cough medicine is made from the inner bark. Jelly and wine are produced from the fruit. The wild cherry was one of the first American trees to be introduced to English gardens in the 1620s.

Ecological Role   The wild cherry tree is an important source of food for wildlife. Birds feed on the berries as do mammals such as the raccoon and skunk. Rodents such as the eastern chipmunk, gray squirrel, and deer mice feed on the cherry pits. Deer mice also store pits during the winter. Many insects pollinate the flowers, gathering nectar for consumption.

KEY POINTS
- The wild cherry is a moderately tall, spindly tree that produces abundant white flower clusters in spring and edible, though sour, cherries in the fall.
- It is easy to identify the tree by the burned potato chip look of the bark.
- The fruits are juicy, bitter, and edible by late summer.

Wild Cherry

Plate 95   WILD CHERRY

NATIVE SHRUBS

Spicebush: *Lindera benzoin*

Description   Growing up to 15 feet, the spicebush has 5-inch-long, dark green, oval-shaped leaves with no teeth. The leaves have a spicy fragrance when crushed. Spicebush has many trunks. The small, yellow flowers bloom in March and April.

Ecological Role   The American robin, northern bobwhite, gray catbird, eastern kingbird, and great crested flycatcher, raccoons, and Virginia opossums eat the shiny red berries. The leaves are consumed by the caterpillars of the spicebush swallowtail and tiger swallowtail butterflies.

Common Elderberry: *Sambucus canadensis*

Description   The common elderberry grows up to 16 feet tall. It can grow in marshes or along forest edges. The opposite, compound leaves can reach 11 inches and have up to eleven leaflets. The tiny, white flowers appear in clusters from May to June and resemble Queen Anne's lace. They produce flat-topped clusters of small, juicy, purple-black berries, which ripen from July to September. The twigs are covered with warty lenticels, or breathing pores.

Ecological Role   The northern cardinal, eastern bluebird, gray catbird, northern mockingbird, white-breasted nuthatch, blue jay, eastern kingbird, European starling, eastern phoebe, American robin, brown thrasher, cedar waxwing, woodpeckers, and the tufted titmouse consume the berries and spread the seeds. White-footed mice eat the seeds and eastern cottontails and woodchucks eat the bark. White-tailed deer eat the leaves and twigs.

Arrowwood Viburnum: *Viburnum dentatum*

Description   This shrub grows to 12 feet. The opposite, dark green leaves have pointed tips and round or heart-shaped bases. The 4-inch-long leaves have spiky teeth and a smooth surface. From May to June, the small white or pink flowers bloom in flat-topped clusters, 4 inches across and produce clusters of blue-black berries.

Ecological Role   The arrowwood hosts caterpillars of the spring azure butterfly and some moths. Many birds, such as the eastern phoebe, mockingbird, American robin, brown thrasher, northern flicker, northern cardinal, cedar waxwing, eastern blue-

Spicebush

Common Elderberry

Arrowwood Viburnum

Plate 96   From top: SPICEBUSH,
COMMON ELDERBERRY, ARROWWOOD VIBURNUM

bird, and the ruffed grouse eat its fruit. White-tailed deer feed on
the leaves. The leaves and flowers sit on top of long shoots, which
were used by Native Americans for arrow shafts.

NONNATIVE SHRUBS

Fragrant Honeysuckle: *Lonicera fragrantissima*

Description An introduced perennial, deciduous shrub, winter honeysuckle, *Lonicera fragrantissima*, is sometimes called sweet breath of spring. It has an extremely lemony fragrance with opposite creamy white flowers that appear in early spring before the leaves. Flowers produce small, red berries that ripen in late spring to early summer.

Ecological Role Honeysuckle berries are consumed by American robins, cedar waxwings, rose-breasted grosbeaks, gray catbirds, northern cardinals, white-throated sparrows, American goldfinches, and mockingbirds. The honeysuckle shrub, a native of China, tends to spread quickly and crowd out native shrubs.

Butterfly Bush: *Buddleia davidii*

Description Introduced from China, the deciduous, perennial butterfly bush can grow to 10 feet tall, and it comes in white, pink, yellow, and purple. The tiny flowers are borne on long, arching spikes, some up to 20 inches long. It is fairly drought tolerant.

Ecological Role Butterfly bushes are planted to attract butterflies and hummingbirds. In Riverside Park at the 79th Street Boat Basin, walk by the butterfly bushes in September and October and you will see hordes of migrating monarch butterflies feeding on the nectar. Although the butterfly bush is an excellent hummingbird and butterfly plant, it can easily escape from cultivation and become invasive because of its hundreds of seeds.

Rugosa Rose: *Rugosa rosa*

Description The rugosa rose, which originated in Europe, is also known as the salt-spray rose. This deciduous, perennial shrub grows to 6 feet tall and has pink, occasionally white, flowers which bear large fruits called rosehips that are filled with seeds. The heavily wrinkled leaves are pinnately compound, with seven wrinkled, oval, toothed leaflets, each 1¼ inches.

Ecological Role When rosehips first appear, they are hard and green. As they mature, they become orange, red, brown, or purple, and soften. Birds and mammals eat the ripened hips, but cannot digest the *achenes* (hard seeds). As a consequence, they

Honeysuckle

Butterfly Bush

Rugosa Rose

Plate 97 From top: FRAGRANT HONEYSUCKLE, BUTTERFLY BUSH, RUGOSA ROSE

disperse them in their droppings. Wild roses depend entirely on birds for propagation.

mushrooms

Artist's Conk: *Ganoderma applanatum*

ETYMOLOGY
Ganoderma: bright skin; *applanatum:* flat

PLACE OF ORIGIN

North America

Description The artist's conk is a large, semicircular shelf fungus, which grows on the trunks of dead deciduous trees, stumps, and logs. Above, it has brown, gray, and tan concentric rings. Below, it is a brilliant white, composed of pores that stain the mushroom a permanent brown color when touched. This characteristic has allowed people to use it as a canvas, etching or drawing on the underside of the mushroom. It can grow as large as 2 feet across and has a rough and woody texture. Normally it is flat, but it can be hoof shaped.

Common Locations Artist's conk can be found in shady wooded areas on both deciduous and coniferous (evergreen) trees.

Notes of Interest Artist's conks grow year-round. Artist's conks can live up to fifty years and are the longest-living mushroom. Cut one in half and count the layers to determine its age. Each layer represents a year of growth.

Ecological Role The artist's conk recycles nutrients from decaying logs for nourishment. Artist's conk will sometimes grow on the wounds of living trees as a parasite. This weakens the wood and makes the tree vulnerable to insects and woodpeckers, which further weakens the tree. Artist's conk is used in tea to aid the immune system.

KEY POINTS

- The artist's conk is one of the largest shelf mushrooms, growing up to 2 feet across.
- Its name is derived from its white pore undersurface, which stains reddish brown when touched; you can draw on it with a stick or even a finger.
- This is a perennial polypore fungus that can live as long as fifty years.
- Oaks, maples, and beeches are some of the host trees of the artist's conk.

Plate 98 ARTIST'S CONK

Chicken Mushroom, or Chicken-of-the-Woods:
Laetiporus sulphureus

ETYMOLOGY
Laetiporus: happy pores; *sulphureus:* yellow

Description This polypore is composed of wavy or flat, fan-shaped rosettes of orange to salmon overlapping caps, 2 to 12 inches across. They are bright yellow below. The tiny, white pores are most visible under magnification. The flesh can be white, light yellow, or salmon colored and looks like chicken. When the mushroom is young, the flesh is soft and tender but becomes firm and dry as the mushroom ages.

Common Locations Chicken mushroom can be found during spring, summer, or autumn in wooded areas in the five boroughs.

Notes of Interest This shelf mushroom can grow to enormous sizes with up to fifty overlapping yellow and orange rosettes. The rosettes can grow over 2 feet wide and can weigh a pound each. It is called a shelf mushroom because it extends out from tree trunks. The chicken-of-the-woods is called a polypore because, rather than having gills underneath their caps, they have tubes. The mouths of the tubes are tiny holes, or pores, covering the underside.

Ecological Role Chicken mushrooms grow on dead trees, stumps, and logs, recycling the nutrients. During summer, they can grow on living deciduous and conifer (evergreen) trees and their roots, parasitizing the trees. This fungus may grow inside a tree for fifty years before it forms the brightly colored fruiting bodies, or mushrooms, that extend from the trunk. As it grows inside the tree, it decays the heartwood at the center of the trunk, creating habitat for decomposing invertebrates. The shelf mushrooms help transform the tree into soil. Inside the tree, springtails, flatworms, and other tiny invertebrates consume the fungus. Outside the tree, the mushroom is fed on by fungus gnats, fungus flies, pillbugs, and fungus beetles. Birds feed on these invertebrates.

KEY POINTS
- A large shelf mushroom, consisting of numerous, overlapping, bright yellow and orange fan-shaped rosettes.
- Chicken mushrooms have a strong smell.
- Oak trees often host chicken mushrooms.

Plate 99   CHICKEN MUSHROOM

Turkey Tail: *Trametes versicolor*

ETYMOLOGY
Trametes: skinny; *versicolor:* multicolo; *turkey tail:* resemblance of this fungus to a fanned turkey tail

PLACE OF ORIGIN

Turkey tail can be found throughout the world. In Japan, it is called Kawaratake, the riverbank mushroom. In China, it is Yun zhi, rain-cloud fungus. In the Netherlands, they are Elfenbankjes, or elves' davenports.

Description   The cap of the turkey tail can grow to 4 inches across. Some have stripes of earthy colors—tan and brown or black and white—while others have colorful yellows, oranges, greens, and blues. Turkey tails change as they age and are most colorful early on before they are ready to spoor (reproduce). Turkey tail fruiting bodies are very thin and pliable. On top, they are velvety to the touch and creamy white and porous on the underside. Turkey tails attach to logs, stumps, and dead deciduous trees along the back center edge of the fan. There is no stem. Although turkey tail is not a perennial, it lives a long time and can overwinter. They are leathery and tough when fresh and hard as plastic when dry or during the winter. Look for them throughout the seasons.

Common Locations   Turkey tails are among the most commonly encountered fungi and can be found year-round in shady, moist woods throughout city parks in the five boroughs.

Notes of Interest   The turkey tail mushroom has many medicinal uses. In Asia, the turkey tail's mycelium (the underground-growing portion of the mushroom) is an approved anticancer drug, responsible for several hundred million dollars in sales annually.

Ecological Role   Turkey tail decomposes dead wood and recycles the nutrients and minerals back into the soil where it is used by other living organisms.

KEY POINTS
- Turkey tail is a common shelf fungus.
- It can be characterized by brown, red, green, blue, and yellow concentric bands.

Plate 100 TURKEY TAIL

geology

Fordham Gneiss

Fordham: named for the part of the Bronx where the rock is found; *Gneiss*: German for banded rock

Natural History Fordham gneiss, formed over a billion years ago, is the oldest rock in New York City forming the basement on which younger rocks were deposited. Fordham gneiss was buried and metamorphosed again with the younger rocks 450 million years ago.

Description It is medium to coarse-grained, gray, metamorphic (formed at high temperatures and pressures deep within the earth's interior) rock and is characterized by alternating light and dark folded bands of minerals. Gneiss has a foliated texture because the minerals have been flattened under great pressure and rearranged in parallel bands. These light-colored minerals include granular quartz and feldspars, alternating with darker bands bearing flakes of biotite mica or elongated grains of hornblende. These are the same minerals that form granite, an igneous rock (formed when magma cools). Gneiss forms when tremendous pressure has been applied to granite, rearranging the granite's minerals into alternating bands.

Common Locations Fordham gneiss can be found in many places throughout the Bronx, and in City Water Tunnel No. 3 excavations in western Queens. From Inwood Hill Park in Manhattan, look north across the Harlem River at the rocky cliff painted with the blue "C" (for Columbia University): This is Fordham gneiss. In the Bronx, gneiss forms the ridge in Riverdale. It also forms the rocky ridge in the Fordham, Tremont, and University Heights sections of the Bronx. Fordham gneiss outcroppings can be found throughout Van Cortlandt Park.

KEY POINTS
- Gneiss is characterized by light and dark bands of minerals.
- Hornblende or biotite mica often gives color to the dark bands.
- Quartz and feldspar make up the light bands of minerals.

Fordham gneiss, with its characteristic alternating light and dark bands, formed more than a billion years ago and is the oldest rock in New York City, commonly found in Van Cortlandt Park and throughout the Bronx.

Inwood Marble

ETYMOLOGY
Named for the northern Manhattan neighborhood where striking exposures of the marble can be seen.

Natural History This white-to-beige marble was transformed from sedimentary into metamorphic rock about 450 million years ago. The New York City area was then at the heart of a collision zone between two tectonic plates, where intense heat and pressure transformed the original limestone and dolomite into marble.

Description Inwood marble is white to beige in color and has a sparkling, sugary appearance. Outcrop of marble once connected Manhattan Island to the Bronx. Marble, which is much softer and more soluble than schist or gneiss, erodes readily and dissolves in water. Erosion of the Inwood Marble helped create the pathways of the Hudson, Harlem, and East rivers around the island of Manhattan. Marble is found aboveground only in northern Manhattan and the neighborhood of Marble Hill in the Bronx. However, below ground, subway and construction workers often find this beautiful, white rock.

Common Locations Isham Park, at the corner of Isham Street and Seaman Avenue, and Inwood Hill Park in Manhattan; Marble Hill in the Bronx. Quarried for over three hundred years, Inwood marble was used for headstones, such as those in the Trinity churchyard cemetery on lower Broadway at Wall Street, dated 1723, 1777, 1795, and 1796. Others may be older, but their dates and inscriptions are illegible. The New York Public Library on 42nd Street and 5th Avenue was constructed of Inwood marble. An arched gateway made of Inwood marble stands at Broadway and 216th Street. This arch, constructed in 1855, originally adorned the entrance to the Seaman-Drake estate. Huge blocks of Inwood marble from a quarry at 138th Street serve as the foundation of the old Custom House erected in 1842 and still standing on the corner of Broad and Wall streets.

KEY POINTS
- Inwood marble is a white, sparkly rock.
- Early settlers quarried this marble in northern Manhattan starting in the seventeenth century.

Outcroppings of the beautiful Inwood marble can be found in two parks at the northern tip of Manhattan Island: Isham Park and Inwood Hill Park.

Manhattan Schist

ETYMOLOGY
Schist: fissile, easily split

Natural History Manhattan schist was metamorphosed from its sedimentary precursor, shale, about 450 million years ago during a plate-tectonic collision. The earth's tectonic plates, floating over the mantle, are in constant motion; they may separate, move apart, or crash together causing earthquakes, volcanic eruptions, and pushing up mountain ranges. Manhattan schist, once largely clay-like shale, was deeply buried and contorted as an "exotic" tectonic plate rode up over North America and became attached to it. Consequent continental shifts pushed the schist up to the surface, exposing some of it as large outcrops.

Description Manhattan schist is a dark gray to silvery, rusty-weathering, coarse-grained rock. Schist is easily recognized by its glittering appearance, which is caused by flecks of the mineral mica within the rock. Red garnet is commonly visible in schist.

Common Locations Manhattan schist is found in many localities and varying depths throughout its namesake island: as outcrops in Central Park, Inwood Hill Park, Marcus Garvey Park, and Morningside Park; from 18 feet below the surface in Times Square to 260 feet below the surface in Greenwich Village. Where schist runs deep below the surface, no tall buildings exist because the bedrock foundation to support skyscrapers is missing. Skyscrapers predominate in Midtown and Lower Manhattan because schist is close to the surface.

KEY POINTS
- Large outcroppings of Manhattan schist can be found in Central Park.
- Glaciers formed the grooves on the surface of the schist outcroppings.

The glittering Manhattan schist formed the bedrock of the island for which it is named. Skyscrapers are built on those parts of Manhattan where this schist is close to the surface.

Serpentenite

ETYMOLOGY
Named after the patterns in the rock that resemble snake skin.

Natural History   A broad ridge of serpentine—a metamorphic rock formed approximately five hundred million years ago when heat and pressure altered rocks from the ocean floor rich in magnesium and iron—forms the spine of Staten Island. Its mineral composition includes fibrous chrysotile (commonly known as asbestos), talc, olivine (green lava grains), as well as other ferromagnesium minerals, which also contain iron and magnesium.

Description   Serpentenite is greenish-black with a glossy, glazed polish. Often mottled with light and dark, its surface has a shiny, waxy appearance and a slightly soapy texture. Serpentenite is generally fine grained and dense.

Common Locations   Serpentenite is found in Staten Island. In Clove Lakes Park, outcroppings of serpentine rock are at the crest of the hills. Serpentenite is visible on an abandoned highway next to the Staten Island Expressway. Todt Hill, the highest coastal point south of the state of Maine, stands 410 feet above sea level on a bedrock of serpentenite, which can be seen south of the intersection of Todt Hill Road and Ocean Terrace. "Todt," is a Dutch word for "dead." The hill was named by Dutch settlers because no plants would grow here. Serpentenite's main component is magnesium, an element that, in high concentrations, will kill most plants. The magnesium in the thin soil covering the serpentenite caused the barrenness of Todt Hill.

KEY POINTS
- Serpentenite is composed of the mineral serpentine that forms as the igneous minerals olivine and pyroxene are subjected to rising temperature and pressure.
- Serpentenite can be cut, polished, and used as ornamental building stones.
- Serpentenite is bluish to greenish gray.

The greenish rock serpentenite forms a broad ridge
across parts of Staten Island.

A hillside of serpentenite on an abandoned highway is visible
along northbound Staten Island Expressway on the right.

Hartland Formation

Natural History The Hartland formation consists of well-layered rocks, which are now metamorphic. Originally they were a mix of sedimentary rocks and igneous basalt flows. Hartland formation is generally considered "exotic" to ancient North America and was attached to this continent during a collision between tectonic plates about 450 million years ago. Rocks of the Hartland formation are roughly similar in age to the Inwood marble and Manhattan schist.

Description The Hartland formation contains a variety of rocks, which include quartz-feldspar gneiss, schist, amphibolites, and marble. This great variety of rocks and noticeable banding are characteristic of the Hartland formation. Quartz veins and migmatite dikes are visible as they cut across the surrounding layers of rock. Migmatite is a rock that forms when granitic melt is "mixed" with solid rock. At Orchard Beach, migmatites were produced by melting rocks 450 million years ago, and younger migmatite was produced by the injection of granitic magma into cooler host rock. The younger granites are conspicuous as coarse-grained, light-colored dikes that cut across older, folded rock units.

Common Locations In New York City, the most dramatic outcroppings of the Hartland formation lie along the shores of Pelham Bay Park in the Bronx. The Hunter Island Marine Zoology and Geology Sanctuary, north of Orchard Beach, includes the northeastern shoreline of Hunter Island, all of Twin Island, Two Trees Island, and Cat Briar Island, where, at low tide, one can walk over these dramatic and beautiful outcrops of the Hartland formation.

KEY POINTS

- Hartland formation is "exotic" to ancient North America.
- Hartland formation is well banded and contains a variety of rock types.

*The Hartland formation, which forms the rocky shores of
Hunter and Twin Islands, Pelham Bay Park in the Bronx,
is made up of various rocks, including gneiss, schist, and marble.*

ORGANIZATIONS IN AND AROUND NEW YORK CITY

American Littoral Society: www.alsnyc.org

American Museum of Natural History: www.amnh.org

Baykeeper: www.nynjbaykeeper.org

Brooklyn Bird Club: www.brooklynbirdclub.org

Central Park Conservancy: www.cenralparknyc.org

EEAC Environmental Education Advisory Council: www.eeac-nyc.org

Green Guerillas: www.greenguerillas.org

Linnaean Society of New York: http://linnaeannewyork.org

Long Island Sound Foundation: www.lisfoundation.org

New York City Audubon Society: www.nycaudubon.org/home

New York City Department of Parks and Recreation: www.nycgovparks.org

New York Restoration Project: www.nyrp.org

Nurture New York's Nature: www.nnyn.org

NYC Urban Park Rangers: www.nycgovparks.org/sub_about/parks_divisions/urban_park_rangers/pd_ur_rangers_events.php

Prospect Audubon Center: www.prospectparkaudubon.org

Prospect Park Alliance: www.prospectpark.org

Queens County Bird Club: www.littleneck.net/qcbc

Riverkeeper: www.riverkeeper.org

Riverside Park Fund: www.riversideparkfund.org

Save the Sound: www.savethesound.org

Sierra Club New York City Group: www.sierraclub.org/chapters/ny/nyc

Staten Island Bird Club: www.sibirdclub.com/

Staten Island's Land Conservation Organization: www.siprotectors.org

Torrey Botanical Society: www.torreybotanical.org

BIBLIOGRAPHY

Amos, William H., and Stephen H. Amos. *Atlantic & Gulf Coasts.*
(Audubon Society Nature Guides). New York: Alfred A. Knopf, 1997.

Anderson, Marianne O'Hea. *Van Cortlandt Park Map and Guide.*
New York: City of New York Parks and Recreation, 2002.

Atkinson, Margaret. *Wolfe's Pond Park, Staten Island, New York.*
New York: City of New York Parks and Recreation Natural Resources
Group, 1990.

Baker, Kevin. *Paradise Alley.* New York: HarperCollins, 2003.

Barlow, Elizabeth. *The Forests and Wetlands of New York City.* Boston:
Little, Brown, 1971.

Barnard, Edward Sibley. *New York City Trees: A Field Guide for the
Metropolitan Area.* New York: Columbia University Press, 2002.

Behler, John L. *National Audubon Society Field Guide to North American
Reptiles and Amphibians.* New York: Alfred A. Knopf, 1979.

Bourque, Jean, Ronald Bourque, and Robert P. Cook. *Birds of Floyd
Bennett Field.* Washington, DC: U.S. Department of Interior,
National Park Service, Gateway National Recreation Area, 1994.

Brill, Steve, and Evelyn Dean. *Identifying and Harvesting Edible and
Medicinal Plants.* New York: Hearst Books.

Brown, Lauren. *Grasses: An Identification Guide.* Boston: Houghton
Mifflin, 1979.

Buff, Sheila. *Nature Walks In and Around New York City.* Boston:
Appalachian Mountain Club, 1996.

Bull, John, and John Farrand, Jr. *The Audubon Society Field Guide to
North American Birds, Eastern Region.* New York: Alfred A. Knopf,
1977.

Burrows, Edwin G., and Mike Wallace. *Gotham: A History of New York
City to 1898.* New York: Oxford University Press, 1999.

Burton, Dennis. *Nature Walks of Central Park.* New York: Henry Holt, 1997.

Carson, Rachel. *A Sense of Wonder.* New York: HarperCollins, 1987.

Chambers, Kenneth A. *A Country-Lover's Guide to Wildlife.* Baltimore:
Johns Hopkins University Press, 1979.

Comstock, Anna Botsford. *Handbook of Nature Study.* Ithaca, NY: Cornell
University Press, 1911.

Cook, Robert P. *Amphibians and Reptiles.* Washington, DC: U.S.
Department of Interior, National Park Service, Gateway National
Recreation Area, 1989.

Cook, Robert P. *Gateway Mammals.* Washington, DC: U.S. Department of
    Interior National Park Service, Gateway National Recreation Area, 1989.
Cook, Robert P. "A Natural History of the Diamondback Terrapin."
    Bulletin of the American Littoral Society (Sandy Hook, NJ). 18 (1989):
    151–154.
Cottam, Clarence, and Herbert S. Zim. *Insects.* New York: St. Martin's
    Press, 2001.
Duke, James, and Steven Foser. *A Field Guide to Medicinal Plants.* Boston:
    Houghton Mifflin, 1990.
Feller, Michael J. *The Gerritsen Creek Nature Trail, Marine Park,
    Brooklyn, New York.* New York: City of New York Parks and
    Recreation Natural Resources Group, 1986.
Feller, Michael. J. *The Kazimiroff Nature Trail, Pelham Bay Park, Bronx,
    New York.* New York: City of New York Parks and Recreation Natural
    Resources Group, 1989.
Fowle, Marcia T., and Paul Kerlinger. *The New York City Aubudon Society
    Guide to Finding Birds in the Metropolitan Area.* Ithaca, NY: Cornell
    University Press, 2001.
Garber, Steven D. *The Urban Naturalist.* Mineola, NY: Dover Publications,
    1998.
Graff, M. M. *Tree Trails in Central Park.* New York: Greensward
    Foundation, 1970.
Hanley, Thomas, and M. M. Graff. *Rock Trails in Central Park.* New York:
    Greensward Foundation, Inc., 1976.
Hiss, Tony, and Christopher Meier. *H2O: Highlands to Ocean.* Morristown,
    NJ: Geraldine R. Dodge Foundation, 2004.
Hoffmeister, Donald F., and Herbert Zim. *Mammals.* New York: Golden
    Press, 1987.
Kershner, Bruce. *Secret Places of Staten Island.* Dubuque, IA: Kendall/
    Hunt Publishing, 1998.
Kieran, John. *A Natural History of New York City.* Boston: Houghton
    Mifflin, 1959.
Kornblum, William. *At Sea in the City: New York from the Water's Edge.*
    Chapel Hill, NC: Algonquin Books of Chapel Hill, 2002.
Kricher, John C., and Gordon Morrison. *The Peterson Field Guide Series:
    A Field Guide to Ecology of Eastern Forests.* New York: Houghton
    Mifflin, 1988.
Levi, Herbert W. *Spiders and Their Kin.* New York: Golden Press, 1990.
Lincoff, Gary H. *The Audubon Society Field Guide to North American
    Mushrooms.* New York: Alfred A. Knopf, 1981.

Lippson, Alice Jane, and Robert L. Lippson. *Life in the Chesapeake Bay.*
Baltimore: Johns Hopkins University Press, 1997.

Little, Edward L. *The Audubon Society Field Guide to North American
Trees, Eastern Region.* New York: Alfred A. Knopf, 1980.

Lopate, Phillip. *Waterfront, a Walk around Manhattan.* New York:
Anchor Books, 2004.

Luttenberg, Danielle, Deborah Lev, and Michael Feller. *Native Species
Planting Guide for New York City and Vicinity.* New York: City of
New York Parks and Recreation Natural Resources Group, 1993.

Mack, Lisa, and Michael J. Feller. *Salt Marshes of New York City.*
New York: City of New York Parks and Recreation Natural Resources
Group, 1990.

Matthews, Anne. *Wild Nights: Nature Returns to the City.* New York:
North Point Press, 2001.

McKnight, Kent H., and Vera B. McKnight. *A Field Guide to Mushrooms.*
(Peterson Field Guides). Boston: Houghton Mifflin, 1987.

Miller, Sara Cedar. *Central Park, An American Masterpiece.* New York:
Harry N. Abrams, 2003.

Miller, Todd. *A Guide to the Birds of Queens.* New York: City of New York
Parks and Recreation Natural Resources Group, 1990.

Milne, Lorus, and Margery Milne. *National Audubon Society Field
Guide to North American Insects and Spiders.* New York:
Alfred A. Knopf, 1980.

Mittelbach, Margaret, and Michael Crewdson. *Wild New York.*
New York: Three Rivers Press, 1997.

Newcomb, Lawrence. *Newcomb's Wildflower Guide.* Boston:
Little, Brown, 1977.

Niering, William A., and Nancy C. Olmstead. *National Audubon Society
Field Guide to North American Wildflowers, Eastern Region.* New
York: Alfred A. Knopf, 1979.

Peterson, Roger Tory. *A Field Guide to the Birds.* Boston: Houghton
Mifflin, 1980.

Petrides, George. *A Field Guide to Eastern Trees.* Boston: Houghton
Mifflin, 1988.

Pons, Luis. *Van Cortlandt Park History.* New York: Van Cortlandt and
Pelham Bay Parks, City of New York Parks and Recreation, 1994.

Pough, Frederick H. *Peterson First Guides Rocks and Minerals.* Boston:
Houghton Mifflin, 1991.

Pyle, Robert Michael. *National Audubon Society Field Guide to North
American Butterflies.* New York: Alfred A. Knopf, 1981.

Rappole, John H. *Birds of the Mid-Atlantic Region and Where to Find Them*. Baltimore: Johns Hopkins University Press, 2002.

Ray, C. Claiborne. "Worms at the Root," *New York Times*, March 7, 2006, Science Times.

Reid, George K. *Pond Life*. New York: Golden Press, 1987.

Rhodes, Frank H. *Geology*. New York: Golden Press, 1991.

Salwen, Peter. *Upper Westside Story*. New York: Abbeville Press, 1989.

Seitz, Sharon. *Big Apple Safari for Families: The Urban Park Rangers' Guide to Nature in New York City*. Woodstock, VT: Countryman Press, 2005.

Seitz, Sharon, and Stuart Miller. *The Other Islands of New York City: A History and Guide*. Woodstock, VT: Countryman Press, 2001.

Shaffer, Paul R., and Herbert S. Zim. *Rocks and Minerals*. New York: Golden Press, 1957.

Shorto, Russell. *The Island at the Center of the World*. New York: Doubleday, 2004.

Sibley, David A. *The Sibley Field Guide to Birds of Eastern North America*. New York: Alfred A. Knopf, 2003.

Skinner, Alanson. *The Indians of Manhattan Island and Vicinity*. Science Guide 41. New York: American Museum of Natural History, 1947.

Stanne, Stephen P., Roger G. Panetta, and Brian E. Forist. *The Hudson: An Illustrated Guide to the Living River*. New Brunswick, NJ: Rutgers University Press, 1996.

Stokes, Donald, and Lillian Stokes. *Guide to Animal Tracking and Behavior*. Boston: Little, Brown, 1986.

Sullivan, Robert. *The Meadowlands*. New York: Doubleday Books, 1998.

Sullivan, Robert. *Rats: Observations on the History and Habitat of the City's Most Unwanted Inhabitants*. New York: Bloomsbury, 2004.

Tanacredi, John T. *Gateway: A Visitors Companion*. Mechanicsburg, PA: Stackpole Books, 1995.

Taylor, Raymond L. *Plants of Colonial Days*. Mineola, NY: Dover Publications, 1996.

Terres, John K. *The Audubon Society Encyclopedia of North American Birds*. New York: Alfred A. Knopf, 1987.

Tiner, Ralph W., Jr. *A Field Guide to Coastal Wetland Plants of the Northeastern United States*. Amherst: University of Massachusetts Press, 1987.

Van der Donck, Adriaen. *Description of the New Netherlands*. Syracuse, NY: Syracuse University Press, 1968.

Waldman, John. *Heartbeats in the Muck: A Dramatic Look at the History, Sea Life, and Environment of New York Harbor.* New York: Lyons Press, 1999.

Whitaker, John O., Jr. *National Audubon Society Field Guide to North American Mammals.* New York: Alfred A. Knopf, 1996.

Willis, Delta, and Michael J. Feller. *Staten Island Natural Areas.* New York: City of New York Parks and Recreation Natural Resources Group, 1991.

Wilson, E. O. *Biophilia.* Cambridge, MA: Harvard University Press, 1984.

Wright, Amy Bartlett. *Peterson First Guide to Caterpillars of North America.* Boston: Houghton Mifflin, 1993.

Websites

www.birds.cornell.edu/

www.fcps.k12.va.us/StratfordLandingES/Ecology/home

http://enature.com/home (The online version of the Audubon Field Guide series.)

http://animaldiversity.ummz.umich.edu/site/index.html (Animal Diversity Web University of Michigan's website, including information and media on many species of wildlife.)

http://museum.nhm.uga.edu (Georgia Wildlife Website University of Georgia's website, including information about many species.)

www.cnr.vt.edu/dendro/dendrology/factsheets.cfm (Tree Fact Sheets at Virginia Tech, Virginia Tech's fact pages for eastern tree species.)

www.treeguide.com (Fact sheets for North American tree species.)

www.botany.wisc.edu/wisflora/ (Wisconsin State Herbarium Database of North American plants. Includes facts, images, and other info.

http://plants.usda.gov (USDA PLANTS Database of North American plants. Includes facts, images, and classification info.)

www.natureserve.org/explorer/ (NatureServe Explorer Online encyclopedia)

http://botit.botany.wisc.edu/toms_fungi/ (Tom Volk's Fungi Website, all about North American fungi.)

INDEX

*The letter "f" following a page number indicates a figure,
"pl" indicates a plate, and "m" indicates a map.*

CREDITS

Photographs by Leslie Day appear on pages 27, 32, 34, 36, 39, 40, 43, 44, 45, 47, 50, 51, 52, 54, 56, 58, 59, 62, 63, 66, 67, 69, 72, 74, 79, 82, 85 (*top*), 95, 97, 98, 99, 102, 325, 331 (*top*)

Photographs by Michael Feller appear on pages 21, 29, 30, 31, 33, 38, 48, 61, 70, 73, 84, 85 (*bottom*), 86, 103, 108, 111, 327, 329, 331 (*bottom*), 333

Photograph by Clodagh Green appears on page 77 (*bottom*)

Photographs by David Künstler appear on pages 22, 37, 109

Photograph by Marjorie Pangione appears on page 77 (*top*)

Photographs by Don Riepe appear on pages 42, 87, 88, 90, 91, 92, 93

Map by George Boorujy appears on page 12

Maps by International Mapping Associates appear on pages 49, 75, 78, 96

Maps by Mark Stein appear on pages 28, 35, 41, 53, 65, 68, 71, 81, 83, 89, 101

LESLIE DAY is an environmental and life science educator at The Elisabeth Morrow School and an adjunct faculty member at Bank Street College of Education. She developed the City Naturalists Summer Institute with the Central Park Conservancy and has a doctorate in science education from Teachers College Columbia University. She and her husband live on a houseboat on the Hudson River in Manhattan.

MARK A. KLINGLER is a scientific illustrator at the Carnegie Museum of Natural History. He was trained at Carnegie Mellon University and Pennsylvania Academy of the Arts. His work has appeared internationally in major scientific journals and popular magazines, as well as museums and art forums across the country.

ABOUT THE TYPE

The text of this book is set in Andrade, designed by Dino dos Santos in 2005. This typeface is inspired by the typographic work of Manoel de Andrade de Figueiredo (1670–1735). The work of Andrade de Figueiredo is among the most impressive examples of type design from the eighteenth century. Updated to reflect contemporary sensibilities, Andrade is a tribute to Portuguese typography.